Composing for Voice

Composing *for* Voice

A Guide for Composers, Singers, and Teachers

Paul Barker

ROUTLEDGE
NEW YORK AND LONDON

Published in 2004 by
Routledge
29 West 35th Street
New York, NY 10001

Published in Great Britain by
Routledge
11 New Fetter Lane
London EC4P 4EE

Routledge is an imprint of the Taylor & Francis Group.

Printed in the United States of America on acid-free paper.

10   9   8   7   6   5   4   3   2   1

Cataloging-in-Publication Data is available from the Library of Congress

ISBN 0-415-94186-5 (hb)
ISBN 0-415-94187-3 (pb)

Contents

v

O fret not after knowledge—I have none,
And yet my song comes native with the warmth.
O fret not after knowledge—I have none,
And yet the Evening listens . . .

—"O Thou Whose Face
Hath Felt the Winter's Wind"
                              —John Keats

Of all composers, past and present, I am the least learned. I
mean what I say in all seriousness, and by *learning* I do not
mean *knowledge* of music.
                              —Giuseppi Verdi, 1723

Preface

This book is designed as a tool for composers and their teachers to help them write in various musical genres for the voice. The primary objective is to facilitate and inspire collaborations between composers and singers, because I am convinced that no book can substitute for such a rewarding practical experience. As a consequence, it is hoped that the book also contains information valuable to singers and actors who hope to work closely with composers. Whether working with singers, singing actors, or acting singers, a composer is confronted with a plethora of competing problems from many disciplines; from questions of vocal technique, stylistic considerations, complexities of performance, and psychological factors, as well as considerations of text and its complex relationship with music. I cannot pretend that this book is universal in its application: the voice is too vast a subject culturally and historically for one person or one book to contain. Nor does it aim to teach those who cannot sing how they might try, except to the same extent an orchestration manual informs composers, say, about the capabilities of string instruments.

I have drawn from my own experiences working with voices as a composer and musical director, and those restrictions inevitably became the parameters that define the content of the book. There is little information here for those who would wish to explore Tibetan "Ghost" chanting, Indian classical singing, or baroque decoration. Indeed, it might prove embarrassing to list the areas that are *not* covered here, but I believe that there already exist books and magazine articles that treat these specialist areas in the detail they deserve. Another important area omitted from the content is choral composition, which deserves a separate and exhaustive treatment for composers.

One aim of this book is to provide a resource where a composer may find information on what sorts of voices exist and which to choose, how to identify vocal expectations, and on the constantly evolving relationship between text and voice. The best resource is to work with a singer. It used to be the norm for composers to work for many years alongside singers and actors in opera houses and theaters, as well as in the concert hall. For reasons discussed later, this is becoming more and more difficult for composers today. Another option is to study the scores of composers from the point of view of the singer, which is now the profession of a coach. It is hoped that this book might encourage composers and singers to begin or continue collaborating in ever new and more fruitful directions.

There already exist many books explaining vocal physiology or describing specific singing techniques, and those interested in these areas are directed to the bibliography. There are also listed some analyses of vocal repertoire, usually exploring how songs or arias might be performed and interpreted. They are all useful for composers up to a point, but they tend to be written from a single stylistic point of view, and aimed at the singer. To my knowledge, at the time of writing, there are no comparative reference works to guide the composer of vocal music, who may have already studied some of the many classic treatises on orchestration and composition techniques. The equivalent manuals for the voice seem not to exist.

Throughout history, there has been little agreement among critics, the public, and the profession about the qualities that make a good vocal sound. In fact, this does not always seem to be a prerequisite for a singing career, as there seem to be many examples of successful singers in all styles who maintain popularity and success despite a general agreement that their voice may have "gone." Patently the same situation is less plausible with instrumentalists. There is even less agreement among teachers about how the qualities of a good sound might be taught, and there are many diverse and even contradictory methods for the teaching of voice itself. Given such dissension, the composer's bottom line might be the ability to make an informed choice about the type of singer and expectations she or he might want to write for. It is a truism to say that you can only learn composing by practicing it, but given the current problems and issues about collaborations between composers and singers in educational music institutions, some pointers along the way might save both time and embarrassment for all concerned. One composer's perfect singer may be another's worst nightmare.

The book uses many quotations, not from a desire to demonstrate any academic virtuosity, but because I am forever humbled at the size of the subject and the importance of certain individuals and their profound knowledge. I am dependent on the knowledge of others to lead me through the wealth and variety of material available. It is also a book of ideas, and I have not tried, nor would I be able, to avoid expressing my own opinion in certain areas. If these ideas are read as statements of fact, then the book fails an additional objective, which is to provoke dialogue in an area too frequently neglected by serious discussion.

My thanks go to Jesus College, Cambridge, where in my formative years I sang as a boy chorister. As a result of the intensity of the experience I soon took up the piano and composition seriously. I was fascinated by voices as a student and have been ever since. I am lucky enough to have played for many inspiring soloists through whom I have discovered much. In particular

I spent some wonderful years playing for the late, great voice teacher, Audrey Langford. The theater has always seemed to me a natural extension of the concert hall, and as a composer I had the luxury of working with some fine singers for intense periods particularly in my own company, the Modern Music Theatre Troupe, as well as others. My thanks go to the innumerable actors and singers who have put up with my demands and particularly for their leaps of faith that I knew what I wanted. Often, I only recognized it after they sang it to me, but those moments of discovery still shine bright in my memory. My gratitude is sincerely offered to those singers named who generously contributed to the chapter, Singers on Composers. Additionally, Susan Rutherford of the University of Manchester, Howard Burrell of the University of Hertfordshire and the soprano Susan Stacey, generously gave much time and consideration with their suggestions. My thanks also go to my editor Richard Carlin for his patience, encouragement, and fine editorial skills. Finally, I lovingly acknowledge my debt to my wife, the mezzo-soprano and teacher Maria Huesca, for her profound insight and knowledge on all vocal matters.

List of Musical Examples

1
The Voice Today:
An Evaluation

This chapter examines attitudes to the voice, past and present. Beginning with the problem of defining the term *vocal writing*, it attempts to summarize the problems concerning composers working with the voice.

Vocal versus Non-Vocal

If we could define the factors that make a piece of music suitable or unsuitable for the voice, we might be in a position to define that which constitutes the essence of vocal material—what makes one phrase "vocal" and another "unvocal"—by common consent. The latter concept is often thrown accusingly at young composers by teachers, and more frequently used disparagingly by singers about composers, absent or dead. Even if a composer were asked today to write deliberately against the nature of the voice, such has the technical and musical ability of singers increased in the last century in some areas that it might not be hard to find a singer who, with application, might conquer it. But perhaps not more than one could do so; and what would motivate that singer to make the effort? There are many instrumentalists as well as singers who become excited at the idea of a seemingly impossible challenge as an impetus to professionally demonstrate their virtuosity. However, the ability to sing a work neither proves nor disproves an inherent "unvocal" quality, which now begins to seem more a concept concerned with generalities than specifics. The fact is that a practical, useful definition of what is vocal is hard to achieve. This is obviously a problem that lies at

-the heart of the objective of this book. Predictably it cannot be resolved in a sentence, nor even a chapter, otherwise this book would not be necessary.

The traditional and obvious response to the problem may be that large leaps of a ninth or more, angular rhythms, extremes of range and dynamics, and competitive accompaniments may appear to be the main opponents to vocalism. Unfortunately, that suggests that neither Mozart nor Beethoven, Verdi nor Paul McCartney qualify as examples of competent vocal composers, because there are countless examples of their trespass of these "rules." More worryingly, it might suggest a serious error in the long depreciation of the vocal music of, for instance, Dittersdorf and Delibes, who remain shining if unsung adherents to such traditional concepts.

The twentieth century produced an explosion of interest in the quality or substance of sound as a basis for musical expression. As regards the voice, this led to composers methodically exploring the outer limits of range and the entire panoply of vocal (and corporal) sound as potentially creative and communicative material. However, if this area is considered unvocal it may be more to do with its association with the infamous concept of the "avant-garde" than the ubiquitous presence it currently demonstrates in the soundtracks of films, cartoons, and in the commercial music of advertisements and the media. There are still singing teachers who are convinced that any time spent by a young singer in the area known as "extended vocal technique" will be harmful or injurious to the voice. That consequence surely might provide a useful definition of unvocal music, were it not for the thousands of voices wrecked in opera houses by singing Wagner, Verdi, and Puccini. It is, of course, misuse or abuse of the voice that harms, irrespective of the composer's aesthetic. The voice of a singing teacher is always present in a singer's consciousness and it is too easy to blame an absent or dead composer when the problem may be in the singing technique. On the other hand, the composer who does not take heed of the lessons of history and ignores the needs of singers may well find difficulty in securing sympathetic performers.

Context may be used to help define the elusive element of what is characteristically well composed, vocally. Any sound emanating from the vocal organ is vocal by definition, but why are some sounds acceptable to singers and others less so? For example, although neglected by composers for centuries, the sound of the human breath became a cliché in musical terms during the last century. Liberated by technology from its essential quality of intimacy or near inaudibility, it became fodder for music as diverse as Serge Gainsbourg's once infamous "Je t'aime" (1969) and Michael Tippett's Fourth Symphony (1977). Also in 1969, Samuel Beckett wrote his sound-theater work, "Breath," which is composed of two identical cries, described by him as an "Instant of recorded vagitus," along with an amplified recording of breath. By the beginning of the twenty-first century, "musicalized" breathing seems almost as ubiquitous a part of contemporary musical "code" as the perfect cadence once was in classical music. While it is doubtful that anyone can yet make a living out of noisy breathing in front of a microphone outside the pornography industry, there are many compositions that exploit different audible techniques, and few contemporary singers who have not had to master some of them. Breathing, it seems, cannot be "unvocal" because of its nature, but it hardly aids a composer in the quest for vocal understanding.

Context of style may dictate more apparently fixed parameters, but only for limited time periods; the traditional considerations of movement regulated by intervals greater than a second, continuous vowel tone as the basis of legato, and melodic line as the begetter of counterpoint rather than its product lie at the very heart of the definition of music by Machaut and Palestrina, although interpreted by each within apparently conflicting social, cultural, or religious ideologies. Unfortunately, the definition of a musical style is only possible *after* a composer has created it, and history tends to demonstrate that each succeeding generation seeks to retaliate against the "old-garde." Once defined, it seems that a style is already passé, from a creative point of view. Some composers have themselves sought to define aspects of what is inherently vocal writing, but their concepts inevitably remain largely allied to their personal musical style, and shed little light beyond for succeeding generations. While this may seem lamentable, it is hardly surprising. Both the creative technique of composition and the art of application of the voice are after all in a state of perpetual flux that will only cease when there are no more composers and singers.

Meanwhile, the context of a specific style sheds some useful information to young composers. Generations were once taught rigorously of the rules of Bach's four-part harmony, as derived purportedly from the composer's chorales. However, the necessary simplifications of a style into a book of rules proved too narrow to encapsulate the master's work, as will be testified by those who, having unethically copied an original, subsequently failed an examination on technical grounds. Nevertheless, analyzing and learning works by other composers is an invaluable way of understanding the discipline of composition. But the question remains as to how a composer then decontextualizes this experience and writes with his own voice.

Contexts of geography also prove variable to the consequences of education and habit. This was pointed out some years ago to me, when I saw some highly educated King's College choirboys demonstrate their aural acuity by repeating with their voice complex chromatic phrases played once at the piano. The same talented group was then presented with some "simple" tunes learned by novices in Java, when beginning to play their sophisticated gamelan instruments. The choirboys were confounded by a division of the scale that evaded the concept of both tones and semitones, although found simple by Javanese children of half their age. The romantic idea of music as the "universal language" of man became a myth at least for me since that experience, and more important what may seem apt vocally in Cambridge may seem inept in Java.

We seem to be reaching the conclusion that there is no universally applicable concept of what represents vocal understanding in musical composition that overcomes the restrictions of style, history, or geography. Nevertheless, some composers are commonly lauded for demonstrating such a mastery, while others constantly attract adverse criticism. An understanding of "vocal technique" may be how a composer unlocks this mystery, but the phrase is loaded with the conflicting contexts already discussed. In the early eighteenth century, the singer-composer Pier Francesco Tosi published *Thoughts on Ancient and Modern Singers,* a treatise that sought in part to define acceptable and non-acceptable vocal practices, which became an important reference source on Italian vocal technique for generations. It is arguable whether such a book might be likely to succeed today, or even whether it is possible to identify and articulate certain elements that we might expect all singers to possess. The composer must confront precisely this problem, when confronted with the *idea* of a voice, rather than an actual example.

The voice, like music itself, is itself constantly remaking itself and evolving. It is not a fixed, self-limiting piece of musical apparatus caught in aspic, perhaps as is a viol, but a living organism with both specific individual identities as well as a hereditary, suprapersonal aspect. Like an Olympic sport, any attempt to define or limit it is doomed to fail because of human nature and the allied creative forces of imagination and willpower. While respecting both the individuality of each voice and the distinctiveness of each composer's language, this book seeks at least to define some of the mutable limits that have been considered good vocal writing, while attempting to avoid oversimplistic or too general answers. It may be a truism to suggest that not all voices and not all techniques are suitable for all composers, yet that does not minimize the difficulties of discovering just what is suitable. It may be possible to acquire an insight or develop an instinct about what is or is not vocal, and to know why.

The more daring the composer, the more fallible may be the result; the more conservative the singer, the more frustrated the composer may become. When a composer risks little, perhaps there is an equally small chance for the singer to be inspired by the music. But when the singer is ready to risk something, then both may begin to fly.

From the composer's view, writing for or against the natural inclinations of an instrument are two equally possible choices. Stravinsky and Tippett both wrote against the idiosyncratic traditions of piano playing in works such as *Piano-Rag-Music* and *Songs for Ariel,* respectively. Piano music tends to reflect the traditional patterns of notes in relation to the five different digits and their conventional relationships. For composer-pianists, these sorts of figurations provoke a strong subconscious and muscular effect, and to write against this requires an effort of will. Vocal idiosyncrasies, traditions, or habits are not so physically obvious as the fingers of a pianist, but to make a decision to write for or against we must first try to define such relationships or vocal traditions.

There is a long and distinguished list of composers who have written against the voice, in one or other of its aspects. Late in the twentieth century, in his improbable opera for solo soprano and orchestra, *Neither,* Morton Feldman repeats slow, high chromatic note patterns for page after page of score. Beethoven's extraordinarily high writing for the chorus tenors in the last movement of his Ninth Symphony may have served as a model, consciously or unconsciously, but Feldman stretches both the endurance of the singer and the audience's nerves with his unrelenting insistence. It is not a question of the altitude of the pitches, but of the composer's use of tessitura, or the average range of the voice in use over a certain span of time. Both composers are unsparing in their technical demands of their performers, in order to gain a particularly extreme emotional communication or response.

J. S. Bach is often accused of treating his voices as if they were string instruments; certainly, considerations of breath and stamina rarely appear either in his music for voice or wind instruments. The effect, where singers are either able to mask or master these concerns, may be an exhilarating and apparently effortless dance between voices and instruments, from a listener's perspective. The singer's real and unique struggle, then, becomes the enunciation and communication of text in addition to everything that is also expected from the instruments. The resolution is to turn the problem on its head, and treat the instruments as if they, too, were voices. The effect can be revelatory: in the most exciting performances I have heard, the care for articulation in the instrumental lines suggests the instruments are articulating text as well as voice. Because their lines often are thematically homogenous with the singer, it is not difficult to imagine the inferred text. The entire music then seems to become a representation of a meditation on the text (see Example 1.1).

This seems to be evidence, at least as far as Bach, that the model for all other instruments was the voice. The art of voice at the time of Bach may have been concerned primarily with flexibility, stamina, and ornamentation— this was certainly true in the opera of the time. Wagner's comment on playing an instrument seems to exhort this idea—"To play an instrument correctly means to sing with it" (Fuchs 1985)—but surely the aesthetic for what was by nature vocal was different for the later composer.

Example 1.1. Bach: *St. John Passion.*

A more contemporary example of how a composer begins with vocal elements and transforms them into instrumental ideas might serve to illustrate some of the more subtle idiosyncrasies between writing for voice and a string instrument. In the summer of 1976, the musicologist Douglas Green discovered that a manuscript draft of the last movement of Alban Berg's Lyric Suite for string quartet contained a shorthand text, which he identified as a translation of Baudelaire's sonnet "De profundis clamavi." Then in January 1977, George Perle discovered a copy of the published score with meticulous annotations by the composer in multicolored ink, which Berg had presented to Hanna Fuchs-Robettin, the woman who inspired the work and to whom it was secretly dedicated. The annotated score unfolds a secret program for each movement and for the work as a whole, identifies numerous musical quotations and cross-references, and clarifies the significance of the implied vocal setting of the finale. Although the composer evidently never intended the sung text to be heard, the quartets that subsequently played the work understandably felt the need to examine this new layer of meaning exposed beneath the surface.

Finding examples of composers writing for the idiosyncrasies of the voice ought to be more obvious. However, it does not necessarily lead to music that is easy to sing, any more than Chopin's extraordinarily intimate insight of the piano renders his music easy to play. Monteverdi, Palestrina, Purcell, Mozart, Bellini, Rossini, Puccini, Richard Strauss, and Britten, for example, can hardly be accused of that. But they did avoid the extremes of physical discomfort as a vehicle for artistic or emotional communication. They all demonstrated knowledge of and understanding of how a singer breathes, how the approach to any note affects the note itself, how the composer's choice of a vowel or consonant must relate to the choice of pitch or duration, and—above all—what was possible to ask of singers within or just beyond the limitations of their own era and style. Composers today might look back at earlier composers with some envy at the creative position of security such a social unity of style must have provided.

The View Back

That there ever was a Golden Age of singing is either historical or mythical, according to different sources. Lucie Manén(1974) wrote that most Italian composers of the seventeenth and eighteenth centuries (such as Caccini, Stradella, and Pistochi) were also performing singers, imbued with an understanding of the laws of the voice. The period gave birth to the Bel Canto "school," which has been the subject of much debate and argument since.

It is generally accepted that the term "Bel Canto" is much misused, abused, and misunderstood today: "The term Bel Canto is generally linked nowadays to an utterly false impression that, in itself, shows the extent to which the great tradition of singing has fallen into decay" (Husler & Rodd-Marling 1976). The Italian term means "beautiful singing," and was first applied to composers such as Cavalli and Cesti, in the generation after Monteverdi, who considered the innate requirements of musical form to outweigh the previously dominating aspect of text. This led typically to graceful, smoothly flowing phrases, supported by relatively simple harmonies. The style was quickly appropriated by composers throughout Europe, and applied to both instrumental and vocal baroque forms. In fact, the philosophy of the style persisted through composers such as Bellini and Donizetti until the second half of the nineteenth century, when it was supplanted by the demands of dramatic realism, or "verismo."

Manén follows Tosi's example, warning against the perceived excesses and imperfections of new practices. She laments that composers of her day were rarely singers, who treated the voice as simply one tone of a certain pitch in various intensities. She also notes the dissolution in singers, reflecting on the schism that has developed between vocal tone and emotion. She attributes this in part to the practice of performing without audiences in recordings, without the apparent need of simultaneous facial and emotional expression. Dynamics have largely replaced changes of mood, another area in which the tradition of instrumental composition has usurped the older tradition of vocal composition. A glance at any Mozart score will confirm he rarely if ever placed dynamics in a vocal part, perhaps because he instinctively understood the difference between mechanical dynamics and true emotive responses. He personally worked with most of the singers he wrote for, and may have considered the articulation of such detail in a score as superfluous. Luciano Berio in the 1960s (e.g. in *Sequenza III*) began to write suggestions of moods into his vocal scores using adjectives and phrases, such as "tense," "nervous," "giddy," or "distant and dreamy," rather than dynamics. The difference with Berio is that they may seem like an annotation to the text rather than demonstrating the symbiosis of emotion and musical tone *through* text.

A generation has passed since Lucie Manén's book was first published, and it is not an unfair generalization to say that today many composers and singers live in different and isolated worlds. For the majority of today's professional opera singers, the most common or best composer is a dead composer; for many composers today, the ideal female sound may be a boy soprano. Given the abundance of alternatives developed over more than a millennium this seems at best restrictive and at worst unhealthy. It is certainly evidence that any idea of "progress" for the art is only temporal rather than qualitative. A living composer for many singers is a threat from beyond their area of skills and experience, where their own competence or perhaps the composer's incompetence, will be cruelly exposed. On the other hand, many singers who do take the plunge and work with living composers may discover a degree of creative freedom rarely attainable in traditional repertoire. Nonetheless, for many composers the world and psyche of the singer is the subject of jokes and mythology: stories of outsized egos and backsides are apocryphal if not mythological, and subject to much general bemusement. Some of the reasons for this "singism" are explored in later chapters.

In the seventeenth century, when opera was in one of its eras of irrepressible growth, a composer could not begin his opera until he knew precisely which singers would be singing it, because he was expected to mold his music to exhibit the individual strengths of the performers so that each might be heard to the best possible advantage. The public evidently clamored for their star singers, and the composer's role was to serve an appropriate dish. This ability to feature the special skills of the singers, while minimizing any technical weaknesses, was considered a great virtue in a composer, and was a natural progression from the baroque practice of allowing singers to embellish their *Da Capo* arias, allowing singers some decorative autonomy.

It was not until Verdi's *Macbeth* (1847) that composers began to fill their scores with more and more details in an attempt to amplify the composer's dramatic conception. Yet, just twelve years separate this new development from Donizetti's *Lucia di Lammermoor* (1835), which is an example of a singer's musical autonomy (see Chapter 5). By the twentieth century, it is not so unusual to find composers insisting that there should be no difference between two performances of the same work by different artists, denying even any interpretive autonomy. This is the antithesis of the tradition of composers providing music as a vehicle for virtuoso display, which seems a long way from the current expectations of some composers. The quest for the score as a masterpiece seems to be the sole remaining romantic inheritance for many composers, and perhaps the hardest to break with. As a consequence composers often over-compose, leaving less and less room for interpretation. The question of whether a score represents the end of the process of composition, or whether a performance does so more completely, is a point of academic discussion. The aware composer will at least provide his own answer by the nature of the score, and the singer will then better be able to judge what is required.

Despite the cyclical rifts between composers and singers (and conductors), there are many recent and notable exceptions of collaborations among composers and singers: The creatively rich relationship between Luciano Berio and Cathy Berberian was echoed in the rich dramatic collaborations between Samuel Beckett and Billy Whitelaw. Other important examples include Benjamin Britten and Peter Pears; Johnny Dankworth and Cleo Laine; Gian-Carlo Menotti and Marie Powers; and Samuel Barber and Leontyne Price. There are many others as well as many composers today who use their own voices in their work: Trevor Wishart, Meredith Monk, Daryl Runswick, as well as more famous examples in popular music such as Paul McCartney and Joan Armatrading. But these remained exceptional among composers in the last century whereas in preceding centuries it was the norm: Monteverdi, Mozart, Schubert, Puccini, Verdi, Richard Strauss, Mahler, and many more created lifelong relationships with certain singers, working alongside them in concert, theater, and opera companies. Moreover, the musical education of many of these composers was at some fundamental level involved with themselves being able to sing—not necessarily to a concert standard, but by way of internalizing musical thought and sound. William Byrd for one wrote famously about the supreme importance of the voice: "Since singing is so good a thing, I wish all men would learne to sing" (Byrd, 1543–1623). In the last century, Wagner's career was in part devoted to discovering and unleashing a unique and superhuman voice, to communicate his unique vision of "Gesamtkünstwerk," which translates literally as "collective art work." It was clear to him where the greatest potential for musical communication lay: "The oldest, truest, most beautiful organ of music, the origin to which alone our music owes its being, is the human voice" (Goldman & Sprinchorn, 1970).

For the majority of these classical composers, the voice was a supreme vehicle of expression, and they spent many years in the study of its techniques, not through books but through daily acquaintance. They put such an emphasis on the voice because they knew that, for most people, to relate to a voice might be easier than to relate to an instrument. The instrumental concert, in which people pay to sit in silence to abstract instrumental music, has only been with us about 350 years. The first public opera house opened slightly earlier. That is a blink of the eye compared to the evolution of song and the voice. Charles Darwin (1871) articulated this point from a scientific point of view: "Human song is generally admitted to be the basis or origin of instrumental music. As neither the enjoyment nor the capacity of producing musical notes are faculties of the least use to man in reference to his daily habits of life, they must be ranked among the most mysterious with which he is endowed." Vocal music dominates everywhere: over 90 percent of popular music is essentially vocal, and similar high figures apply to ethnic or folk music.

Moreover, there is historical justification for seeing an understanding of the voice as a key to learning about other instruments: that is what all composers of the past have done. However, in earlier eras, there was some basis of agreement, forever evolving and reforming, about the basis of musical style (at least nationally or geographically) and an understanding of the changing fashions of singing along with certain vocal expectations. In our global society, a visit to any CD store will confirm the extraordinary availability of music of the last millennium across many cultures. In our hunger for merchandising human culture, the line of development for the new has been splintered into a minority group, and singers are similarly able to specialize into any historical or geographical niche. The universality of music as a fundamental means of human expression has never been more evident, and the voice has always been the primary vehicle. However, the plurality of means of that expression has never been more diffuse.

The paradox is that despite the commonality of the human voice, and 200 years of scientific exploration by laryngologists, there are still many mysteries about the physical apparatus that endows a voice with potential and the distinguishing factors that produce greatness. Perhaps the situation is not so far removed from the almost mythical status of string instruments by Stradivarius and Amati, which also seem to defy modern scientific analysis and reproduction. Bunch (1997) notes, "Because singing is a common musical outlet, the complexities of the vocal mechanism and the high degree of coordination and the amount of energy necessary for artistic performance are often overlooked, taken for granted, or not understood."

Twentieth-century fashions and trends have inevitably broke with many traditions, and resulted in composers finding themselves beached on instrumental islands without appropriate voices to write for, and even unable to sing for themselves. Frank J. Oteri's interchange with composer John Adams, published in the *New York Times* (2001), is revealing in this respect:

> OTERI: You've written a lot of vocal music, three evening-length music theater works, the two operas and Ceiling/Sky, Harmonium for chorus and orchestra, The Wound-Dresser, and now El Niño.
> ADAMS: And I don't know how to sing. I can't carry a tune. It's true!

Many composers may well feel that their instinct is good enough, but Adams's comment is evidence of a seismic shift in the experience and objectives of many composers. How and why this has occurred might help clarify the function and reality of what it is to be a composer—or a singer—today.

How We Got Here

The voice was once the instrument to which all others aspired. The Renaissance, through the eyes of the church, saw the voice as perfection and so began the development of modern instruments to emulate one or other of its aspects. For instance, the string instrument's ability to blend emulated a choral sound, and the recorder or later flute emulated the purity of a boy soprano. For Vaughan Williams (1934), the voice remained at once primeval and sophisticated, a singular representation of a stable force of identity and communication in an ever-evolving species: "The human voice is the oldest musical instrument and through the age it remains what it was, unchanged; the most primitive and at the same time the most modern, because it is the most intimate form of human expression."

The orchestral sound created by Vaughan Williams in his famous *Fantasia on a Theme of Thomas Tallis* owed more than just the theme to his composer-ancestor. In that famous work, he invokes the choral-cathedral ambience that was the daily norm for composers for more than a thousand years, even before Ambrose and Gregory began collecting and collating the disparate chants of the early Christian era. When Minnie Ripperton sang those extraordinary phrases in "Loving You" (circa 1975), she might not have had Gregorio's Miserere as a conscious reference point, but the soaring top C in the solo part of the earlier work had left its indelible mark on dozens of generations in the intervening years, in spite—or perhaps because of—the Catholic Church in Mozart's day, which jealously prohibited copying or performance of the work outside of the Vatican (see Example 1.2). "Loving You" echoes the Miserere with spine-tingling scale of six notes down from the G "in alt," (G7), starting a tone higher than the highest in Mozart's famous "Queen of the Night" aria, in *Die Zauberflöte* (see Example 2.8). However it

Example 1.2.   Gregorio Allegri: *Miserere Mei.*

changes its form, the music of the past seems to reverberate in the present and will doubtless continue to do so in the future.

Singing was once the foundation of a musical education, and thanks to theoreticians such as Boethius, continued to be so for at least a millennia. As the importance of the symphony orchestra grew, slowly and subtly, the emphasis for many composers shifted. Some, like Schubert, Wagner, and Mahler, still held the voice supreme, and later composers, such as Bartók and Janáček, developed their music from a study of their native spoken language and folk songs. The line of development between music and language has always been symbiotic, as was noted by Eisenstein (1946): "Intonation, i.e., the 'melody of speech,' is the foundation of music."

But by the early twentieth century many classical composers began to see the orchestra as the supreme test of their creative ability. The advent of electronic and digital tools has given them even more options. Popular music has itself undergone a revolution: the sung voice has always been the main vehicle for the most popular music, but I suspect a lower ratio of people today have heard the unamplified human voice in song than at any time in history. As a result, audiences expect voices to be loud, even when whispered, and opera companies try to satisfy this demand by emphasizing volume above vocal quality, or by introducing amplification. The paradox is that there are many popular singers sustaining careers today with tiny voices who would not have been able to succeed in a purely acoustic era. Steve Reich has gone on record as stating that he would not consider working with an unamplified voice. On top of this confusion over volume, the contemporary vocalist is confronted with more technical demands than ever before and an ever-increasing list of stylistic and generic categories to absorb and respond to.

Despite this confusion of means and objectives, the voice remains the *sine qua non* of music. Even inside the most arcane areas of contemporary music, the voice appears and seems to emphasize its own preeminence. Two acknowledged masterpieces of *musique concrète*, Stockhausen's *Gesang der Jünglinge* from the 1950s and Jonathan Harvey's *Mortuos Plango, Vivos Voco* (1980–99), gain much of their communicative power not through the manipulation of ring modulators or through the concept of spectrum analysis, but through the deliberate and calculated contrast with technology of the voice of a boy soprano. Of Stockhausen's *Gesang der Jünglinge,* Steve Reich (*The Wire,* March 1991) said: ". . . But what makes the piece great is the Jünglinge—the kid's voice. That's what makes the piece vibrant, not the electronic oscillators."

Despite the emphasis on the voice in today's music, the proportion of time students spend dealing with vocal matters has perhaps never been less. This reversal of historical trends is encapsulated in today's higher-education system. Few serious music students or composers I have encountered in any country have ever been given even an option to study how to write for the voice as a part of a music degree. Orchestration and music technology are "de rigueur," but the voice is largely left in the dark and singers are sequestered safely into their own department away from any risk of contamination with instrumentalists, let alone composers. This system implies to young composers that the voice is not worthy of serious curriculum study.

Moreover when a composer does seek out a singer in an institution, they will often find the singer totally immersed in a nineteenth-century technique, or even earlier, and deaf to the possibility of other cultural or historical criteria. Those singers who embrace a more contemporary vision may not be taken seriously by the prevalent opera culture, which still often remains the core source of income for a career classical singer.

Academics tacitly support the rift: twentieth-century musical analysis is dominated by systems that concentrate entirely on instrumental music. The systematic analyses of Schenker and Reti, the psychological analysis of Meyer, and the "set-theory" analysis of Forte concern themselves almost entirely with instrumental music. The synthesis of words and music with the voice is largely left alone, perhaps because it is too complicated. At best this suggests to students that music for the voice is not to be taken so seriously, from any academic point of view. In my own education at the university, I heard proposed more than once the idea that the addition of words "cheapens" music in its structural purity, inferring that it is not worth a serious composer's attention.

In the following chapters, I hope to open a window into the means by which a composer can utilize the most primeval medium, at the same time savage and sophisticated, of the human voice.

2
How the Voice Works: A Composer's Perspective

To speak of the voice as a complex instrument is an understatement. Cornelius L. Reid (1965) makes the interesting point that the best school of voice occurred at a time before the physiological aspects became visible scientifically and began to be explored. It was in 1855 when Manuel Garcia II, a famous singer turned voice teacher, rigged a set of mirrors and a light source into something he called a "laryngoscope." It allowed the observation, for the first time in history, of the functioning of the vocal cords in a living subject and marked the beginning of vocal science. The scientific approach to vocal production has provoked much debate among singers and teachers, because, while later scientific developments have provided valuable insight into how the sound is produced, the information is of less practical use for a singer, because the mechanism of the larynx is not under volitional control.

The most lucid summary I have encountered is by Kurt Adler (1965), a great coach and accompanist, who describes the working principle of every musical instrument, including the voice, in three parts:

1. *The Energizer:* physical source of power; in the voice it is the respiratory system.
2. *The Vibrator:* turns energy into sound waves; in the voice it is the vocal cords contained by the larynx.
3. *The Resonator:* amplifies and modifies the sonority or timbre; in the voice it is mainly the shape of the mouth and throat, the head sinuses and cavities, and ideally most of the body.

The acquisition and application of muscular control skills in all of these areas provide the basis of any singing voice. To acquire these skills is not a simple thing in itself because, uniquely, the physical structure of the voice continues to change with the body it inhabits throughout life. Moreover, the mastery of these skills does not in itself produce a singer, which requires less tangible and perhaps less teachable assets, that might be termed psychological disposition, presence, personality, and ego combined with probably an inordinate amount of single-mindedness, stubbornness, and commitment.

Uniquely, the voice is a dual-purpose instrument, and any scientific study of its function must take into consideration both its ability to sustain tone, as any other instrument does, and produce the sounds we associate with words. The singer's training is naturally divided between these two functions, and most disagreements with regard to teachers and audiences may be ultimately traced back to a predilection or preference for one over the other.

The quantity of air required to sing is often greater than that required for speech. Moreover, because the act of breathing is an automatic function, a singer must master effective control and understanding of the breathing apparatus until the methodology is internalized, and any bad habits eradicated. The act of breathing causes the diaphragm (a muscular partition between the upper and lower bodies) to descend and the ribs to expand providing a space to be filled by the expanded lungs. There are three breathing techniques. *Clavicular* breathing, whereby the upper parts of the chest are raised while the diaphragm is drawn in, is detrimental to any singing technique. *Abdominal* (sometimes called diaphragmatic) breathing takes place when expanding the lower area of the lungs, while the chest remains passive and the lower ribs are without perceptible movement. Although the technique is acceptable for less demanding music, it is limited in its efficiency as regards the building and sustaining of pressure in high phrases. The name *Intercostal* breathing implicates the active use of the ribs. With this technique the breathing apparatus expands to utilize its fullest resources and receives assistance through an outward movement of the lower ribs. This movement fills the lungs to capacity. The effect of Intercostal breathing is to create a feeling of expansion around the entire middle of the body, including the small of the back and sides, as well as the abdominal wall. The distinction between Abdominal and Intercostal breathing is of crucial importance in the breathing out, control of force (which produces variations of dynamics), and steadiness (or the avoidance of tremolo). Typically in action, a singer may breathe in very fast and breathe out very slowly, developing an extremely athletic musculature that permits these actions.

The air is passed from the lungs to the "vocal cords," in fact two strips of cartilage, about one half inch across (less in women), which may be vibrated together. They are enclosed inside a fleshy box, which projects forward from the neck of men, often called the "Adam's Apple." A singer may control the tension of the cords to affect any pitch within the physical compass.

The upper part of the throat, along with the mouth and the nose, act as sounding boxes to amplify, color, and enrich these vibrations. In its most relaxed state, the uninterrupted passage of air through vibrating cords produces a long vowel sound somewhere between "A" and "O." Through the intervention of tongue, teeth, and lips, this sound may be modified to produce a change of vowel or a consonant. Many teachers credit the sinuses and cavities with an additional propensity to enrich vibration, although some scientific experiments do not support this belief.

One of the problems facing a singing teacher is that the instrument lies hidden within the player, and many of its functions are nonvolitional. This may account in part for the many uses of imagery and psychological suggestion that different teachers use to activate the person-instrument. This in turn has given rise to a large body of myths and stories about singing teachers, which the advent of the scientific approach has failed to dissuade.

For those interested in more detailed physiological explanations in the working of the voice, the bibliography offers a selection of excellent books that deal with the matter in the detail it deserves; for instance, Husler and Rodd-Marling (1976) and Bunch (1982) amply repay serious study.

The Break

"The voice" is a conceptual contradiction, except as an abstract idea: it signifies not one instrument but many. Before the current generic division of voices into the five main categories of soprano, contralto, tenor, baritone, and bass, each voice has been itself divided many times. The tenor voice alone, during the nineteenth century, was further refined as to type with the following definitions: eroico; drammatico; di forza; robusto; lirico spinto; lirico; di grazia; di mezzo carattere; leggiero; and tenorino.

Even an individual's voice is rarely one instrument. Many see the voice as naturally divided into three different registers of chest, middle, and head. The training of a voice, to a large extent, is the attempt to create the same strength and smoothness of tone throughout these registers. This was one basis for the development of the Bel Canto school. There are many exceptions: in the popular form of singing, often cruelly termed "Can Belto," typically a female singer has the extraordinary ability to produce the punchy, earthy bottom sound up through the range. Like the Italian tenor "sound," it is open to abuse, but is often impressive and powerful, as any fan of Shirley Bassey or Whitney Houston understands instinctively.

The concept of vocal registers perhaps needs further explanation. When a typically inexperienced singer sings up a scale, there are one or frequently two areas where the voice breaks, after which the voice continues with a

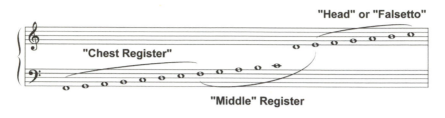

Example 2.1. Vocal Registers.

different quality. The objective of much singing technique is to smooth out these breaks and effect seamless transitions between the three areas, which have been termed "registers." The same function occurs in both female and male voices, however the male falsetto is distinct in its quality and maintains its own identity and character as an extension to the lower registers, typically for high "floated" notes. The falsetto male range attains power mainly in the male alto or countertenor voice; the distinction between these two names is predominantly historical in origin.

Example 2.1 illustrates a typical, or better, *average* dispensation of the registers in a bass-baritone voice. An octave higher might represent the female soprano version. Individual voices always vary according to the placing of the middle register as well as the extremes.

For a description of the functioning of the registers, it would be difficult to be more precise than Nadoleczny (1937):

> The concept of register is understood to be a series of consecutive, similar vocal tones, which the musically trained can differentiate at specific places from another adjoining series of likewise internally similar tones. Its homogenous sound depends on a definite, invariable behaviour of the harmonics. These rows of tones correspond to definite objectively and subjectively perceptible vibration regions on the head, neck, and chest. The position of the larynx changes more in a natural singer during the transition from one series of tones to another than in a well-trained singer. The registers are caused by a definite mechanism (belonging to that register) of tone production (vocal fold vibration, glottal shape, air consumption), which allows for a gradual transition however from one into an adjoining register. A number of these tones can actually be produced in two overlapping registers. But not always with the same intensity.

Cornelius Reid (1975) offers a shorter, more compact version:

> As a vibrator of a given length and thickness cannot tolerate excessive tension and responds by breaking so, too, the voice will break off and crack when the chest register ... is forced too high. When such a break occurs the distinctive tone quality which suddenly appears is that homogenous quality recognized as a falsetto.

Singers have named the three registers according to the subjective sensations they produce. The lower register produces a feeling of vibration in the chest and lower neck and is termed the "chest" register. The upper register is termed the "head" in the female and the "falsetto" in the male, because the vibrations are sensed high in the head. The "middle" register is sometimes termed "mixed," containing vibrations akin to both areas. Many years of research in the area has led to many vexed disputes over terminology and its semantic relevance, but these details are now generally accepted.

In certain techniques the break between registers is exploited for effect. The Swiss yodel is an extreme example, as is the abused cliché prominent in much popular song, where the interval of the break is minimized to emulate a theatrical sob interpolated into the legato line. With a little effort, most singers can learn to emulate this device even in pitch areas where there is no natural break. (More on this technique is discussed in Chapter 5, in relation to Dolly Parton's song, "I will always love you," made famous by Whitney Houston.)

Vocal Categories

The average ranges of the 8 principal voice types are shown in Figure 1. (Appendix 1 should be referred to for more detail of voice types and examples from operatic roles.)

Although this remains the basic guide agreed on by most textbooks, like most generalizations it does not transfer easily into individual voice types. First, the untrained voice usually cannot be allotted a category based on its range or sound. Second, that there is more overlapping between voice types than Figure 1 suggests the following: high sopranos may well display notes below those of a contralto, some of whom may have cultivated an extension to allow them to sing high soprano notes. The same is applicable to male voices. The composer writing for a specific singer is best advised to ask about range, and not simply refer to a diagram such as this. The composer writing for a choir should not assume that sectional ranges are as extended as for individual solo voice types.

Rather than range, it is the characteristic sound or timbre of a voice that will suggest its category. The rich upper harmonics of the tenor voice display a quality easily distinguishable from the baritone in the same range; consequently their music is transposed one octave higher on the page. Husler and Rodd-Marling (1976) make the important distinction between the sound character of a voice formed by the processes in the larynx, which is not to be confused with the vocal quality, which is determined by the proportions of the vocal folds.

Another factor in determining category is where the middle or gravitational center of a voice lies. When a singer peruses a score, the tessitura

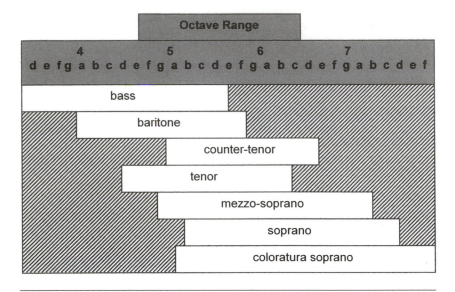

Figure 1. Categories of Voice.

of the music, where the majority of the notes lie, is just as important—or even more so—than the occasional extremes. The mezzo-soprano voice for instance may, with some Rossini and Verdi roles, be almost indistinguishable in terms of range from the soprano range (see Figure 1). The central range of the mezzo may be only two or three notes below the soprano range, but the general tone color may be significantly warmer or darker. The countertenor voice is generally found in a well-developed falsetto extension to the baritone voice. It is unique in its exclusive use of a single register, although the accessibility of baritone notes compliments the richness of the timbre. Coloratura sopranos often have access to their chest register, whereas some sopranos may not, although this is by no means predictable.

It is also worth pointing out that Figure 1 does not represent nature's rather more individual approach to vocal elasticity, which allows some voices to traverse across many of the vocal categories. Therefore, these vocal divisions should be taken merely as rationalizations.

Although there exist a multitude of subdivisions for each voice, the primary division acknowledged by singers is whether the voice is lyric or dramatic by nature. A lyric voice generally is best at agility and flexibility of line, whereas a dramatic voice carries a higher degree of intensity or weight, often at the expense of agility. The structure (width and length) of the vocal cords are said to be directly responsible for this distinction, in the degree of tension they produce and the measure of activity in the breathing organ.

Legato and Leaps

The legato line is the other major obsession in training a voice. Derived from Gregorian chant, through Palestrina, perfected by the Bel Canto school and through Puccini into Frank Sinatra, the vehicle for emotional expression is considered to be the vowel, and an uninterrupted continuation its most concentrated and powerful exploitation. The challenge appears when clear articulation is an equal goal. In Italian, there are seven vowels (see Kurt Adler's [1965] book for an explanation), and the consonants remain largely unmodified, so the singer's job may seem more simple than in English or French, where there are several variations in sound of the vowel written as "e" and many compound vowels or diphthongs. In music where line is the goal, a singer will often rehearse each phrase "purely" with vowels only. The consonants will be practiced by "dropping them in" over the same line, consciously minimizing any interruption of the voiced vowels, or the flow of air.

One of the most revolutionary of composers in vocal development was Mozart. His achievements would have been more widely acknowledged had he thought it to write or publish his theories, but unlike Wagner, he concentrated on his craft itself. Before Mozart, many composers nurtured the line for singers by moving in relatively small steps within one register, always enclosing any slightly large interval by movement in the opposite direction both before and after. Mozart's instincts and close association with singers (comparable in intimacy to Haydn's profound knowledge of his orchestra) led him to exploit enormous leaps, often between extreme registers. In all cases, the security of the harmony produces a clear target for the singer, whose vocal cords must change shape in an instant. Imagine a car suddenly moving between first and fourth gears to realize the athleticism required. The effect is both dramatic and exhilarating.

Example 2.2, "Come Scoglio," sung by the character Fiordiligi in Mozart's *Cosi fan Tutte,* gives an example of this technique. Mme Ferraresi del Bene was the original Fiordiligi in Vienna, and it is said that this aria was partly inspired by Mozart's animosity toward her (Hughes 1972). It is a parody in homage to the ostentatious display aria, and the effect is comic. Fiordiligi professes to be "as solid as a rock" in her feelings, and expresses outrage at Dorabella's suggestion that she may someday feel differently. Her vehement denial in this aria serves as a prelude to her change of heart later on, in advance

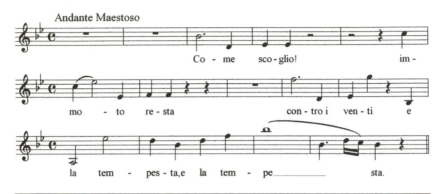

Example 2.2. Mozart: *Cosi fan Tutte: Come Scoglio* (Fiordiligi).

of Dorabella's own flip-flop. Fiordiligi's position is regal; she professes to be unassailable. Her U-turn is the very stuff of high comedy, although she remains deadly serious in her formidable character.

Despite its difficulty, this passage demonstrates an innate understanding of vocal technique allied to dramatic characterization. Despite the athletic leaps, disconnectivity is not the objective in this music. However, the singer's job may often be to connect the apparently disconnected, and in Mozart the underlying harmony and phrasing gives a sense of direction, allowing difficult leaps to be taken "downhill." The difficulty for the singer is the required precision of pitch changes across registers, while maintaining the same tone color and legato. This requires tremendous stamina and control.

Technically, the compositional tool used behind these leaps is simple: extending the melodic intervals by an octave maintains the lyric quality but emphasizes the drama. Virtuoso leaps are a trademark of much of Mozart's writing for sopranos, even beyond obvious opera examples, for example in the *C Minor Mass* and many of the concert arias. They also appear in many of his instrumental works, for example the clarinet concerto and slow movement of his piano concerto K466. The theory behind this technique of jumping between registers was first expounded in the Bel Canto school, as described by Lucie Manén (1974, 11): "For describing events with little emotional content and in a neutral mood, the human voice uses exclamations in its lower range. As soon as the individual changes the emphasis of what he speaks or sings, the pitch of the voice changes. It rises with increasing emotional content." Abrupt changes of range then suggest abrupt changes of emotion, which here translate as an incisive insight into the irony of Fiordiligi's words, belying her unstable feelings.

Example 2.3. Wagner: *Die Walküre:* "Brünhilde's Battle Cry."

These vocal leaps became an obsession with succeeding composers, such as Wagner and Strauss, in turn leading to the German Expressionism of Schoenberg and his disciples. In Example 2.3, "Brünhilde's Battle Cry" from Wagner's *Die Walküre*, the leaps that bestride an octave have a very different effect than those found in Mozart. They create the effect of a superhuman cry proclaiming Brünhilde's power, designed to inspire her listeners with awe. Although this part requires a very different sort of singer from the one who would tackle Fiordiligi, from the singer's point of view the difficulties encountered are the same, and require similar athleticism and control across her registers, and the same, serious, deadpan delivery. Nonetheless, the effects of the two examples are at either end of the scale of comedy and tragedy.

Strauss's *Four Last Songs* sum up a lifelong adoration of the soprano voice (see Example 2.4). On the page it might seem to resemble Bellini in its floridness, but the speed is Andante, and a full romantic orchestra supports this extraordinary fluid line. Unlike Examples 2.2 and 2.3, here the leaps are astonishingly beautiful and mesmerizing in their effect. Whereas Fiordiligi and Brünhilde might flaunt their virtuosity, the singer of this song must make it sound fluent and easy to the listener, apparently denying its undeniable difficulty.

Writing in 1963, Victor Fuchs (1985, 156) defined the term "modern music" correctly as relative rather than stylistic. He wrote that as a young man he sang songs by Richard Strauss for the composer himself. In this context his ensuing warning of the dangers of so-called "modern music" seems paradoxical, but his words still convey the real fear felt by many

Example 2.4. Strauss: *Four Last Songs; Beim Schlafengehen* © 1950 by Boosey & Co., Ltd. Complete Edition 1959. Reprinted with Permission.

singers and teachers with regard to the unknown: ". . . in tackling modern music, a singer jeopardizes his tone and his legato."

Fuchs is certainly not alone in his concern for vocal health, and the risks involved in singing non-legato are also emphasized by the eminent laryngologist Norman Punt (1967, 54):

> Singing legato (that is smoothly, without breaks, flowing) is much less harmful to the larynx than staccato methods, which should therefore be avoided except when the score compels. One has heard staccato passages which represented a series of glottic shocks. So-called coloratura sopranos are frequent offenders.

These two quotations shed some light on the confusion that abounds over the responsibility for vocal health. Whereas Fuchs implies that composers, in their cavalier disregard for the "natural" act of singing, ask for dangerous (unspecified) vocal actions, Punt is merely admonishing the specific technique of using the *Coup de Glotte* to attack notes. Above the vocal cords are two membranes called the False Vocal Cords, which may be used to begin a sound "explosively," in an action somewhat similar to a cough. Although the technique has been used in the past by many fine singers, it is largely discredited now and is responsible for some vocal injury.

It seems sometimes that composers are blamed with their "modern music" for a great number of crimes against singers. The question of whether a composer's conviction to his or her vision is of more or less value than a

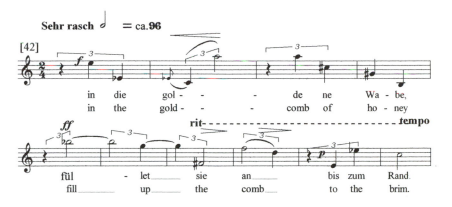

Example 2.5. Webern: *Drei Lieder,* Op. 25, No. 3. Copyright 1956 by Universal Edition. A. G. Wien. Copyright renewed, All Rights Reserved. Used by Permission of European American Music Distributors. LLC, sole US and Canadian agent for Universal Edition A. G., Wien.

singer's conviction to their art perhaps should be articulated. Patently the answer remains subjectively the property of the questioner. To a great extent, singers and composers depend on each other, and if more composers made it their business to understand singers, perhaps more singers might return the compliment. Contemporary (classical) composers are unique as a profession, in that all their major competitors are advantageously dead. The living composer in that field is a minority, and therefore suspect; too easy a prey for teachers and singers insufficiently technically equipped.

Example 2.5 by Webern may appear at first as an extreme case, potentially challenging the singer in its leaps between registers, speed, and apparent atonality. However, the excerpt needs contextualizing in the song and within the cycle, and perhaps within the vocal tradition from Mozart: the phrase provides the climax of the last of three short songs; the poem is an exultant paean to love and fertility, as close to unrestrained ecstasy as anything in Webern, and here the leaps of register reflect both the extreme and volatile emotions exposed and analyzed in the earlier excerpt from Mozart (Example 2.2). The line owes more to the Bel Canto tradition than the avant-garde: emotionally the difficulty is climactic and textually justifiable, and once mastered, the line dances with an infectious energy. Even the intervals, which are essentially major and minor sevenths with minor thirds, demonstrate an internal logic, that may, with a little practice, become almost instinctive. Without minimizing the skill and imagination needed to perform this passage, it is too easy to forget how sheerly daunting the difficulties of Fiordiligi (in Mozart's *Cosi fan Tutte*) and Zerbinetta (in Strauss's *Ariadne auf Naxos*) are, for instance, to singers embarking on the roles for the first time.

The middle of the twentieth century was a time of wild experimentation and even Dionysian enjoyment, creatively, and many composers felt an urge to create their own personal language without recourse to tradition or models. Today's composer lives in a different world, perhaps a more conservative one, where the ostensible norm of cultural shock for succeeding audience generations has been replaced by apathy. However, the myth of the dreaded modern music composer lives on in the minds and hearts of many teachers and singers today.

Then again, perhaps the fear of the new is a normal part of all aesthetic evolution. Mathilde Marchesi (1821–1913) was a teacher of Nellie Melba (1861–1931) and other international star singers of the time, and she wrote positively of "modern music," admonishing the fear prevalent in her own time:

> It is argued, that because modern vocal music consists of long and declaimed phrases, without florid passages or embellishments, it is unnecessary (so it is said) for the singer to cultivate the mechanism of the voice, as it tires the vocal organs and causes loss of time to the pupil. As regards the fatigue of the vocal organs caused by practice, that depends entirely on the ability of the professor and the intelligent docility of the pupil. As to all that concerns the technical requirements of the long and declaimed phrases of modern vocal music, the true facts are quite at variance with these statements (Marchesi 1970).

Air and Breath

This is perhaps the most hotly debated aspect of voice production that has produced a plethora of diverse opinions. Fuchs (1985, 73) notes: "Opinions on breathing differ more widely than on any other topic in singing, which is itself the most controversial branch of music study." Reid (1965, 160) expands on this point:

> No single phase of singing has received more attention from theorists than the subject of breathing. There are those who believe control of the breath is the cornerstone upon which a correct technique is founded; there is a second group equally vehement in declaring control of the breath to be a damaging practice functionally; and yet another school of thought holding that it does neither good nor harm.

So it seems breath control may be essential, harmful, or irrelevant to voice production! The theorists agree to disagree in this fundamental area. If singers and teachers cannot find a common viewpoint, how is the composer to understand the choices involved in writing for a voice?

Most writers appear to agree, at least, with the idea that the voice may be classed as a wind instrument. Manén (1974, 12) summarizes the prevailing view:

> The human voice can be classed as a wind instrument. The basic sound is produced at the level of the larynx, and has a rich spectrum of harmonics. The basic sound is then filtered or reinforced by the larynx, the pharynx, the mouth, and the nasal passages. This action intensifies some harmonics by resonance; other harmonics are silenced according to the acoustical condition of the filters.

Fundamentally, a singer needs to breathe, of course. The "how" of breathing may be left to the individual or teacher, but the "where" may be a compositional concern. As with any wind instrument, a low note needs more breath to articulate than a high one. The fissure between the vocal cords on a high note is greatly reduced compared to the lowest notes, and this is of course amplified through all the voice types. High voices can typically sing longer phrases than low voices for this reason. However, the velocity of air passed through the gap creates the effect of volume or intensity, and obviously affects the need to replenish breath; a loud phrase may not be sustained for the same duration as the same phrase sung softly.

The efficiency of the singer's breathing does not necessarily reflect on the quality of the voice, but rather on its functionality with regard to flexibility, expressivity, and color. The oboe, for example, is uniquely efficient in its demands of breath control among wind instruments. Only a small volume of air is required to vibrate the double-reed instrument, enclosed completely by the embouchure. The lips of a flautist, by comparison, barely touch the mouthpiece, and the breath may be released equally freely. The oboist has as great a need to release breath away from the instrument as to inhale. Different sorts of singers and sound productions relate to different ways of managing air. It is not a requirement for all singers today to always produce the most "pure," classical sound. There are occasions or even styles in which a certain breathiness or huskiness will communicate more directly, as in close-miked music such as with Bing Crosby and Simon and Garfunkel. On a more subtle level, colors of the voice may also be managed with control of the breath. Understandably, there are singers whose personality and training have maintained their path exclusively in pursuit of the pure vowel sound, one aspect of the Bel Canto school. Such a singer may be ill-advised to tackle pieces such as Schoenberg's *Pierrot Lunaire,* unless she is willing to explore a new world of technique. Indeed, the actress for whom Schoenberg wrote that score was not a classically trained singer, and for her, it may be assumed, communication through text and voice could happily circumvent the entire tradition of Bel Canto.

The problem with voices, as regards a composer, is that the current nomenclature for categorizing voices has remained largely unchanged for too long. One of the most radical changes, historically, was the creation of the mezzo-soprano, sometime after Mozart. When a composer writes for a violin, for example, s/he generally can be sure of certain basic parameters of the instrument. However, the word soprano has become so all encompassing as to be merely an average, as impossible as the proverbial "two-and-a-half children." Although the word was perfectly adequate for Mozart, within his defined era and style, the reality of an "average" soprano simply does not exist today. Instead they come with other handles, identified by their association with composers (Rossinian, Wagnerian, Handelian), styles (baroque, folk, or contemporary), or within their "Fach"—by now a fairly arbitrary categorization of voices and character types created in Germany in the last century, at a time when opera houses really were factories, producing to an inexhaustible demand. Every succeeding generation of composers has asked ever more of singers, while the systemic thinking of the "Fach," based on old repertoire, has remained largely unchanged.

The demands on performers have increased relentlessly. Singers in earlier eras could create a career out of a repertoire of music by living or recently living composers, whereas this would be most unusual for the student today fresh from their years of training. Moreover, it is hardly unusual for singers currently to be able to cross what were once stylistic barriers. Jazz, popular songs, improvisation, operas, and recitals, as well as acting itself, are all potential areas for work for singers, with or without microphones, and many are able to move freely from one area to another, with the required adaptation of vocal control and color.

The composer who writes for a soprano is perhaps doing the equivalent of writing a concerto for a wind instrument; there are so many more decisions left to be made! It is a dangerous path to tread, although not necessarily without successful precedents. When Ligeti wrote his score, *Aventures,* he admits he was young and idealistic. The difficulties of the score were so great that the biggest problem at the time was trying to find singers willing to tackle them. Similarly, the Feldman opera *Neither* (see Chapter 1) was, to my knowledge, not recorded in his lifetime. Both these composers wrote without a singer as a model in their mind, but both have since found numerous performances by a new generation of singers, better equipped to take the difficulties in stride, in the same way that the famous solo bassoon opening of Stravinsky's *Rite of Spring,* which was once considered all but unplayable, has since become expected from every orchestral player.

The composer who plans every breath for the singer denies the individual singer a characteristic idiosyncrasy, which, of course, may be intentional. Most good teachers, and audiences, might agree that if a singer breathes correctly, most audiences will not notice how many breaths are taken in a phrase, while all audiences will notice when a singer appears to be out of breath. Daryl Runswick's score for amplified soprano, *Lady Lazarus,* is among a small number of scores that stipulate that no breaths are to be taken by the singer except where marked. He uses the singer's breath, both ingressively and conventionally, to produce sound, and the amplification allows the smallest sounds to have an effect without concerns of volume and the concomitant stress. Many composers, such as Berio and Wishart in the last century, have exploited the effect of singing on the in-breath. For some singers it may be an exciting discovery, a new technique to add to their portfolio, whereas for others, the fear of the unknown and risk of damaging their instrument will prevent them from taking such a new path.

Dynamics

Mythically or historically, the high altar of the Bel Canto school was expression. Technically speaking, this meant that their singing was based on the use of exclamatory vowels to produce colorings appropriate to the mood or the emotion that the music and text were meant to express. Manén (1974, 11) explains, "For expressions of pleasure, the natural expression is 'ah.' The exclamation 'ee' denotes disgust and hatred, whilst 'oo' denotes fear and horror. These are the basic exclamatory vowels."

At least up to the eighteenth century, the vocal qualities most prized of a singer were (after accuracy), colors of tone, flexibility, and range. In contrast, careers of opera singers today are often literally sacrificed to the God of Volume; size is everything, and the pushing of the inadequately trained young voice toward this goal has led to many premature retirings, or worse. It is unclear when the shift in priorities took place. It may be assumed that Wagner was the first to push the limits in this respect, but this would seem to be a misunderstanding according to Viktor Fuchs (1985), whose words interestingly make a tangible and logical connection between the aims of the Bel Canto school and Wagner's own apparently revolutionary ideas:

> So many singers forget that in dramatic singing it is not the volume of voice that is decisive, but the skill in using one's energy. Cosima Wagner, Franz Liszt's daughter and wife of Richard Wagner, who for many years after his death educated the next generation of Wagnerian Singers, always declared: "The real strength is based not on force, but on expression." (107)

Jens Malte Fischer has challenged Cosima as a reliable guardian of her husband's practices and ideas on the voice, yet there may at least be room for debate here.

The demand for increased volume may have begun with architects and the building of the new public theaters such as La Scala in 1778. The crescendo became the focal point and climax for opera audiences with Rossini's thrilling and innovative use of it in *La Gazza Ladra,* and the high note became emphasized as the operatic climax of Beethoven's *Fidelio.* Verdi's demands for bigger orchestras and heavier scoring certainly continued the trend along with new open-air public arenas in the late nineteenth century, which continued into the twentieth century with the development of new technologies.

It is difficult to imagine the effect of the ever-growing orchestra on nineteenth century audiences, when the orchestra provided some of the loudest sounds heard by man, and it was inevitable that the demands of the human voice would grow in parallel. An orchestra today may seem tame to some in comparison to many rock concerts, and perhaps that is a contributing reason to a continuing decline in the orchestra's popularity. Meanwhile, for many singers the battle to sing in front of audiences of thousands has been won by technology, and an audience's animal need to manifest a sound as a tangible entity has long been democratically available to all, with the aid of a microphone. Amidst this revolution, the opera houses continue with their ancient nineteenth-century traditions, either as oases of "culture" or as anachronistic monoliths, depending on one's point of view, but they feel the need to compete with young audiences' expectations of volume. Perhaps the battle is a little absurd, or else has already been lost, but meanwhile there are sufficient numbers of inexperienced young singers to present themselves as willing sacrificial victims. The appetite of the God of Volume is insatiable.

Few voices are capable of truly dramatic changes in dynamics, equal say, to a trumpet. Furthermore, a "large" voice may be impossible to make smaller, if, as is often the case, it has been "designed" or "trained" solely to produce tones able to penetrate large auditoriums over massive orchestras. A "small" voice is by nature more agile, and may be able to define infinite gradations of subtle coloration as well as dynamics. For this reason the opera singer who can achieve magic in a song recital is a rare breed.

"Dynamics" is not a pure science, because everything depends on the context. Just as an orchestra more easily masks a fortissimo cello than a violin at mezzo forte, higher voices tend to penetrate further than lower ones. Pianists who accompany flutes learn quickly to adjust to the comparatively weak lower octave, and the same may be true with some voices. Questions of balance in orchestration and vocal matters require detailed analysis of each unique musical situation and some knowledge of models, as well as good instincts.

Mozart largely omitted dynamics for his vocal lines, placing them only in the orchestra. He also omitted crescendo and decrescendo markings. When he wrote a score, he expected to work and rehearse individually with the singer, so what need of writing such mechanical and abstract concepts as piano or forte? Perhaps, because of their shared culture and education, he largely trusted the instincts of singers, to this extent. Puccini, on the other hand, seems to have reversed this practice and painstakingly writes in every nuance of rubato as well as dynamics. He, too, worked personally with his singers, but if he trusted any of their instincts, it is not evident in the score. Perhaps, on one level, he was already aware of the dissolution of cultural norms, and was compelled to create a musical language that enabled him to define and control every detail and shade. Perhaps, too, their contrasting scores reflect changes in the publication market, in that the later composer was consciously writing for a publisher and performances on the world's stage.

However, both composers follow the ancient axiom of a rise in pitch indicating a crescendo and increase in tension, while a fall in pitch suggests a decrescendo and decrease of tension. Climaxes, where exploited, occur at the summit of rising phrases, and releases are descents from these summits. The whole of Samuel Barber's *Adagio for Strings* is the simplest demonstration of this vocal technique in instrumental form. It was originally written for string quartet, but the four individual players could arguably not always sustain the volume and intensity sufficiently at the extreme pitches in the climax, and the version for string orchestra is now most common. There is something to be learnt here about exploiting extremes of range, whether for voices or instruments.

When a composer writes against the axiom that a rise in pitch corresponds to an increase in emotion, it may be for a very special reason. The pianissimo, high "floating" note, is often a singer's magic moment when an entire audience may find their breath suspended. Although the effect can be applied to an infinite number of emotional situations, there is no denial of the axiom; rather we are reminded that some emotional responses are contained within us, precious and intimate, while others burst through in their need to be communicated.

In Mozart's *Die Zauberflöte*, Pamina sings *Ach ich fühl's* to Tamino's turned back. Tamino has sworn neither to speak nor to look at her, as his trial. Pamina does not know of this, and cannot understand his silence; she is heartbroken. She pleads to him in her aria, which becomes the testing moment of his trial. The phrase beginning at bar 14 is one of the most difficult and telling phrases Pamina sings (see Example 2.6). It requires great breath control to perform, even if a breath is taken, as it often is, before "mehr." The final rising phrase to the top B flat is repeated but at half speed; it is the moment at which Tamino would break his promise if he were going to. The more quiet the repeated rising phrase, the more difficult and the more expressive and telling. The writing is difficult in the extreme, but justifiable dramatically. It may take much more strength to

Example 2.6. Mozart: *Die Zauberflöte: Ach ich fühl's* (Pamina).

sing restrainedly than loudly, in many cases. The absence of words for the melisma does not denote mere decoration, but transcends the text as a supplication.

The internalising of extreme emotion became something of a stylistic fingerprint in French "Melodies." Example 2.7 presents two examples, one from Debussy and one from Fauré; the Debussy is coquettish and charming, while the Fauré hints at something more intimate and personal.

Both composers approach their climax with a typically French anticlimactic diminuendo, against the tradition of a rise in vocal pitch inferring a crescendo. Yet the emotional response of each composer is distinct and personal, appropriate to their view of the text.

Flexibility and Stamina

Vocal stamina is best understood in comparing a singer to an athlete. Both need to train their muscles to operate in a highly efficient way, and sustain their performance. The endurance of long performances and demanding vocal lines requires a highly tuned instrument allied with mental stamina. Any singer with any voice is required to develop stamina, which is too often confused with volume. Vocal flexibility may be understood in two ways: the ability to move along the spectrum of dynamics and to move rapidly between notes as in a coloratura passage.

A large voice is rarely flexible. Although there are exceptions, such as Christine Nilsson (1843–1921), Kirsten Flagstad (1895–1962), and today Jessye Norman, the musculature required to sustain intensity and volume is rarely able to be agile, for the same reason that few 100–metre sprinters excel at a marathon. However, even the greatest composers ask the impossible sometimes. Mozart's aria *Oh, zittre nicht,* the first Queen of the Night

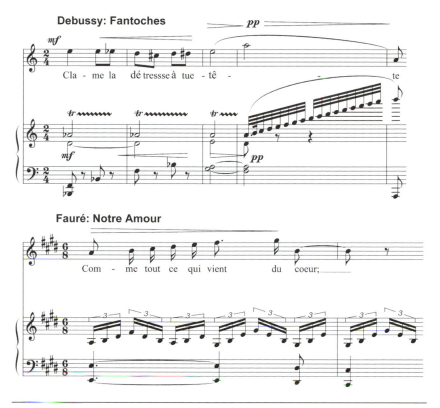

Example 2.7. Debussy: *Fantoches;* Fauré: *Notre Amour.*

aria from *Die Zauberflöte,* is an interesting example (see Example 2.8). The opening recitative is a tour de force of sustained dramatic tension and declamation, all in middle voice. Mozart perhaps intends us, even in the context of a comedy, not to doubt the Queen's potential menace and power, while also to have some sympathy with her character. In the second famous section, she displays through her coloratura as incandescent and wild a nature as Mozart was to create in any of his operatic characters. We can feel no sympathy here, only awe. From a vocal point of view, few singers today are equally adept at both sections, so extreme are the demands of range and color. Dramatically, however, it serves to enrich her "schizoid" regal character.

Perhaps the vocal divide was not so great in Mozart's day, and in our pursuit of size we have created a vocal schism that simply was not an issue with the original Queen of the Night.

Example 2.8.   Mozart: *Die Zauberflöte: O, zittre nicht* (Queen of the Night).

Berlioz noticed and commented on the effect of continually larger opera houses and concert halls on voices. Berlioz (1853) expressed the view that opera houses were too large and concert halls for orchestral and choral music also placed new demands for the solo singer. Jenny Lind, one of the greatest singers of the period, filled such spaces without abandoning the ideals of Bel Canto, through the cultivation of tonal intensity rather than sheer volume.

Wagner—after stripping away all his Teutonic mythology and dubious philosophy—was a disciple of Mozart. He shared the desire to push the voice further than ever before, and he declared and justified his intentions in print. It should be remembered that these composers did not work in an ivory-tower vacuum, but worked every day intimately with singers on every level. Wagner's demands on his singers may have been as great in his day, in intellectual and physical demands, as Brian Ferneyhough's today, although I suspect Wagner's daily experience with singers gave him a practical advantage. Typically, a Wagner "Helden" singer's uncomfortably long apprenticeship ends at middle age, after which they sing little if anything else for just a few years. Such singers may abstain from singing for several days before and after a single performance; performances are carefully separated by an adequate number of days to recuperate. This extreme almost religious fanaticism is only possible where remunerative circumstances can sustain it. Wagner created the possibility through the sheer force of his unerring creative personality. Sadly, few if any contemporary composers and their artists are able to command this autonomy or purity of purpose.

Today the situation for singers is even more extreme for those who work in opera. Although some houses employ amplification for specific repertoire, the trend to praise quantity above quality, borne partly out in the public's experience from recorded music played at high volumes, has led to a universal expectation for vocal volume. It is not surprising that so many composers in the twentieth century chose not to work with such voices, given the over-evident association with a tradition long eclipsed, founded on a misconstruction of the ideas of Wagner and Berlioz.

Composing Between the Notes

Because of the historical and analytical emphasis on pitch in works of extended tonality, serial methodology, and new complexity, many composers today understandably have as a principal objective the organization of pitch. Sounds then become primarily vehicles for pitch-driven arguments, the value of which is ascertained by their interrelationship. In respect to composing for the voice, some attitudes in popular music and jazz are much more sophisticated. These composers may be concerned about events *between* the notes, especially where the performer maintains some creative input. The use of quartertones and microtones in jazz and soul or "bending" notes (on electric guitars in some rock music) to accentuate the dissonant relationships of "blue" notes are characteristics that refer back to the origins of jazz in the blues. Both jazz and popular singers often exploit a unique capability of the voice to link subsequent pitches through a variety of connecting relationships and techniques. Although portamento and glissando are two specific ways of describing these relationships, the two words cover a multitude of different stylistic approaches, and they seem hardly sufficient to define the variety of different ways that voices are able to connect one pitch with another.

The glissando and portamento has been an important compositional device at least since Bellini and Donizetti, but their location has been kept alive through tradition, rather than in notation (see the Donizetti section in Chapter 5). Later romantic composers such as Richard Strauss occasionally notated them into score, such as in his lied *Wie Sollten wir geheim,* Opus 19, No. 4. Composers such as Ravel, Debussy, Puccini, and Gershwin have explored various effects and contexts of the device, although not always notating them. For instance, the Debussy excerpt from *Fantoches* (see Example 2.7) infers a portamento through the final descending octave, in counterpoint with the ascending glissando-type figure in the piano; more radically, the ascending octave glissando traditionally floated on the final word ("standin' *by . . .*") of Gershwin's "Summertime" (and sometimes a return descending octave as well) and does not even appear as a change of octave in the score, whereas the word "standin'" which begins the phrase is notated as a glissando down a tone between E and D. (A notated example by Ravel is discussed in Chapter 5.)

Recently, composers such as Penderecki, Ligeti, Xenakis, and Crumb have increased the compositional currency of the glissando, but the straight line joining two pitches hardly does justice to signify the wealth of potential variation. Furthermore, the straight line is a visual misinterpretation of an event, which derives much of its variety of character from the seemingly infinite possibilities of curvature.

Defining Portamento and Glissando

Considerations that may entirely alter the nature and effect of a portamento or glissando can be categorized in various ways. A simple legato liaison between notes implies no interruption of the air and a swift muscular movement of the larynx articulating the change of pitch; the movement or action is without perceptible duration, and without reference to any notes in between. A glissando infers that every microtonal pitch between the two notes should be articulated with equal emphasis for the duration of the first note, whereas a portamento is a "lightened" version, which sketches in some of the pitches, maintaining emphasis on the outer notes. Furthermore, a portamento is typically articulated quickly between the two notes, whose duration remains imperceptibly altered, although in reality some time is "stolen" from the first, and rarely if ever the second.

Rising and Falling Glissandos

It is a point of conjecture that the falling glissando preceded the rising version, at least in the classical repertoire. Falling between two notes is arguably easier to effect, because the velocity of breath must increase to maintain the same volume at a lower pitch. The effort required in producing a smooth glissando often instinctively involves a crescendo, which would be contrary to the nature of reducing breath to maintain a dynamic through rising pitches. Falling glissandos seem to be more common on the whole, and the rising glissando frequently occurs, producing a "floated" higher note, as in Gershwin's "Summertime" (already discussed).

A descending glissando allows the possibility of a simulated "glottal" attack or a sudden change of register on the second note. This is not common after a rising glissando.

Consider the three excerpts in Example 2.9. The first suggests that the voice spends literally no time on the first note, because the entire length of the quarter note is designated as a glissando. In practice, this is very

Example 2.9. Delay and Curvature in a Glissando.

difficult, because the singer is not allocated any time to assert or define the first note. The second, depending on any tempo indication, might more clearly represent how a singer approaches such a notated glissando, the first single pitch being designated two distinct functions: determining the pitch and duration of the glissando. The third is even less clear in its objective, and open to more interpretation. Assuming variables of tempo to be irrelevant, the singer is presented with several possibilities for the duration of the two functions of the first note, and several choices as to the curvature of the ascent. For instance, it may be interpreted as a fast ascent for the start of the octave, slowing down toward the goal; or it may begin as a slow ascent building in velocity; or it may be a smooth glissando for a (unstipulated) duration, without apparent changes of velocity.

Variety of Attack on the First or Second Note

Any specific articulation on the first note may have an effect on the second. An accent on the first may suggest a decrescendo through the glissando, with repercussions concerning the direction, whereas an accent on the second note will infer a crescendo. An accent on the second note will affect the curvature of the glissando, to heighten the gesture, and is similarly affected by the direction. As already mentioned, it provides an option for a simulated "glottal" attack or sudden change of register, where, in fact, the last microtones are skipped, and a sudden and dramatic jump is made to the last note. This technique is less common after an ascent.

The Placing of a Crescendo

The use of crescendo and decrescendo before, during, and after the glissando will vary the forms of attack and the curvature.

Example 2.10. Johnny Dankworth: *Blue Portfolio.* (Suite for Soprano, Flute and Piano commissioned by the author in 1983.)

Intervals

The interval itself will characterize the liaison. Generally they may be defined in five types: a semitone or tone; a fourth or fifth; an octave; compound intervals between two vocal ranges; extreme intervals crossing the three vocal ranges. A glissando between a small interval is not necessarily less dramatic or difficult than a large interval, rather each will produce a sequence of choices and problems to be overcome by the singer, according to the context.

The Duration of the First Note

In addition to the dual functions of the first note already mentioned, if the first note is an acciaccatura or an appoggiatura, the singer may instinctively choose a simple liaison or a portamento, according to the emotional objective or context, unless the composer stipulates a specific approach. An ascending interval may suggest an accentuation derived from the blues. The excerpt from Johnny Dankworth's *Blue Portfolio* (1981) repeats the technique with expressive emphasis in a very idiomatic way (see Example 2.10).

Classically trained singers often require help in navigating a glissando, because much of their training may be spent avoiding the pitfalls of scooping up to a note as a result of poor technique (although it is a device frequently employed to emotional effect in jazz to expressive effect), or simply through an effort to avoid poor intonation. Many singing teachers, however, sensibly employ exercises with glissandos for a variety of technical objectives. Some vocal techniques apply the principal of a portamento as the foundation of a legato. An example of this extraordinarily fluid sound may be heard on recordings of Edita Gruberova, particularly in Glière's *Concerto for Coloratura Soprano and Orchestra,* Op. 82.

Furthermore, the glissando is a ubiquitous part of the interpretation of music from the romantic period onward. In music, often of a dramatic nature (composed by Verdi, Strauss, or Puccini, for example), an experienced singer will use the end of the first note of a cadence figure to move the voice to the last note, effectively anticipating it. Along with a crescendo and even a ritardando, this has the effect of heightening the cadential tension and prolonging the tension/release effect. According to the skill of the singer, it may sound like a poor intonation problem, as emotionally hackneyed, or artistically refined. This is rarely if ever notated in the score itself, and is equally applicable from intervals of a semitone to a perfect fifth. If the two notes of the cadence are the same, there is an old trick of restarting the second very slightly below with a rising microtonal glissando to emphasize the change of harmony. This technique is much abused, and equally applied across the musical/stylistic spectrum of popular music. The difference between artistic success and failure in its use depends on the taste, judgment, and skill of the performer.

There are several additional musical contexts in which the vocal glissando plays an important part. The Mexican folk song known as "Corrido" and the Latin American "Bolero" traditionally employ the glissando, as does much music for Barbershop Quartets. There are also several compositions that would repay serious analysis in this respect:

1. Boulez: *Le Marteau sans Maître* frequently uses glissando and portamento, annotated as to the specific intention.
2. Britten: *Dirge* from *Serenade for Tenor, Horn and Strings,* where each repetition of the nine strophic verses is connected by an ascending octave glissando.
3. *Salce, Salce* from Verdi's *Otello* (see Musical Example 5.6c).
4. *Strange Fruit,* as recorded by Nina Simone (widely available); the glissando appears toward the end of the song and is remarkable in its technical and emotional control.
5. *Somewhere, Over the Rainbow,* from *The Wizard of Oz;* the rising octave that begins the song is affected because of the fluid "m" connecting the vowels. It is almost impossible to navigate without at least the hint of a portamento.

One final note: this section describes a technique as a simulated "glottal" attack or abrupt change of register in preference to the suggestion of a real glottal attack that in overuse will harm the vocal cords.

Extended Voice Techniques

This somewhat abused phrase cannot be considered a style in itself, but it signifies an area of both curiosity and concern, or even fear, for many singers and composers. All instruments in the twentieth century were exploited or recreated anew for their sonic capabilities. Notable pioneering examples include Cage's works for prepared piano, Crumb's works for electric string quartet, and Bruno Bartolozzi's book, *New Sounds for Woodwind* (1967) and its categorization of multiphonics. The voice has also been subjected to imaginative explorations, from all stylistic areas. Jane Manning (1998) admits to "bristelling" when asked to explain the term "extended vocal techniques," which she understands as the composer's need to create a rational notation of everyday sounds we might otherwise instinctively recognize in other contexts. In this respect, the trend may be seen as a logical continuation of a process engendered by Verdi's *Macbeth* (1847), when he attempted to notate a fuller dramatic conception of the vocal performance. However, the variety of approaches created in the twentieth century was vast, and is deserving of a book in itself. The following list merely catalogues some famous examples and executants associated with the development. Although each exploits the voice from a different parameter, they all share in common a playfulness in the world of vocal sound beyond the Bel Canto principle of the pure vowel as *the* vehicle for emotional expression. It is perhaps in this regard that the epithet and intention of an "extension" may be best understood.

Composers' curiosity and delight in this area has perhaps been equally matched by a reluctance on the part of many singers and their teachers to explore it. It is perhaps understandable that a singer, whose entire training may have been devoted to the control and expression of music through pitch-related vowel sound and the consequent subjugation of non-vowel sounds, may feel uneasy or ill-equipped to deal with such material. From this point of view, it might be thought of as similar to asking a violinist to play a work on a percussion instrument. Although the development may seem logical to many, change in itself for any skilled worker represents a form of threat, or a step into the unknown. Many singers, through their personality and philosophy, happily embrace the new challenge, and find that the new techniques can coexist with their traditional skills, while others may wish to turn away. For the same reasons, there will be some teachers who will not permit their singers to work in an area they consider demeaning or damaging, while others acknowledge the logic behind the idea of an "extension."

Here is a fairly random selection of some famous and established examples of extended vocal techniques.

Cathy Berberian *Stripsody*

This comic work exploits, with the aid of a graphic score, the onomatopoeia that proliferated in the United States in comics such as "Batman" and "Superman" in the middle of the twentieth century. It is, as suggested by the composer when she introduced her own performances, intended to permit the audience to laugh.

Luciano Berio *Sequenza III* and *Visage*

The vocal "Sequenza" is, as mentioned in Chapter 3, an exploration of emotive states, specified adjectivally and notated phonetically. *Visage* was edited in a recording studio from many hours of improvisation by Berio's then-wife, Cathy Berberian. It is a veritable compendium of sounds associated with a woman's life, from birth to death. Perhaps it may be understood as a contemporary sonic re-enactment of Schumann's song-cycle, *Frauenliebe und Leben,* consciously attempting to expand the composer's possible sound world.

Peter Maxwell Davies *Eight Songs for a Mad King*

Davies states in the album notes from a recording of this work: "The sounds made by human beings under extreme duress, physical and mental, will be at least in part familiar. With Roy Hart's extended vocal range, and his capacity for producing chords with his voice (like the clarinet and flute in this work), these poems presented a unique opportunity for me to exploit these techniques and thus to explore certain extreme regions of experience." The work was first performed by Roy Hart, who continued famously his exploration of voice into his theater companies in the UK and France.

Arnold Schoenberg *Pierrot Lunaire*

The seminal work, discussed in Chapter 5, uses *Sprechgesang,* between speech and song, in a style of vocal delivery that recalls the principles of melodrama, and returns to the singer an unusually large degree of interpretive and even creative autonomy for the period.

Karlheinz Stockhausen *Stimmung*

The composer demands the controlled production and amplification of harmonics, that are available from any fundamental pitch. In this case, the work is based around a single chord of the ninth on the root of B flat, which is to say B flat rising through F, B flat, D, A, and C. The harmonic up to the 24th from any of the pitches are required from each singer, produced on a long vowel sound, and the harmonic is articulated and emphasized by fractional changes in the position of the mouth, the tongue, and the lips. There is a strong relationship here to Mongolian overtone chanting. While the production of lower harmonics is easy enough for most singers to control, Stockhausen found it might take singers up to six months to master control and accuracy of harmonics higher than the ninth.

There are many other composers and performers working with extended vocal techniques in all musical styles. They include:

Laurie Anderson; US multimedia performer
Björk; Icelandic pop diva
Joan LaBarbara; fabled US singer and composer
Bobby McFerrin; http://www.bobbymcferrin.com
Meredith Monk; in her multi-media performances and many
    recordings
Diamanda Galas; fabled US singer and composer
Shakira; Colombian pop diva
Joseph Shambalala; South African singer famous through the group
    Ladysmith Black Mambazo
Yma Sumac; singing in some extraordinary recordings from the mid
    twentieth century
Tom Waits; US pop legend
Trevor Wishart; UK performer and composer

3
Voice/Text/Music

A composer's knowledge and understanding of the relationships among voice, text, and music is crucial to his understanding of how to write for the voice. In this area, a singer acts most like a composer, dealing with the codified sounds of a language in order to communicate. The choices a singer makes regarding intelligibility, expression, and emphasis are often a refining of similar decisions an able composer confronts in the creative process.

Text and Music

Henry Purcell, in his Preface to *Dioclesian,* gave this description of the relation of music and text:

> Music is the exaltation on poetry. Both of them may excel apart, but surely they are most excellent when they are joined, because nothing is then wanting to either of their proportions; for thus they appear like wit and beauty in the same person.

Purcell's elegant view remains potent, but by no means expresses the gamut of compositional strategies and shifts of perspective that have occurred over the intervening years between his writing and our reading. The relationship of text to music remains perhaps the most fascinating, rich, and rewarding area of creativity, open to infinite diversity of representations by composers, and a constant source of marvel or irritation for singers. Purcell's music for voice often exemplifies a perfect balance between musical and textual expressivities, combining to suggest a third language of communication, greater than the sum of its parts.

For other composers such as Monteverdi, the ideal balance between text and music was not always one of equality: "Let the word be master of the melody, not its slave" (cited in Morgenstern 1958). Monteverdi was writing to promote his theories of *seconda prattica*, the *stile moderno*, represented by Rore, Marenzio, and himself, where text dominated the music, against the *prima prattica*, in the Netherlands school of vocal polyphony, typified by the works of Willaert (codified by theorist Zarlino), where music dominates text, in the *stile antico*. During the seventeenth century, champions of the *stile moderno* often used this quote from Plato to attack the *stile antico:* "The melody is composed of three things, the words, the harmony and the rhythm . . . and the harmony and the rhythm must follow the words" (cited in Strunk 1978).

Monteverdi's ideal relationship, borne out in his mature music, demonstrates the composer's understanding of the singer's perspective, the underlying and persistent need to communicate words. The singer is the vehicle for the realization of the marriage between text and music, although Poulenc cleverly pointed out that that marriage is itself a rather more complex issue: "The setting of music to a poem must be an act of love, never a marriage of convenience" (quoted in Bernac 1977). Sometimes a singer may find himself or herself as an arbiter between the need for clarity of language or musical expression, when their relationship is forced in any way, either by textual or compositional insensitivity, or simply questions of technique, in which notes interfere with verbal comprehension and vice versa.

The composer writing for voice today encounters a continuous series of choices. The first is whether to use a text or not. The composer who chooses not to must choose one or more sounds, the simplest example being a vocalize, or devise their own language or sound vocabulary, perhaps using extended voice techniques or onomatopoeia. There are compelling examples of both, from Glière's *Concerto for Coloratura Soprano* to Cage's textless songs (e.g., *A Flower*) and Cathy Berberian's *Stripsody*. While it is a rich vein to mine, it remains significantly thinner by example and scope than using an actual text.

The composer who uses a text may write one, be given one, choose one, or collaborate to devise one. It is the composer's emotional involvement, intellectual grasp, and physical understanding of the text that will inform their music. Language as it is sung is more complex than either written or spoken language. Consciously or intuitively, a singer operates on emotional, intellectual, and physical levels simultaneously, all of which are areas in which music may be said to affect or intrude. Assuming enough time is spent simply thinking about the text (Brahms professed to first memorizing his chosen poems as a necessary step in the process of composing a song), one of the first issues is the enormously complex one of intelligibility.

The composer must choose a language to work with, but will it be a language known locally or internationally? Several languages may be possible simultaneously, aiming perhaps at a wider or a more confused audience. Conversely, a minority language contains strong local reverberations, which may be of importance. The ultimate minority language might be a "dead" language, such as Latin. Using such a language may have two consequences. When executed deliberately, as in Stravinsky's neoclassical choral works, the use of a dead language potentially frees an audience from the instinctive need to hear and understand words and allows the music to dominate their conscious listening, unimpeded by linguistic meaning. Alternatively the lack of verbal understanding may distance the audience from the material sufficiently to create the effect of coldness or aloofness, resulting either in a Brechtian theatrical coup or mere disinterest. Certainly, an audience's frustration at hearing a language they profess to know but which is presented unintelligibly may be immense. Sometimes this may be the fault of the singer, but all too often it is the fault of the composer.

The composer using a living language should clarify her/his attitude or position to the language and its writer. If linguistic comprehension is an objective (as opposed to the post-modern, deconstructive attitude often adopted by many composers of the 1970s and 1980s), then there are a series of consequences affecting all rhythms and pitches, derived from a study of how the words might be made intelligible in a musical context, with an appropriate voice. This is the core of traditional songwriting historically, and curiously sometimes seems the least interesting aspect for some composers. The symbiotic welding of text to sound remains today a comparatively unresearched, somewhat mysterious alchemical process. Historical anecdotes at least demonstrate the polarities of opinion, perhaps not without some additional irony in evidence with Heine ("Where words leave off, music begins") and Aristophanes ("For music, any words are good enough.").

However, a deeper analysis of specific examples will give a greater understanding of techniques that composers have used to wed music and text. For example, compare the approach taken by Ravel in his sensuous setting of *Scheherezade* with Berio's more analytical approach to language in his setting of *O King*. Ravel's music sensuously and psychologically penetrates the verses of Tristan Klingsor (aka Léon Leclère), to the point where it may be difficult to perceive the words apart. It represents a culmination of traditional song structure in that respect. This seemed to fit with the poet's own aesthetic:

> My poems are like sketches . . . A poem should be that already; a point of departure for a song or a melody . . . Perhaps that is why I have had the good fortune to please musicians. You see, I attempted not merely to be a rhymer, I attempted to be a rhythmist. Rhythm, in poetry, music, and in painting, is the artist's foremost resource. (cited in Pronger 1965)

In his *O King,* Berio's work uses only the words "O Martin Luther King," but the words are not apparent until the very end. The composition moves from abstraction to concretization of language, by way of a thoughtful mediation on sounds, words and their meaning, to create what may be understood as an elegy in memory of the dedicatee.

Poetry, as opposed to prose, is generally seen today as a heightened, enriched form of verbal communication. Whereas there is a case for seeing it historically as the primary area of collaboration between composer and writer, there has been a trend in the last few generations for composers to demonstrate a suspicion toward the form, and choose prose instead. This view of poetry, tending toward the artificial, is spurious according to some commentators. Janáček's quest for a "rough" language in opera, Hemingway's aggressive stripping away of textual redundancy, and Allen Ginsberg's in-your-face expletives may seem to be sideswipes at a tradition of "high" poetry typified, say, in the erudite works of T. S. Eliot. But for Martin Heidegger there was another, perhaps more compelling context for perceiving the necessity of a more universal aspect to poetry: "Poetry proper is never merely a higher mode of everyday language. It is rather the reverse: everyday language is a forgotten and therefore used-up poem, from which there hardly resounds a call any longer" (quoted in Chatwin 1988, 303).

Language, whether poetry or prose, is itself hardly a concrete medium. At best it is an imprecise form of communication; one of the strengths of great writers such as Shakespeare is their flexibility or ambiguity, which is why every age must reinvent their relationship and understanding of his work. A similar process, identified by John Koopman, has been in operation for some centuries with the development of classical music, as well as "standards," the more enduring songs of popular music:

> The ambiguities in old scores serve a useful if unintended purpose by allowing successive generations to bring new, vitalizing insights and interpretations to them. Modern composers, by lessening the future infusion of imagination, may be limiting the opportunity for their works to grow with the ages.

Sometimes music can be seen to undermine this ambiguity and render something complex merely inane or banal. This may well be the reason why some songs are rarely performed; despite a superficial attractiveness, they appear lifeless, or without character. Carl Orff's choral Triptych, including Carmina Burana, took the opposing principle of non-ambiguity to great popularity; it seems to nullify any concept of enrichment of text, with its musical straightjacketing. Despite the use of a dead language, the Latin, like the music, remains definitive, immune to debate or significant variation of interpretation. There is little room for textual ambiguity in this music, as there is also a reduced role for musical interpretation, as a comparison between recordings might illustrate.

Although music itself may be said to be even less precise in its "meaning" as a language, it can sometimes evoke layers of subtlety where there seem to be none. There are abundant examples of this in Schubert's settings of apparently mundane verses, where the musical inspiration transcends and transforms the apparently innocent or naive material. According to Peter Porter (2001):

> Vocal music, as Stravinsky observed, needs syllables, and poetry is, at least in one sense, a marvelous concatenation of syllables. But the case isn't as reductive as that. Both composer and poet require good ideas: the rest is craftsmanship. Great music has been written to fine poetry and not just to doggerel, but the impulse must be the composer's. Bach set Picander's provincial rhymes in his Passions as enthusiastically as he did the Gospels, and Schubert's inspiration was as readily engaged by spooky ballads such as von Collin's *Der Zwerg* (The Dwarf) as by anything of Goethe's.

There is a theory that the greatest poems and plays refuse to become fodder for musicalization, indicating that perhaps these texts render a musical setting irrelevant. Similarly, the most banal texts may disguise their paucity of content by their musical presentation. Haydn's selection of librettos perhaps betrayed this, yet Purcell excelled despite the awkward and illogical libretto of *Dido and Aeneas,* with his musical setting.

Banality may itself be deliberately chosen for its own musical purpose. This may have been the logic behind the choice of Milhaud's *Machines Agricoles* (settings of agricultural machinery catalogues), and the song cycle by Poulenc, titled *Banalités.* For some, such as Ned Rorem (1996), inconsequentiality helps explain the very existence and function of popular song: "[Edith Piaf] knows the secret of popular song (the secret Bernhardt knew so well) which is expressivity through banality, the secret of knowing what must be added where. This formula can apply only to "'popular' artists: They interpret mediocre works by completing them.'"

Composers such as Bartók and Janáček hammered their music out of the unique rhythms and cadences of the sound of their own language, which they deliberately studied. I do not know whether Purcell and Monteverdi pursued such linguistic and musical analysis consciously, but all four composers physically fused their language setting into their music in ways which few if any fellow journeymen have equaled since. The unique rhythms and accents of their syllables and the coloring of specific words imbues their music with an individually rich and rewarding sound-world, accessible to those who both understand the language or not. If this uniquely communicative symbiosis between language and music is the aim of a composer, the singer must be helped—not hindered—through the composer's technique and sensitivity. Without the full technical support of poet and composer, singers have to work harder, look deeper into their own creativity, if the song is to be brought to life. This was one of the first lessons Stanislavsky taught in his opera studio:

> For your exercises it is important to choose a good text. This is of great help to a young singer. From this point of view Rimsky-Korsakov will provide you with taste and fine discrimination. Chaikovsky, on the other hand, often chooses weaker verse. Take for example his "He loved me so . . ." The music, to be sure, makes up for the triviality of the poem, yet if you listen carefully you will sense all its thinness, so it requires more effort on the part of a singer to make something out of the verse and endow it with some worthwhile meaning (1998, 18).

Stravinsky once suggested that performers might benefit from less respect and more love toward the compositions they perform. His remark may have been aimed at "historical" performances of music that attempt to realize faithfully every literal detail of a score without considering the composer's intention or objective in the sense of the inferences of the score. Composers' attitudes toward their poets or librettists demonstrate a similarly complex area of concern, and different composers have exhibited various degrees of love and respect toward their creative colleagues. The examples in Chapter 5 illustrate this wide range of possibilities, from Wolf's reverential attitude where repetition was forbidden and the poem was virtually sacrosanct, to that of Schubert and Eisler who from differing starting points felt no compunction to edit, reorder, or change texts even by writers such as Goethe and Brecht. Whether a composer today follows one course or the other does not in any way necessarily reflect the quality of the collaboration, but represents instead how the composer is best able to function.

Text and Voice

Inevitably the discussion of meaning in musical text settings centers around opera, but certain principles and axioms are equally applicable to all forms of vocal music. In this respect I refer to Edward T. Cone (1982), who suggests that any song is an opera in miniature. Roland Barthes and Constanin Stanislavsky offer two opposing views of the weight and importance of linguistic as opposed to musical meaning. Barthes wrote in his IMAGE-MUSIC-TEXT (1977):

> The "grain" of the voice is not—or is not merely—its timbre; the significance it opens cannot better be defined, indeed, than by the very friction between the music and something else, which something else is the particular language (and nowise the message). The song must speak, must write—for what is being produced at the level of the geno'song is finally writing (185).

Stanislavsky offered the countersuggestion: "The music, in fact, is the dramatic content of an opera, provided in a ready-made musical form. It is in it, and in it alone, that one has to look for the nature of the action" (1980, 170).

Barthes' comments were made in relation to Benveniste's concept that language is the only semiotic system capable of interpreting another, and goes some way to explaining how it achieves this, within limitations. Stanislavsky (who trained as an opera singer and directed opera for the Bolshoi before his more famous formulation of acting technique) addressed his comments to performers. The two quotations seem to suggest a conflict about where the meaning of musical text-settings may be found: Barthes seems to find it in the friction between the music and "something else," whereas Stanislavsky finds it entirely in the music.

A libretto shares something in common with a play: the words chosen illustrate points of view that may or may not be taken at face value, and are also affected by their context. Directors, actors, and academics also stress the importance of subtext, and much time may be spent searching for it. When music is added to words, the aspect of meaning is simultaneously both simplified and made more complex. To some extent, a composer's music is a coded elaboration of both subtext and context. However, the important word here is "coded," and the "understanding" of that code is by no means simple, as it often tautologically involves language itself.

Where, then, does the "meaning" of an opera, for instance, reside? The question is only possible if we accept the idea that language can interpret other semiotic systems. If not, the meaning would have to lie in the libretto, which might suggest that music can be no more than a frame or a decoration to the meaning. Patently this is not the case for opera; the fusion of words and music at the highest level of, say a Wolf Lied or a Duparc chanson, appears to create another independent form, where the two elements become inseparable or symbiotic. This may be no less true in many great songs that have become "standards," which are merely less formally controlled in performance details than classical music.

Opera does not only combine text and music, but a plethora of visual and dramatic elements as well. When synthesis is achieved, the sum may become even more than the many parts. But here I discover the limits of language; even if a composer was able to describe in every detail how he or she would ideally like to see a performance of his or her opera, it would not help define its "meaning." Theater is essentially a collaborative form, and all the creators and performers themselves must contribute to the end result. The performance must then contain more "meaning" than the score. Whether that "meaning" can ever be expressed fully except through performance, or a single performance, is at least debatable. And whether that degree of collaborative meaning is always applicable for all composers, is also questionable; it did not seem appropriate to Rossini, who wrote in a letter to his friend Guidicini in 1851: "The good singer should be nothing but an able interpreter of the ideas of the master, the composer . . . in short, the composer and the poet are the only true creators."

The relegation of performers to servility or their elevation to co-creativity with the composer goes to the heart of a dialectic on the nature of classical music performance practice, at least since the time of Beethoven and the elevation of certain compositions to "masterwork" status. Interestingly, the issue is sidestepped in the popular music world, where "cover" versions often provide the performer with undisputed freedom to create an individual interpretation of a song. It may be argued that Rossini's point of view reflects a dictatorial ideology, with its roots in a Platonic philosophy, in which creativity remains the sole responsibility of the high priests of culture. This point is well made by Eric Salzman (Sept. 2001):

> The great irony is that these views derive from German idealistic (or Platonic) philosophy which elevates music to the highest form of the arts because it is the purest and most perfect art and because it represents some kind of transcendent condition that speaks of the essence of things. "Great" works of art (the concept of "Great Art" and "Masterpiece" is an essential part of this view) therefore must challenge and eliminate other kinds of art and the job of the artist is to create these perfected essences and archetypes. This essentially Germanic view, mystical and cultist, has come to dominate classical music everywhere in Western culture. It is a view that, like organized religion, promotes dogma, priesthood, and a certain kind of near fanaticism that opposes anything that challenges its authority. It also leads to an idealization of essences (mystical states, death, sacrifice, terror) as well as to hierarchies and domination. It violently opposes non-idealistic art as dirty and unworthy. It particularly opposes what we might call the Aristotelian view that idealized essences made in heaven do not exist and that real artistic culture is the ongoing sum of all the works and experiences that go to make up culture."

Idealism has its attractions, though. Purcell's quote at the beginning of this chapter reflects an ideal that has served for many generations of songwriters. And in our time, Stockhausen (1989) has tried to identify the qualities of being a singer in a way that few might not wish to aspire to, however hopelessly: "If singing is to be more than empty twittering, singers must be filled with a divine spirit, transmitting a profound joy in life and a sense of assurance to all their listeners." Experience Bryon summarizes more practically the role of the singer and suggests a new way of understanding where "meaning" lies in an opera (Bryon 2000):

> There are two main ways in which the performer has appeared in the history of opera. The first is as a depicter of the perfect organization of the text. They have consequently been instructed not to get in the way of the words or the music and to let these flow through them. In these instances the performer becomes a vessel, or a puppet to the composer and the librettist, or (as in more modern times) to

the director. The texts, or the direction of the texts, were assumed to hold the meaning and the performer's job was to be a vehicle for that meaning which they were encouraged to depict. The second role of the performer is similar to an attraction in a circus show. In this role the performer defies gravity with feats of high notes or clever ornamentation; the meaning is in the very novelty of the act. In these eras, the critics traditionally blame the singer for becoming unruly and ruining the sacred drama.

Konstantin Stanislavsky was one of the first widely received advocates for the idea that meaning happens in the act of performance and that the performer has a responsibility and influence over this meaning. Bryon continues:

> The Integrative Performance Technique is essentially . . . [my] . . . response to the historical question of originated meaning as manifest in an ideal mythical and primal notion of the voice, and the hundreds of years of assumption that says that the texts of score and libretto hold the meaning of the drama. The Integrative Performance Technique aims to challenge the practitioner to question the assumptions that are placed on their practice and pedagogy of the performance art, and explore new ways of working and creating opera. This thesis is a proposal of a new way, as a response to the history, and as a development on the Stanislavsky system, an application of post-modern critical thinking, but ultimately an expression of the desire to empower the performer and therefore the performance of the texts.

For Stanislavsky, music often became the means by which he could conjure dramatic "truth" for the actions and intentions of his pupils, as opposed to relying on the cerebral processes enactioned by words. Implicit within his statement lies recognition of the limits of interpretation that language alone can produce, and through the music, or through the actors' personal or shared interpretation of that code, can come an understanding of the meaning. And if I have read the subtext of Stanislavsky's words correctly, the meaning of the fusion between text and music is in Barthes' "grain" of the voice, in the performer, at the time of performance. The "friction" of which Barthes speaks "between the music and something else" is more than merely the text in a song. How much more than in a collaborative art form such as opera? The concept of "grain" of the voice in opera surely refers to the "voices" of all the performers combining with the designers and the director, through the moment of performance. This idea is a contradiction to Rossini's beliefs, and flies against the composer-as-god role, too often assigned by those ideologically bound to Plato in their view of music and art.

Most of the music we hear is recorded, fixed and immutable, straitjacketed or crystallized into an "ideal" form. One of the greatest recording artists in the twentieth century was, perhaps, von Karajan, who would seem to be a direct inheritor of Platonic theory of artistic dictatorship. But the fundamental importance of ambiguity, which endows art with the breath of life, is negated in this way. The value of ambiguity over absolutism is fundamental to the existence of art and its mutable influence is ultimately subjective, in terms of language. Perhaps this is what lies behind this intriguing quotation from Billie Holiday (1956):

> I can't stand to sing the same song the same way two nights in succession, let alone two years or ten years. If you can, then it ain't music, it's close-order drill or exercise or yodeling or something, not music.

The quest for subtextual truth is at best an act of divination, but when the original text is not used, it is probably best treated as merely an intellectual exercise. Some of the pitfalls of translating opera libretti and song text can be glimpsed at here.

In earlier centuries, an opera's libretto was written in the language of the country in which it was to be performed. As opera became more international, composers found the need to make translations for the new audiences. The libretto translation industry was hardly less prolific than the contemporary voiceover or subtitle industry for English-language films today. This suggests that opera composers traditionally assumed that their audiences expected to be able to understand the words in performance. Some libretti became so well known in the eighteenth century that dozens of different composers would use the same text, in the same way that new versions of old films are always being made today. However, several factors developed during and since the nineteenth century that radically changed this model. First, some composers began to write music that organically grew out of the sound of the language. Debussy and Janáček, for example, in contrasted ways, molded their music from characteristics of their own language, and their performances always lack something in translation, if unwisely attempted. Second, there developed the corpus of works known as "standard" repertory, which later traveled every continent. It was not possible to sustain the translation of even those works that might have been considered translatable into the many languages required. Third, during the last century, nationality and language within each country became less polarized. In Texas today, more than half the population has Spanish as their first language. In some cities in the UK, Punjabi is the first language at many schools. Assumptions about nationality, language, and cultural norms have never been so precarious as now, a result of the continuing process of globalization.

Composers such as Stravinsky (*Oedipus Rex*), John Buller (*The Bacchae*), and Philip Glass (*Akhnaten*) have deliberately written operas in languages that cannot be understood by any audience: Latin, Classical Greek, and Ancient Egyptian, respectively. Perhaps these examples, each solving different compositional problems with ostensibly similar solutions, represent the view that although an opera's music may depend on its text, the "meaning" of the text can sometimes best be left to the music without the complicity of the audience's linguistic faculty. But that is only possible where the directors and performers can contribute to a "meaning" that may be considered to be the ultimate "message" of the work. Whether these examples all succeed equally is not relevant to the argument. The setting of otherwise "dead" languages in opera seems to be a phenomenon, albeit relatively rare, of the twentieth century, in its own illusive search for meaning in the marriage between music and text.

The search for meaning in opera has always been enriched or confused by the plethora of art forms involved. But I would suggest that these basic principles apply to a greater or lesser extent wherever music meets and interacts with language.

In summary, both music and words are imprecise forms of communication. The level of precision will depend somewhat on the depth of the interaction of the composer, the singer, and the audience. There are also many models for the relationships between music and text. Some composers have offered clear-cut (some might say, unyielding) instruction as to how the two should function together. For others, ambiguity remains a potent creative factor, resulting in the possibility of different degrees of interpretation. One thing is certain: if the composer is unsure of his or her objectives in relation to textual clarity, the singer is left to resolve the confusion. Any lack of understanding of the workings of the voice will deprive the composer of the ability to communicate his objectives to the performer.

The singer always gets the last word.

The Nature of Language

The intelligibility and understanding of language itself is the basis for the study of all literature and drama, as well as the subject of one of the twentieth century's greatest philosophical preoccupations, as articulated by writers such as Noam Chomsky. Some texts, such as an agricultural machine catalogue set to music by Milhaud in *Les Machines Agricoles,* are avowedly one-dimensional in intent, i.e., information lists. Other texts, such as a Shakespearean sonnet, are full of rich ambiguity or even conflict; a skilled actor can read the same sonnet twice to create two opposing meanings. Language is as infinite in its application as human imagination, where it was born. Poets such as Mallarmé concern themselves with the sound or resonance of a word or a syllable rather than with its semantic meaning, while those such as Rilke delve into the subconscious, exploring psychological associations. Language is our most subtle and therefore abused communication tool (a fact well understood by politicians and judges). Composers should bear in mind how close the magic of ambiguity lies to the frustration of confusion for an audience. Audiences and critics are often too quick to criticize the incomprehensibility of the text, instead of their own incomprehension, for their discomfort with some musical works.

For John Keats, there was a moment of joyous discovery when he perceived that language's quality of ambiguity was a source of strength and understanding:

> At once it struck me what quality went to form a Man of Achievement, especially in Literature, and which Shakespeare possessed so enormously—I mean Negative Capability, that is, when a man is capable of being in uncertainties, mysteries, doubts, without any irritable reaching after fact and reason.

The other consideration of the nature of language is less philosophical: What is required for its intelligibility? All languages have their own innate rhythms, cadences, and melodic structures, and while some languages are rigidly proscribed, others are more flexible. To be unaware of these features or to ignore them is to rob a listener of the possibility of comprehension, as well as inflict a disservice to the author. However, it is often suggested that listening to words and hearing music are two very different and not necessarily complimentary skills. Certainly there is scientific evidence showing that the processes occur in different areas of the brain. Composers have devised all sorts of tools to ease this congestion of concentration. The classical aria, from Mozart to Stravinsky, generally exploits three contrasted musico-linguistic relationships, placing them in what seems to be a logical order:

1. Recitative, where a linear text is delivered, usually without repetition, and text comprehension dominates musical concerns. Usually there are a greater number of words and syllables than different notes.
2. Arioso, where a text may be repeated several times but the music is developed continuously, creating developments of mood. This is a preparation for the final climax.
3. A final section, perhaps an Aria, where single words are elongated on a single vowel predominate perhaps over several lines or pages (melisma), or words are even eschewed altogether in favor of "Ah."

There are too many examples of this technique to be cited here, but may be found in Mozart's *Cosi fan Tutte* (*Come Scoglio;* Fiordiligi); Gounod's *Faust* (*The Jewel Song;* Marguerite); Verdi's *Ernani* (*Ernani, involami;* Elvira); and Stravinsky's *The Rake's Progress* (*I Go to Him;* Anne Truelove).

Even the baroque *Da Capo* aria exhibits this same basic structure, in the embellishment of music with a text from the first section repeated as the third. Embellishment or decoration in this style was not considered merely a decorative adjunct, but contributed to the musical and emotional structure of the work. It also allowed for the singer to offer an entirely individual, creative contribution.

Whether there is a place for this sort of rigidly structured form in the future is a question for contemporary composers to address. Regardless of their future fate, these structures expose at least some of those contrasting relationships between language and music, and furthermore integrate them with a sense of emotional or dramatic direction, by allowing audiences to engage with text and music with different emphases.

The Nature of the Singing Voice

Just as there are many books illustrating the physiognomy of the singing organ, there are widely accessible analyses of speech for the purpose of understanding diction and explanations of the phonemes that underline our languages. Certainly a basic understanding of the universal phonetic alphabet can aid a composer's work (see Appendix 2 for a list of reference works on this topic). There also are rules to understand and refinements to be made for each voice type. Appendix 1 also carries a description of these general voice types.

The invention of the "Fach" was a tradition crushing every voice into an existing category for the sake of an opera-factory culture based on a "standard" repertoire. Because so few contemporary operas have entered this repertory, the concept of the "Fach" remains embedded in traditional repertoire and does not reflect developments over the last few generations that many composers recognize. Because of this, a singer is perhaps best written for as a person rather than as a type. Mozart, composing before this standardization process became ossified, frequently rewrote passages or entire arias for new casts, a practice often scorned by composers today. He took great care when writing for his soloists, but knew where to draw the limit of their influence. In 1780, he was commissioned by the Elector for Munich to compose *Idomeneo*. Anton Raaff was to play the title role, and Mozart discusses his relationship with the singer during the creative process in a letter to his father:

> I have had a good deal of trouble with him about the quartet. The oftener I fancy it performed on the stage the more effective it seems to me; and it has pleased all who have heard it on the pianoforte. Raaff alone thinks it will make no effect. He said to me in private: "Non c'è da spianar la voce-it is too curt." As if we should not speak more than we sing in a quartet! He has no understanding of such things. I said to him simply: "My dear friend, if I knew a single note which might be changed in this quartet I would change it at once; but I have not been so

completely satisfied with anything in the opera as I am with this quartet; when you have heard it sung together you will talk differently. I have done my best to fit you with the two arias, will do it again with the third, and hope to succeed: but you must let the composer have his own way in trios and quartets." Whereupon he was satisfied. Recently he was vexed because of one of the words in his best aria—*rivigorir* and *ringiovanir,* particularly *vienmi a rinvigorir*—five i's. It is true it is very unpleasant at the conclusion of an aria (Kerst & Krehbiel 1965, 19).

A singer's voice type is not dictated by the extremes of its range, but rather through the singer's favored tessitura, wherein lies her or his maximum comfort and stamina. When writing to exploit the range and strengths of a singer, the composer will need to spend some time listening to the singer, as well as asking questions, rather than referring to a description of generalities. This section on the other hand, is an attempt to understand language from the singer's first point of reference, its sound. The composer needs to be aware of the sounds that singers must master, and how techniques such as vibrato potentially affect linguistic, musical, and communicative functions. For a singer, the main areas for consideration are vowels, diphthongs, consonants, and sibilants. The training of a singer involves understanding of how these different sounds are produced, and how they may best be projected or made homogenous.

Vowels

Different vowels affect the sung voice in a variety of ways, especially in different ranges. For instance, the long "ee" vowel creates a tension in the back of the throat, restricting the flow of air, which may become painful or dangerous on high notes. Singers consciously and unconsciously practice vowel modification to different degrees to compensate for problems like this. At extreme high pitches the result is unintelligibility, which may reflect no fault in the singer who wishes to maintain a good voice. The same is true, in some respects, with extreme low notes. Some say a long "a" is the most universally easy vocal vowel, while most perhaps prefer the short "o," with the muscles at the most relaxed. If a fluid line with intelligible text is an objective, composers should develop sensitivity to the most appropriate syllables for the pitches within a phrase, particularly at extremes of range. Appropriateness may be a combination of many factors, including emotive words, syllabic stress, and the category of vowel sound.

Vowels may be classified according to where in relation to the different position of tongue and lips the sound is created. The most open vowel, requiring least muscular control, is the "a"; "e" and "i" necessitate slight changes of the tongue position, with an ensuing tension at the back of the throat, whereas "o" and "u" require a progressive rounding of the lips. Each vowel may be

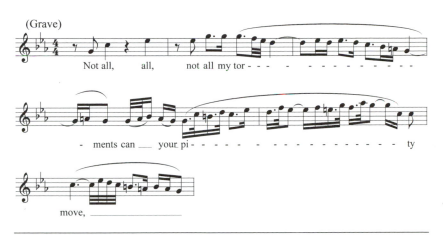

Example 3.1. Purcell "Not All My Torments."

further divided into a long and closed or short and open vowel. However, sung words often make demands contrary to spoken words, so that a short vowel when spoken, such as "bin," may be indistinguishable from "been," the distinction depending entirely on the relative duration of the notes.

"Not All My Torments" by Purcell (Example 3.1) clearly demonstrates some of these choices. The repetition of the first two words is a compositional choice for emphasis; the choice of TOR-ments, PI-ty, and MOVE for the extended melismas clearly observes syllabic stress on emotive words. The vowel sounds on the first and last melismas are open and relaxed, but the long "i" vowel in "pity" will cause some tension for the singer as she rises up to the extreme notes, creating a tension that, if controlled, will increase the emotive nature of the supplication, but could be spoiled by vowel modification or lack of control. (Nearly all Purcell's songs seem to have been written for soprano.) Without risk, little can be gained, but Purcell was a master of knowing how far to push a singer toward such risks. Strauss's choices of vowels as melismatic vehicles are usually safer, to enable the singer to negotiate the less directional, more perhaps decorative or ecstatic sentiment (see Example 2.4). He tends to avoid the tensions that Purcell deliberately used, favoring more open vowels for his coloratura melismas.

Purcell may take risks, and Strauss may be practical, elegant and heartfelt, but these do not remain the only options for a composer such as Wagner:

> An understanding of the vowel, however, is not based on its superficial analogy with a rhyming vowel of another root; but, since all the vowels are primarily akin to one another, it is based on the disclosing of this ur-kinship through giving full value to the vowel's emotional content, by means of musical tone.

> The vowel itself is nothing but a tone condensed: its specific manifestation is determined through its turning toward the outer surface of the feeling's "body"; which latter—as we have said—displays to the "eye" of hearing the mirrored image of the outward object that has acted on it (Goldman & Sprinchorn 1988, 206).

Wagner's vision, somewhat tortuously expressed, places him firmly in the tradition of the Bel Canto school, where the vowel was honored supreme as the carrier of vocal thought. By contrast, Janáček (1922–23) offers a more challenging goal, derived from the quest for "verismo": "On stage, it is not always the best word for vocalizing that we require; we need the everyday word, its melodic turn, torn from life, misery congealed, despair in sharp relief. Real life is needed in opera." Janáček's vision reflects a need to reinvent the language of the operatic medium into the reality of his time, whereas Strauss's seems to look back nostalgically to a past made ever more elusive by its passing into memory.

Diphthongs

Diphthongs are the transformation of one vowel to another by use of a transient, unstable middle section. The word "my" is a simple example of a diphthong between two vowels, although triphthongs exist:

(m)   a.......   (ae).....i

The classical singer approaches such a word, if on a held note, by maintaining the first vowel until the very last moment, minimizing the middle section in order to arrive at the last and the final moment. Popular singers such as Frank Sinatra exploit the nature of colloquial American speech and deliberately spend maximum time on the middle transition, merely acknowledging the outer sections. (Hear, for example, Sinatra singing *My Way.*) Similarly, popular singers sing through sung consonants such as "m," "n," and "ng," especially at the ends of words and phrases, where classical training emphasizes the purity of the vowel, minimizing the length of these ending voiced consonants. The two singing styles remain polarized even in a culture where the "crossover" between musical styles is long taken for granted. Certain composers, for instance George Gershwin and Leonard Bernstein, often used a written language that represented colloquial rather than classical speech patterns. With such extremes of interpretation available, composers might at least consider indicating their preference of detail in this area.

Italian composers deal with diphthongs in a creative way. In *La Bohème,* Puccini sets the words in such a way as to define pure vowels from diphthongs (see Example 3.2). Sometimes, to achieve a special effect, Verdi consciously changed the rules of pronunciation. In his *Otello,* he changes the diphthong

con grande espansione

Il pri - mo bo - cio dell' A - pri - le è mi - o

Example 3.2. Puccini: from *La Bohème.*

in "paziente" into a pure vowel, turning a three-syllable word into a four-syllable word, to emphasis Iago's deliberate power over Otello; in *La Traviata*, Violetta sings "re-li-gi-o-ne" as if it were a five-syllable word, instead of the four with the diphthong "io," to underline her weakness.

Consonants

Consonants are objects that potentially obstruct the free flow of air, through deflecting, hindering, or interrupting it, and thus intrude on the vocal line. They may be classified as voiced, when they carry with them some remnants of voiced sound (such as "b," "g," and "d") or unvoiced (such as "p," "k," and "t"). These unvoiced consonants may be termed "plosives," because they are produced by a quasi-explosive release of pressure between two adjacent areas of gum, tongue, or hard pallet. The action may be mimicked on any vowel by suddenly opening the throat under pressure, called a glottal stop. Some teachers will not allow this sound, considering it dangerous, and indeed, too much pressure may, with poor technique, inflict swollen nodules on the cords, incapacitating a singer for months or worse. Scientists measuring human sneezes discovered air speeds frequently exceeding 500 mph before leaving the body. I do not know whether this speed is approached by plosive consonants, but I have sadly witnessed singers temporarily disabled by these intrusive objects when carelessly placed, often in multiples (e.g. "liked," "picked," etc), at high tessitura. The effect is comic when not pathetic.

Even in *Messiah* there are passages in which performers by tradition move the underlay of syllables to avoid crucifixion by consonant. The seemingly

first_____ fruits of them_ that____ sleep

Example 3.3. Handel: *Messiah.*

innocuous phrase shown in Example 3.3 disguises problems enough for a fluent English singer, but for a less fluent speaker the negotiation of the diphthong "ir," the sibilant "s," the plosive "t," another sibilant "f," and the modified vowel "r" in between the last eighth note of "first" and the first vowel of "fruits" can produce some extraordinary and unintentionally comic effects.

Just as vowels operate differently in different languages, consonants often metamorphose their character. For instance, Italian consonants are famously softer than English or German, and are produced much more at the front of the mouth. Judging the singer's pronunciation of any text requires a linguistic understanding of the requirements, or a change of cultural viewpoint. In (Mexican) Spanish, "D" and "V" tend to be heard as the opposite of their English equivalents. Consonants remain the biggest impediment to a smooth legato in English and German.

Sibilants

Sibilants are unvoiced by definition, when the breath passes with a fleshy vibration or intrusion. To modify a sibilant to affect a legato is to transgress its nature, from an "s" into a "z," or an "f" into a "v." Sense may not prevail. When line or phrasing is a priority, sibilants should be placed to affect minimum intrusion. Of course, this is largely the job of a singer, but a composer should be aware of these constraints when attempting to create a legato passage.

Luciano Berio, in his deconstructional methodology (*Sequenza III, A-Ronné*, etc.), exploits these phonetic concepts by placing them in the foreground of the singer's vocabulary, isolating them from conventional "meaning" or semantic structure. It is worth reiterating that Berio's frequent

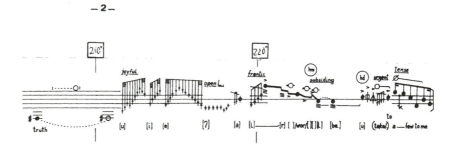

Example 3.4. Berio: *Sequenza III.* Copyright 1968 by Universal (London) Ltd, London. Copyright renewed. Used by permission of European American Music Distributors LLC, sole US and Canadian agent for Universal Edition (London) Ltd, London.

use of adjectival emotional states creates another direct layer of communication for the voice, bypassing conventional dynamics with their codified traditions.

Vibrato

If there is a single factor about the voice in the twentieth century that has provoked immense controversy, it is vibrato. Vibrato is a function of the diaphragm that allows a minute, and ideally controllable variation of pitch at a certain tempo relative to the music. When singers have prioritized volume, at the request of their agents and managers, this often becomes out of control. There are few popular singers, except perhaps the very early Joni Mitchell and Joan Baez, who do not selectively use the vibrato at least to "emote" at the end of long expressive notes. The assumption that some in the early music fraternity made—that the vibrato was absent throughout the baroque era—may be academically verifiable. However, if so, it may be the only time in the history of the world that musicians agreed on something, and that seems unlikely. The case for the ubiquity of this "white" sound in earlier times is certainly brought into question by a statement made by Pomponius Festus about 2000 years ago: "Vibrissare est vocem in cantando crispare. (The vibrato is a singing style when the voice shakes backward and forward.)" (Reid 1950).

Reid (1950) gives one of the most complete analyses on the subject of vibrato I have ever read. He says that when periodic fluctuations of pitch taking place during the sustaining of a single tone, there are three results: vibrato, tremolo, and wobble.

Vibrato occurs when the changes of pitch do not enter the consciousness of the listener. Early theoretical works dealing with the subject of vibratory pulsations were written by such eminent authors as Marin Mersenne of France and Christopher Simpson of England, both of whom lived in the seventeenth century, and the Italian Francesco Geminiani, an eighteenth-century theorist. All historians, outstanding musicians, and performers, they praised the expressive capacities and general merit of the vibrato in instrumental playing and demonstrated that the "livening" of a tone by introducing a vibrato movement was a very early development of instrumental technique. It might be remembered how early instrumental developments mimicked the voice in tribute, which remained the model for all instruments. Leopold Mozart, Amadeus's father, declared that "nature itself suggested it to man." This suggests a general recognition and acceptance of the vibrato as an artistic medium at a time long thought of as being hostile to its use.

The vibrato was, for the aficionado, a natural and untaught aspect of vocal production, ensuring flexibility, longevity, and expressivity. It was the consequence of a sound vocal technique, but never the objective. It implies a consistency and regularity of pulsation. In contrast, tremolo and wobble are injurious and the result of strain or an inadequate technique. Vibrato cycles repeat slower than a tremolo but faster than the wobble, regardless of volume, whereas tremolo and wobble may be affected by intensity. It is the amplitude of the wavelength that is governed by intensity for a vibrato. The tremolo is conspicuous with a rapid pulsation and deficiency in amplitude. Reid emphasizes the unrelated nature of vibrato and tremolo, and cites unbalanced muscular control leading to strain as the cause of tremolo's "throatiness." Synchronized tongue and jaw movements often betray this poor technique, the result of a muscular constriction. The wobble is the result of a noticeably slow pitch change whose width and unevenness of amplitude and periodicity are its distinguishing features. It is caused by driving and forcing the vocal registers beyond natural boundaries.

Reid has even analyzed the regularity of periodicity in pitch fluctuation, assigning to vibrato a figure of 6.5 times per second, regardless of volume with absolute consistency; tremolo 8+ times per second, and wobble down to 4 per second. He further states that tremolo and wobble change in relation to loudness in periodicity but not in amplitude, whereas vibrato reacts to loudness in terms of amplitude but not in periodicity. Pitch and loudness govern the amplitude of the vibrato, where there is an automatic adjustment between volume and amplitude, allowing perhaps a semitone of perfect gradation in between. Pitch is one of the governing factors determining the amplitude of the vibrato by reason of the fact that the voice shows an inclination, even when the intensity is held constant, to narrow the pitch slightly as the scale is descended. In the lower octave of the voice there is relatively little fluctuation even when singing full voice. There is, therefore, much greater opportunity for increasing and decreasing the intensity in the upper portion of the voice, and for creating a much wider variety of emotional expression, than is possible in the lower range. Composers who write well for the voice always take this into consideration.

There is much confusion, understandably, between the concepts of vibrato, tremolo, and wobble. Many composers and audiences today fear the dreaded generic "wobble," and the desire to create the flat-toned, boyish sound is the basis of many great contemporary choirs. Unfortunately, the requirement negates the natural production of the voice and may produce tension and strain. For at least some singers, singing without vibrato is an unnatural and tiring technique. It would be fruitless to press for a revolution in taste, but the range of what is acceptable might be wider if composers recognized the restriction felt by many vocalists with a good technique, who are forced to sing for long periods without this natural, controllable asset. Ask a string quartet to play together for long without vibrato and you expose every possible flaw. Unfortunately, the reality among many of today's singers of contemporary choral music is fear that if a suspicion of a vibrato is found, they may lose their job.

Text Effect

Singers who have to take into account all of these vocal considerations may, perhaps understandably, give less attention to the importance of the text. The work involved in interpreting the text, while still maintaining vocal perfection, cannot be underestimated. Sometimes the demands of diction, dramatic or emotional truth, musical style, and even acoustic considerations compete with vocal objectives, and it takes a master vocalist to maintain balanced concentration in all these areas. A singer's relationship with text defines, to some extent, the kind of singer. Modifications of vowel sounds often result from the more extreme labor of classically trained singers, perhaps because of the exploitation of extremes of range or virtuosity; in any case, the emphasis on purity of vowels always obviates the problem. Some concert and opera audiences are able to overlook such weaknesses, accepting them in the context of the "holy grail" of vocal perfection. On the other hand, singers from the acting world often retain their actorial understanding, control, and passion for textual characterization. Although their voice may not display a classical perfection of line, the emotional energy with which the text is delivered may often amply compensate to a different audiences' ears. Occasionally a singer from either background brings such charisma to a performance that these considerations may both be accorded second place to the sheer communicative force of delivery.

Nudity and Performance

When something is memorized it is "learned by heart." This phrase "to learn by heart" is very revealing. To put your heart into something rarely suggests a lack of intellectual effort, whereas to "apply your mind" might be possible without engaging passion. The essential difference between an instrumentalist and a singer is most visible when performing by heart, and lies between the performer and the audience. A pianist and a cellist are largely obscured by their instrument. It is not a question of size; even the piccolo, when played from memory, demands some contortion of the body in the form of an extension, drawing some of the audience's gaze toward the instrument. However, when singers perform by heart, they are—comparatively, metaphysically, and symbolically—naked. They are their instruments; there is no intermediary. This nakedness allows a wealth of social, historical, cultural, and personal values to be made available to a discerning audience. Stature, clothes, movements, gestures, expressions, and attitudes can affect an audience subconsciously, not necessarily in harmony with the objectives of the music. As a result, by inference as well as by fact, the concert platform with a singer is as much of a stage as the theater.

Concerning clothes, a woman on stage has a far wider variety of choice than a man, and is thus more open to criticism. In comparison, the male classical music "uniform" is an anachronistic subterfuge in the concert hall, bordering on dishonesty. European orchestras adopted the evening suit of tails in the nineteenth century to reflect the same attire as their audience: it was on some level an attempt to minimize the distance between the musicians and their audience. As the culture of the nineteenth century was maintained at the heart of the repertoire of orchestras and opera houses, the performers continued wearing the "traditional" clothes, while their audiences donned Levis, ensuring a separation and a distance between audience and performer that was the opposite of the traditional objective. Classical music and opera are still suffering from the effect of this reversal in status and it has led to misleading assumptions about class identity.

Why should these matters concern a composer? Because to understand something of the psychology of a singer is to understand better the voice in relation to an instrument. Composers frequently and unwittingly enter this arena if not naked themselves, certainly unprepared. Multiple functions are frequently asked of instrumentalists and singers in contemporary music. For example, vocalists may be required to play a percussion instrument. It is worth considering that a drum for a cellist has a completely different relationship with the performer than for a singer; for the cellist it may be a second visual obstacle between the player and the audience, whereas for the singer, it perhaps becomes an additional part of his or her costume. While there need be no effect on cello or voice, the singer might perceive the extra object as an intrusion into the intimate relationship with the audience. The same may also be true to some extent of additional actions, such as clapping or finger snapping.

To be a performer necessitates a degree of ego; to be a naked performer, or a singer, necessitates an additional degree of exhibitionism. For many singers, the apotheosis of their art to which they aspire is typified in the overripe romantic Puccini style of singing appassionato, or "with the heart." Not all composers (nor all singers) admire this, but in the context of the demands on a naked performer, the desire to be heroic may be understood if not sympathized with. Conversely, the singer who works with Steve Reich needs to be hardly less committed to the music, but the approach may be more objectified, less solistic, more as "one of the band." Some singers intuitively are repelled or attracted by these opposing demands, and few if any are able to straddle between the two planets of technique and temperament involved.

This may go some way toward explaining why the "breed" of contemporary singer seems so far from the traditional one, and why comparatively few vocalists manage to work equally in both worlds. "Classical" music has only recently become predominantly (that is, statistically) a historical art form, and many of the traditions, etiquettes, and attitudes of its illustrious past perhaps threaten its currency as a living medium. Some singers such as Cathy Berberian and Meredith Monk have consistently challenged the old aesthetic. Berberian's humorous "Stripsody" concerns itself with the twentieth-century culture of the comic strip and onomatopoeia, and her programs exhibited a reinvention of popular music by composers, such as The Beatles, long before the word "crossover" became common currency. Monk has approached the voice inventively through movement and the stage. Both singers reinvented the ambience and aesthetics of the concert hall, and thus appear more nakedly as singers closer to our own time, rather than wearing the obsolete weight of a revered tradition.

On the other hand, as long as the teaching of the voice continues to be essentially concerned with a core, traditional repertory, where most (statistically) work exists, there seems little chance of the status quo being challenged. As a result, many performers display the same weakness as Hans Christian Andersen's famous Emperor: they may have been told they are wearing New Clothes, but the garb of past centuries is all too obviously apparent, obscuring more contemporary objectives. The composer who is able to work with a singer who is truly naked, in that respect, may find greater reward and clarity of expression.

Text Underlay in Scores

At the risk of stating the obvious, reading vocal scores is the best way to learn how to write them. Yet, because I have never encountered a summary of the traditions and details about the underlay of text in scores, this would be the place to attempt it. This section deals mostly with English, but many of the rules apply to other European languages, or Latinizations of, say, Russian and Greek. A composer attempting to set a language foreign to his or her tongue would do well to study relevant examples in score.

There should be no indications between the notes or pitches for the singer and the text underneath. All dynamics, tempo markings, marks of expression, and other indications should be placed above the leger lines, to clarify the relationship between text and music.

Singers begin to sing any syllable on its first vowel, so preceding consonants will instinctively be placed just before vowels, as if written with acciaccatura. It is rarely necessary for a composer to articulate this except when special emphasis or color is required. Polysyllabic words are divided with hyphens, whereas a single syllable prolonged over more than one note will carry an underscore ahead of it to visualize the prolongation.

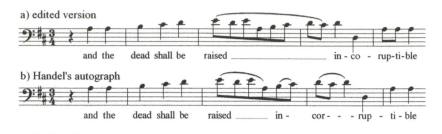

Example 3.5a and 3.5b. Handel: from *Messiah.*

Example 3.5a illustrates the traditional use of slur or phrasing lines that link together the groups of notes that share the same vowel. It also represents one of the many attempts to regularize Handel's occasional lapses in word setting (see Example 3.5b).

Polysyllabic words are split in various ways. Where there is one consonant between syllables, the consonant is left with the first vowel, except where the root of a word or part of a word would be obscured. Hence not "re- dee- mer," which obscures the root word "deem," but "I know that my re- deem- er liv- eth."

Where there are two or more syllables in between vowels, there are rather more considerations involved, as in "in- cor- rup- ti- ble." Two separate consonants intervene with the first two syllables and they are thus divided between the consonants; the repeated "r"'s between the next syllables, and the two plosive syllables that succeed are also divided similarly; the final syllable treats "l" as if it were a vowel, an idiosyncrasy of English. It would be more logical to place the "b" at the end of the previous syllable, but this would disguise the root of the word and leave the final syllable as "le," which bares no visual relation to the idiosyncratic and perhaps indivisible "ble" that is a common word ending.

Some words such as "power" and "every" are arguably either monosyllabic or bisyllabic for the former, bisyllabic or trisyllabic for the latter, from a composer's point of view. The composer might save unnecessary confusion by indicating clearly where the second syllable occurs or by abbreviating the words as to define them definitively, as in "pow'r" or "ev'ry." However, other words, such as "cruel," may seem to remain obstinately bisyllabic, despite a tendency to ambiguity in speech. Context of historical time, poetic meter, and phraseology are the determining factors in these optional areas, and reflect the composer's sensitivity, care, and taste.

There is an abiding tradition that leaves notes unbarred together that do not belong to the same syllable. Thus, in recitative, with much text and each syllable a single note, the visual representation is of a forest of trees, in various

Example 3.6. Puccini: *La Bohème*.

degrees of maturity. There is logic here, in terms of clarity of information for the singer, but the more complex rhythms of some contemporary composers would seem to militate against the tradition.

Example 3.6 can be compared with a score by Ravel, such as "Placet futile" from "Trois Poèmes de Stéphane Mallarmé" (see Chapter 5). Puccini abides by the tradition of separating vowels with unbarred notes, whereas Ravel fearlessly writes as if for any other instrument, his primary objective perhaps in making the compound rhythms clear to the eye. The relationship of each syllable to music may be clearer in the Puccini. However, Ravel uses phrase marks instead of slurs that join together melismatic vowels. The Puccini excerpt also carries a floating "a" vowel between two adjacent notes (sua), the sound being incorporated smoothly into the preceding vowel. In some editions of the Ravel, the French multi-syllable words are not hyphenated, with each syllable written without breaks under the appropriate note.

Punctuation, such as commas and periods, should be placed after the last letter of any word, before any prolonging hyphen or underscore. Any capitalization in the original, such as at the beginning of each line of poetry, might be respectfully reproduced in the text, even though the visually intended effect may be nullified in musical form.

To summarize:

- Divisions of syllables in text underlay should respect roots of words but clarify idiosyncrasies of pronunciation.
- Prolonged syllables may be indicated with a dotted line when a part of a word, or a continuous line when the word is complete.
- Syllables should not be subdivided into phonemes except to indicate special emphasis.
- There should be no indications visually interfering with the relationship of the text and the music.

- The tradition of separate stems for syllables may render complex rhythms illegible.
- Phrasing marks may clarify musical and textual objectives, but breathing, as with the bowing of string instruments, may be considered a separate function.

Singing and Speaking

The relationship of the singing to the speaking voice is often clouded by misconception. Our self-awareness as a small child develops at about the same time as our speech, erroneously leading us to consider that the voice is essentially a tool for verbal communication. From the day of our birth we actively explore the vocal apparatus with gurgling, crying, apparently random or even melodious sounds. Moreover, unlike language these are sounds that do not have to be learned. The purpose and function of speech is social, whereas singing in this most early sense "is no more than the unmeaning outflow of an innate mythico-lyrical disposition," according to Husler and Rodd-Marling (1976, 95).

In fact there is mounting evidence that musical communication (if it may be determined so) not only predated the formation of speech for our species, but that long before Homo sapiens or even our more distant ancestors existed, a similar tendency toward sonic curiosity was practiced in other species, according to Roger Payne (2001):

> Music is far, far older than our species. It is tens of millions of years old, and the fact that animals as wildly divergent as whales, humans and birds come out with similar laws for what they compose suggests to me that there are a finite number of musical sounds that will entertain the vertebrate brain.

It may be reasonable to accept that our primary voice is in fact the singing voice, and that singing may never be developed from speaking, which is our secondary voice. The voice is born with us, after which we learn to articulate sound.

Stockhausen (1960, 44) distinguished five degrees between speech and song:

1. Parlando, where tone and speed imitate colloquial speech
2. Quasi parlando, where the curve of the pitch oscillates, but with fixed duration of syllables and intensity
3. Syllabic song, where all the parameters are exactly proportionally set
4. Melismatic song, where the musical parameters become dominant, and tones predominate over syllables
5. "Pure music" performed with the mouth closed

While these categories between "comprehension of speech" and "comprehension of music" are illuminating in the context of Stockhausen's discussion of the music of Boulez and Nono, they also present certain problems. Although such a systematic gradation between speech and music might seem an attractive compositional stratagem, it fails to acknowledge the different perspectives of singer and audience.

There are three perspectives from which speaking may be compared to singing. From the point of view of the singer, speaking is the opposite end of the spectrum from singing. Singers think of speech as modified noise, whereas singing traditionally has the ultimate objective of purified tone. From the point of view of an audience, the process of understanding language occurs in a different part of the brain to following music, with the consequence that there is usually an imbalance between the two when they are presented concurrently. From the composer's perspective, there is at least theoretically an infinite line of development between the spoken word and the sung word, incorporating rap, sprechgesang, crooning, and recitative in various degrees of emphasis. Moreover, beyond the extreme of speaking, there is noise itself: modified noise without a linguistic objective, which is an area that became widely available to composers in all styles during the twentieth century. Beyond the extreme of singing lies the ultimate purification of tone, where the unbroken vowel sound is the carrier of a vocalize. From the perspective of the dominance of music or text, the line of development now appears to be a circle (see Figure 2).

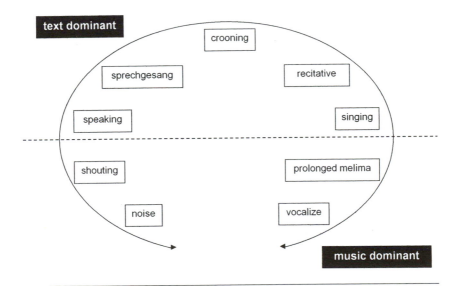

Figure 2. Dominance of Music vs. Text.

The line dividing dominance (and therefore comprehension) of text or music is in reality more flexible than it seems. For instance, it is possible to shout but still have the sense of the words conveyed, but some shouting in a dramatic or musical context may be beyond words, as in a scream, or be deliberately distorted, emphasizing the intended aggression, as in, for instance, punk rock and heavy metal music. A single work will often move between two or more areas, and cross between dominance of music or text. Prolonged melisma (e.g. *O had I Jubal's Lyre*, from Handel's *Joshua*, or *Alleluja* from *Exsultate jubilate*, K 165, by Mozart) may in time obscure its linguistic root, and become a miniature vocalize in its own right. From the other end of the spectrum, Steve Reich, in an early studio work called *Come Out* (1966), took the words "Come out to show them" from a voice recording of a street gang member in Harlem, and phase-patterned the voice very slowly over itself. The work lasts about 13 minutes and contains well over 600 repetitions of the same phrase. One effect on the listener is to move from the area of speech dominance to the area of musical dominance. Gradually, the phonemes, especially sibilants and plosives, become liberated from their syntax, and the listener inevitably looses consciousness of the voice as human, of words as in a language, and is able to perceive the sound as abstractly as a symphonic or a percussion work. "Most people do some kind of singing when they speak," Reich told Alan Rich of the *Los Angeles Times*, "more than they realize."

As regards the vocal instrument itself, the classical objective of the sung voice to seek the purification of tone is often superseded by artistry, charisma, or star quality. Few would use the description of "purity of tone" to describe the later recordings or performances of opera diva Maria Callas. Similarly, singers from all styles may burn out their voices through various excesses, but through application and sensitivity to the material, despite the prevalence of noise over tone, singers such as Rod Stewart and Nina Simone also remained professionally and creatively active and successful. Others, such as musicians like Louis Armstrong and actors such as Rex Harrison, arrived at singing through circumstance rather than vocation, and learn to transform what may be seen technically as a weakness into an original idiosyncrasy. With these voices, selective noise remains crucially the strongest factor in vocal identity, style, and communication.

Figure 2 does not account for the various relationships that exist between the voice and music. In this respect, the musical context has played a crucial role in composition for the spoken voice. One of the most ancient forms is melodrama. The word originally suggested a spoken text with musical background, as in Greek drama. The form was popular during the eighteenth century with composers such as Georg Benda, J. J. Rousseau, and W. A. Mozart, among others. J. J. Rousseau's melodrama *Pygmalion*

(1762; first performed 1770) made vogue stage plays in which the action was generally romantic, full of violent action, and often characterized by the final triumph of virtue. Mozart's famous number operas are *Die Entführung aus dem Serail* (1782) and *Die Zauberflöte* (1791), but in those, the spoken word did not occur simultaneously with accompanying music. Significantly in this respect, Beethoven included dialogue over orchestral music in his own singspiel opera, *Fidelio* (1805), which (like Mozart's *Die Zauberflöte*) was originally commissioned by the actor and impresario, Schikaneder. (Incidentally, the term "melodrama" was used extensively in England in the nineteenth century as a device to circumvent the law that limited legitimate plays to certain theaters, which diluted its original meaning.) The sung voice was traditionally a place for heightened or extreme emotion in opera, whereas the spoken voice conveyed action. Claude Debussy reversed this convention in his opera *Pelléas et Mélisande* of 1902; the vocal writing eschews the use of virtuoso performance feats to convey dramatic intensity. It offers one of the most remarkable moments in all opera when, at the long delayed peak of the drama, Debussy defies every rule of musical theater when the orchestra stop playing, the singers stop singing, and the climatic "Je t'aime" is spoken. Twentieth-century examples of the true music melodrama, where the words are allotted at least a rhythmical relationship with the music, are found in Richard Strauss's setting of Tennyson's *Enoch Arden*, Stravinsky's *A Soldier's Tale*, Poulenc's *Babar the Elephant*, Prokofiev's *Peter and the Wolf*, and Walton's *Façade*, as well as in a more developed form in Arnold Schoenberg's *Pierrot Lunaire, A Survivor from Warsaw*, and H. K. Gruber's *Frankenstein!*—which develops the special role of "chansonnier."

The contrast between the spoken word (with or without accompanying music) and the sung word remains the pivotal structure of much contemporary musical theater. Although the traditional division between action/dialogue vs. reflection/music remains prevalent and successful (*Oliver, Cabaret, The Sound of Music*), through-composition has long been experimented with (*Company, Les Miserables*). In some, such as Bernstein's *West Side Story*, the spoken word, both accompanied and not, seems to fuse with the sung word in an astonishing variety of ways.

In popular music, too, the synthesis of the spoken word with the sung word has had an important trajectory: "Scat" singing liberated certain phonemes from language to create a new sound vocabulary, perhaps begun by Satchmo (Louis Armstrong) and more recently developed further by Bobby McFerrin. The later development of "doo-wop" singing (The Ink Spots, The Silhouettes, and The Marcels) began in the 1950s. It was then succeeded in the 1970s and 1980s by rap and hip-hop (Pete DJ Jones, DJ Hollywood, "Love Bug" Starski, Grand Master Flash, Afrika Bambaataa, and Kurtis Blow.) Later styles included ska, reggae, rap, and dub-poetry (Linton Kwesi Johnson, and Jean "Binta" Breeze). They all maintain a direct connection to the spoken word with music, which was originally defined as melodrama.

The presence of both speaking and singing on stage or in the concert hall provokes a series of philosophical, dramatic, and technical questions. Philosophically it raises the question of the relationship between song and speech: whether the character is aware of their singing or speaking, and whether the voice is their own, their character's, or the voice of the writer, composer, or director. Dramatically it necessitates a demonstration of the contrasting emotional states of speaking and singing: without the presence of speaking we might accept the ostensible "normality" of the singing voice, but the presence of both leads us to necessarily provide an answer as to why one is appropriate at one moment, while the other is more appropriate at the next. We might just forget to ask the inevitable question of why words are being sung at all unless we also hear them spoken.

Technically, although the singing voice might be thought of as an extension to or development of the speaking voice, the experience of actors and singers suggests that the two modes of vocal delivery remain independent. Many classical singers refrain from talking for long periods before a difficult performance, because they are sensitive to the adverse effects of speaking. The ubiquitous tool of our time, the telephone, has long been known as the creator of many vocal problems, because we do not speak on the phone as we would face to face. Apparently, we overcompensate for the lack of visual communication by exaggerating certain speech habits. This seems to be in line with the ideas of Lucie Manén when she lamented the lack of facial and emotional gesture when singers perform in front of a microphone without a visible audience (see Chapter 1). Singing has an effect on the speaking voice, and vice versa; most people who talk immediately after singing will discover that their speaking voice will have raised itself a few pitches above the norm. Singers who train insufficiently in speaking may suffer from similar laryngeal problems to actors unaccustomed to singing.

Edward T. Cone (1974) coined the concept of a composer's "voice" as equivalent to the idea of a musical "persona," a surrogate for the empirical composer, who projects "the illusion of the existence of a personal subject" behind or within a work of art. As a "role" assumed by the artist, a persona (originally a "mask" in ancient theater) suggests for Cone "that all music, like all literature, is dramatic; that every composition is an utterance depending on an act of impersonation which it is the duty of the performer or performers to make clear." For Cone, the "vocal persona" expresses itself "at least as much by melody as by speech, and as much by tone-color as by phonetic sound." Cone was specifically concerned with the classical Lied, but his ideas have far-reaching consequences.

The very act of listening to a singer invokes a complex psychology from the audience. There is in fact a bewildering plethora of voices, and it may never be totally clear as to their origins at any one time. The character, the singer, the composer, the writer or poet, and the director all have their own voice, yet ultimately it is the performer's voice we apparently hear. When that voice itself seems divided into separate voices for singing or speaking, the various possibilities of "ownership" are not merely increased by one but are in fact doubled.

The connection between the spoken and traditional singing voice is perhaps more theoretical than real, as an auditory experience. Developments in the last century have both accentuated and narrowed the gulf. Operas by Alban Berg and Aribert Reimann amplify the super-human aspect of the traditional singing voice even beyond Wagner, with the role for the orchestra similarly providing both an interior commentary and a competitive tension between sheer audibility of voices and instruments. The early development of "crooning" was a result of the inability with early microphones to faithfully deal with the full-powered singing voice. One of the first of these artists was Rudy Vallee who, in a time before electronic amplification, made a personal trademark of the megaphone he used to extend the carrying power of his voice. Bing Crosby, Frank Sinatra, Peggy Lee, Tony Bennett, and many others were later artists in the crooning style, requiring faultless diction, subtle nuancing of text, and a seamless line with a light, ostensibly unstudied tone production. The apparent effortlessness of their vocalism was predicated on the use of electronic amplification, and their accompaniment, be it a band, small instrumental "combo," or piano, was astutely arranged to be supportive without being competitive. Composers began to write specifically for this style, and audiences reacted enthusiastically to the "normality" that the intimacy conveyed. Although undreamed of by Verdi, the concept of "verismo" here seemed to find its ultimate vocal style, paradoxically as a result of a technology unsophisticated by today's standards. It has been noted the "conversational naturalism" of the microphone singer represents a rebirth of the text-centered singing manner favored by the Florentine Camerata. This and other interesting ideas are developed in Henry Pleasant's book, *The Great American Popular Singers*. Between the two extremes of singing and speaking, an infinity of vocal possibilities has been exploited, to the extent that there has been a blurring of the intention between dramatic literature and musical composition. It might be possible to trace the inherent musical qualities of poetic text as controlled by the experimental novels of James Joyce (*Ulysses* and *Finnegan's Wake*), or the playwright Samuel Beckett (the "mouth" monologue *Not I* and the textless *Quad*) through a complete circle to the literary, philosophical, and dramatic ramifications of works by Luciano Berio, such as *Sequenza III*, *A-Ronné*, and the *Sinfonia*. Furthermore, the redefinition of the concepts of what is philosophically justifiable as music by John Cage inevitably led to a redefinition of what is essentially vocal. In poetry, too, the refocusing on the performance aspects of poetry (Roger McGough, Adrian Mitchell), which has a far older tradition than its literary history, has reaffirmed some aspects in the musical arena. In this light, the old definition of the voice between merely spoken and sung, which lies at the root of melodrama, seems almost naive and has certainly been overshadowed.

4
The Singer and the Actor

Composers may work with singers who can act and actors who can sing. Sometimes a single performer embraces both disciplines with equal mastery, but more usually the performer concedes to a feeling of inferiority in one or the other, at some level. Actors and singers may or may not be predestined, share personality traits, or demonstrate similar practical considerations about performing. But certainly as a result of their too-often separate training and education, their differences often become polarized. This chapter is an attempt to clarify some of their differences and similarities as they might affect a composer intending a collaborative relationship.

Differences Between Singers and Actors

Singers and actors are both obsessive, but their obsession lies with different areas. A singer typically strives every day for "the" sound of his or her voice. After achieving this, if there is any time and energy left, the singer focuses on singing the right note at the right time. An actor typically strives every day for "the" truth of the character. After achieving this, if there is any time and energy left, the actor focuses on learning the lines. Creativity in a singer or an actor is achieved when they are able to transcend these restrictions and become the vehicle for the music or drama, replacing their self-consciousness with a full awareness of the moment of performance, endowing the breath of life to their work.

As a result of these different obsessions, singers may bring a finer precision to pitch and rhythm, but actors may have a sense of discovery and experiment that will permit them to do things with their voices that singers might find contradictory to their primary obsession. The actor's willingness to explore unknown areas of the voice contrasts with some singer's innate conservatism. Moreover, the actor who cannot read music but has a good ear and an open imagination may be able to achieve with relative ease the kind of effect a trained singer might strive for months to duplicate. But, of course, with an actor, notes and rhythms may change in detail every time; the composer who is obsessed by the performers reproducing the correct notes and rhythms may not have the time and energy left to deal with the other wild but exciting challenge. It is finally a question of how much control to exert, or of redefining the limits of musical ambiguity within a style, which composers must answer for themselves. But the challenge of composers working with actors is both exciting and rewarding, perhaps because of this wildness and the inherent risks. Because actors sometimes understand the mechanics of performance more consciously than singers (perhaps as a result of their education with the emphasis on their creativity rather than *re*-creativity), they may be able to sing and play instruments, acting the part of a musical performer; even demonstrating, apparently, a lifetime's devotion to their craft. The corollary of a singer's acting without the aid of "their" sound identity is perhaps more rare. Some singers find the experience of talking on stage frightening for the same reason.

Bertolt Brecht gave this description of the actor's job when singing:

> The actor must not only sing but show a man singing. His aim is not so much to bring out the emotional content of his song (has one the right to offer others a dish that one has already eaten oneself?) but to show gestures that are so to speak the habits and usage of the body. (Willett 1978)

This is an extreme theoretical view, akin to Stravinsky's denial of music's ability to express anything, and one that Brecht later contradicted:

> Lotte Lenya, one of Brecht's most famous actor/singers and wife of Kurt Weill, recalls a conversation during rehearsal with Brecht that took place just after the war: "Now at that time, there was a big to-do about epic theater—everything was epic, everything was Entfremdung (sic)—alienation. I said, "to hell with that, I'm singing "Surabaya Johnny" the way I always sang it' . . . right in the middle of it. I stopped for a second and said, "Brecht, you know your theory of epic theater—maybe you don't want me just to sing it the way I sang it—as emotional as "Surabaya Johnny" has to be done?' . . . He said. "Lenya darling what ever you do is epic enough for me.'"(Willet 1978, 248)

The actor-singer offers a synthesis and range of techniques, ability, and expression that may seem limitless. Many great works have been inspired by great actor-singers, such as Schoenberg's *Pierrot Lunaire*. It was written for an actress and cabaret singer, Albertine Zehme, who commissioned it and gave the first performance in costume. It is a unique and powerful invention, defying generic classification, and with many stylistic heirs. Peter Maxwell Davies's *Eight Songs for a Mad King,* Walton's *Façade,* H. K. Gruber's *Frankenstein!,* and Ligeti's *Aventures* and *Nouvelles Aventures* give witness to the richness and diversity of its progeny, all exploiting text, voice, and implicit or explicit drama with a certain dangerous wildness and risk-taking. Not all were written for actors, but all require singers some of the skills an actor brings.

Today it is a truism that many singers can act, and many actors can sing. They are all at least potentially naked exhibitionists, and tend not to shy away from a little competition. On the occasions I have had the opportunity to create companies using both actors and singers, I have witnessed how each group slightly refocuses their work to accommodate the apparent competition from the other side. The result is usually better acting and singing from all. Only when both disciplines work side by side are they able to transcend these tacitly accepted limitations.

The singer typically arrives at first orchestral or stage rehearsal knowing not just the text but the notes as well. This may have been a private process, or one in which a coach has helped. On the other hand, the actor typically arrives at a first rehearsal perhaps not even having read the text, if it is a new work, on specific instruction from the director. The fear may be that by learning the text too soon, a deep subconscious relationship may be created between the actor and role, which may be inappropriate to the director's objectives. Such is the elusive ambiguity of language that the director needs to make a mark on a virgin surface, for fear of irrelevant layers of meaning taking priority. In this context, the language of music appears to be less ambiguous, because so many of the director's decisions appear to have already been made by the composer, and what remains is to interpret the composer's indications. However, given the approximation of our musical language, there is usually plenty of scope for interpretation or ambiguity there. Here, then, are two very different sets of expectations and attitudes as to what precisely constitutes a rehearsal for singer or actor, and thereby we may infer that the intentions, objectives, and mindsets of singers and actors are equally diverse. It is also possible to perceive here how the striving for power through the ownership of ideas in a play is more firmly perhaps in the hands of the sole director, whereas an opera requires two directors, one for music and the other for drama. However, there are many other authors to a stage presentation, including choreography or movement, stage-design, costumes and lighting, as well as the author and the composer.

Actors and singers rely on instinct to differing extents, but not usually as much as children. I have heard a children's choir begin with a four-part chord that bears no relation to the atonal clusters preceding it, with every voice on pitch. Luckily, the children had never been told how difficult it was, so the problem never arose as it would with an adult group who might logically be able to explain why they could not do it, and seek to avoid any risk of failure. Both singing and acting are essentially creative and imaginative processes, and children may display, as in this case, a victory of instinct over reason, empowering them to achieve something a group of adults might reason to be impossible. H. Wesley Balk (1977) offers an explanation of why the education of a musician may rob the adult singer of this instinctive understanding, and create a predisposition toward conservative tendencies, in contrast to an actor:

> Musicians transfer their music-making, right-hemisphere skills to the management and control of the left hemisphere, where the logical, disciplined, reason-orientated capacities can guide the musical-fantasizing energies. Perhaps, like all attempts to control freedom, creativity and fantasy, a system of over-control sets in. The logical and, in this case, repressive left half of the brain overcompensates in its control efforts and stifles the rest of the right half functions to some extent even as it controls the musical capacities. The actor, on the other hand, is a simpler case. The element of discipline which is so necessary in music, and which presumably creates the need for right hemisphere subordination, is lacking (some might say sadly lacking) in theater. In acting there does not seem to be the same need for a complex, controlled discipline, and so there is no need for the left hemisphere to exert its control (20).

Too often, it seems, the educational process seems to be concerned with narrowing down choices or possibilities and restricting imagination. It is not an uncommon experience for composers, when working in creative workshops with groups of children of mixed ability, to discover that the young violinist who has had only a couple of years tuition will much more readily explore and discover the sound world of their instrument than the more advanced student. The concepts of "right" and "wrong" seem to play a fundamental part in the instruction of young musicians far more than with young actors, and music can too easily become a vehicle for certain personalities to express their instincts for obedience and correctness at the expense of imagination and expressivity.

The most important word shared by drama and music in English is "play." It is the noun that defines the central object of dramatic work and as well the verb that expresses the fundamental musical activity. It is also, as many educational psychologists may try to prove, the technique by which we begin to learn about the world around us. The *Concise Oxford Dictionary* offers yet more definitions: "the state of being active, operative or effective; the ability of freedom of movement in a mechanism; light and constantly changing movement; to amuse oneself by engaging in imaginative preference." Many composers may be able to see some of their own work in all these terms, and yet the inherent playfulness of the act of composition too often leads to a deadly serious pursuit of correctness. Actors seem to be free, at least to some extent, of this rigorous desire to acquire brownie points, acknowledging instead an inherent and nebulous instability as a foundation of their work. Actors who perfectly speak their lines without intention, energy, or focus may well be as common as the flawless musical performer who lacks any personality or insight. However, I suggest that such an actor may be more aware of the missing element in a performance, even if temporarily unable to combat it, whereas the poor musician may not even be aware that anything is missing.

H. Wesley Balk (1977, 3) also illustrates the contrasting direction of emphasis between singers and actors, when he says that the singer's only recourse to "truth" lies in an understanding of the score, whereas the actor aims foremost to communicate with the audience. The singer's motto is "In score we trust," whereas the actor's is, typically, "Honor that which communicates." Moreover the singer onstage has two directors who are attempting to put forward their own view of the score. The Music Director's work precedes the Stage Director's, giving the former some advantage. If there is any discrepancy between the two directors, the singer is left in an impossible position, because it is not in their power to arbitrate, only perhaps to compromise. The lines of authority are at least less complex in the theater, with only one director's vision to subsume.

Singers are often pejoratively termed re-creators, a sort of bureaucratized copying machine that no actor might wish to aspire to be. The singer's path to the stage is preceded by instruction from singing teacher, music coach, language coach, music director, choreographer, stage director, and conductor, and always accompanied by an orchestra, every step of the way. There appears to be little room for the singer's individuality here, and with such a diversity of input, it may understandably require all of the singer's attention simply to retain the proliferation of information offered. On the other hand, the actor will often find him or herself rehearsing and performing, accompanied by nothing but silence. This imbalance, denying a singers' primacy in creative terms, is exacerbated by their education: much time is spent working on their instrument and developing their abilities to decode music, but their training in theatrical techniques is often perceived as a secondary, additional skill rather than an equal part of their armory. Similarly, actors with good voices often find their gift "useful" in certain situations or roles, but may often feel they are relying entirely on their natural instincts, which may feel inadequate next to their continuous development and self-analysis as an actor. In the last generation or so there have been many books published to help the actor understand the technicalities of voice production, but unfortunately, for the singer, there exists no comparable body of technique to prepare them for the special performance problems of music-theater.

In some ways then, the roles of singer and actor seem to be diametrically opposed:

- The singer understands words as lyrics, the actor perceives them as inferring action.
- The singer battles to memorize various instructions, whereas the actor may rely upon an ability to improvise both in rehearsal and even in performance.
- The singing voice reflects, in most cases, the professional identity of the performer, whereas an actor strives to find an individual voice for each character.
- The singer works within a highly restricted framework of time decided by the composer and controlled by the conductor, whereas the actor has to supply an internal timing mechanism, and allow the external timing to be influenced by it.
- The singer is accompanied, often on every syllable, by an encouraging, kaleidoscopic wall of orchestral sound, whereas the actor works against perhaps the theater's fifth wall: silence.

Despite these differences, singing and acting share different aspects of the same skill: within a limitation of time, they are both the creators and generators of communication through sound. Sound was, even in the recent past, a far more important vehicle for the communication of words than text, and of course remains the only medium to convey whatever it is that music can be said to convey. Patsy Rodenburg (1993) sums up the giant hierarchical shift from sound to text: "[I]t is fair to say that in our schools the written word has triumphed over the spoken word. Literacy has had a far greater impact than oracy" (23). Perhaps the same is true with music, where educationally the written note holds supreme over the sounded note. In composing terms, what it looks like on the page has more analytical "meaning," or potential for much academic justification, than its sound. This is obviously a contradiction because music is by its nature ephemeral, and the score remains a mute shadow requiring the giving of life that only a performance can realize.

Speaking comes before writing, just as making sounds must precede the need to write them down. Yet because of educational imbalances we now universally seem to value the latter over and above the former. If this is the case, we have moved far, far away from the study of the sound of a language influencing the sound of a country's music (Verdi, Bartók, Janáček, etc.) simply because we are desensitized from the primacy of sound and focus more on the text or the score. In this light, the famous "avant-garde" works of James Joyce—*Finnegan's Wake* and *Ulysses*—experiment with the sounds of words—were nostalgic rather than revolutionary, harking back to a time when the sound of language was preeminent. Joyce's peppering of the text to allusions of Classical Greek literature offers a clue here, as the Greek language was an integration of musico-linguistic techniques, drawing together, rather than separating the acts of speaking and singing. Incidentally, Joyce had an excellent voice and once considered becoming a professional singer, and many other important figures in twentieth century theater were also trained singers or instrumentalists, such as Stanislavsky and Meyerhold.

In Classical Greece, "melos" indicated both lyric poetry and the music to which it was set, and the word became the root of our word, "melody." The fusion of words and music into an indivisible whole is a common occurrence in many ancient societies. All children learn tunes with words, and thereafter are able to remember the tunes. Moreover, most children when singing prefer to simultaneously move their bodies in time to the music. It is, perhaps, an instinctive need for them to not separate these activities, and celebrate their creativity or playful energy in this symbolic unity. Similarly, the sung choruses in Classical Greek theater were not performed by an immobile crowd, but were simultaneously choreographed in their movements. There is ample historical evidence of unity between drama, music, and movement, yet we persist in teaching speaking, singing, acting, and dancing as if there was no connection between them. Worse still, the practitioners in any one category are often encouraged to see their own craft as superior. Singers may be the worst offenders in this regard, as a result of the "stand still and sing" school of the worst traditions of romantic, starry opera.

The challenges and the rewards of composers working with actors and singers are great, and indeed lead beyond that into all cross-platform, artistic collaborations. The synthesis of music and words is the work of both singers and actors. On the stage, this synthesis potentially expands to combine the arts of sight and sound and movement with the word. For a composer, there can be no greater challenge, nor any greater reward.

Similarities Between Singers and Actors

Both the actor and the singer's work is magical in that nothing is visible, and everything is hidden. Appearances are often deceptive, and the greatest art is often that which conceals art. The theatrically physical movements of a virtuoso pianist, violinist, or rock guitarist, may play an undeniable part in the effect the performer has on an audience. Some performers consciously or unconsciously develop this aspect of performance, learning through experience how to manipulate an audience response. Others might consider such aspects frivolous, vulgar, or irrelevant: but to play a string quartet with a minimum of gesture also requires a stern discipline. Actors and singers demonstrate all these extremes, but their instrument is their body. The actions of singing or speaking may appear "natural" and unforced, as a mother soothes a child, or strident, dramatic, and overtly emotional. Both extremes are the result of learned technique applied to an appropriate context.

We are excited when a voice is pushed to the point of danger, just as we watch trapeze artists and tightrope walkers with bated breath. If the weightlifter fails twice to lift the weight, we are the more ready to applaud his success on the third attempt. We are less inclined to believe our eyes if we detect no strain, even if it was easy. The perception that film actors talk "naturally," whereas theater actors suffer from the "training" of their voice may be the result of the performer's achieved objective and the contrast between two opposite genres. In the end, both the "natural" and the "super-human" aspects of acting are the result of analysis and applied technique. The same confusion is often made between the "trained" operatic voice and the "natural" pop or folk voice. Whether technique is ostentatiously displayed or cleverly disguised, it is always learned either from instinct or study, or both. The novelist Salman Rushdie (1999) seemed to understand this perfectly: "The solutions to the problems of art are always technical. Meaning is technical. So is heart" (303).

Stanislavsky (1998) expressed some envy toward the work of the singer from the actor's perspective:

> How lucky you singers are. The composer provides you with one most important element—the rhythm of your inner emotions. That is what we actors have to create for ourselves out of a vacuum. All you have to do is listen to the rhythm of the music and make it your own. The written word is the theme of the author but the melody is the emotional experience of that theme" (22).

The Synthesis of Music, Dance, and Drama

For classical musicians, instrumental music has sometimes seemed more sophisticated than vocal music; perhaps this reflects an era in which interest in technology seems to outweigh interest in the natural world. This attitude is mirrored in the changes that occurred in scoring for voice and instrumentalists over the centuries. In the dominant vocal music of the Renaissance, little or no information regarding dynamics was given in scores. It is hardly likely that there was only one dynamic in this time, any more than there was only one tempo for music before the invention of the metronome, and it is not unreasonable to suggest that the words that were set, implicitly along with the music, suggested the manner of performance to the performers, in terms of dynamics. In the following centuries as instrumental music began to take precedence (as a result of what we may now see as the beginning of the technological revolution still in progress today), composers needed to make explicit what was before implicit, and the concept of musical dynamics grew as a sort of shorthand or code for the more complex and subtle association of word and emotion with intensity long associated with music for the voice.

The technological need to codify and explain all things soon affected vocal music, with the emergence of the Doctrine of Affections. It was an attempt to codify the relationship between music and words, from a quasi-emotional point of view. Musical clichés or conventions were said to relate by their nature to certain modes of speaking, but this resulted in a monothematic restriction of mood (or affect), wherein each emotion might be isolated from contact with any other. This became the basis for much Baroque music.

Meanwhile, the continued abstraction of music from the written word required a more scientific level of information retrieval at the disposal of the instrumentalist. However, the representation of dynamics in musical scores betrays their ancient association with textual sources. However detailed, they require more than merely an obedient replication of changes of intensity of sound from a performer. If they are to become an organic part of the life of a work of music, the dynamics of a work or a passage come about through an understanding, at some level in the performer's mind, of the presence of a tension; an obstacle that must be acted upon to release or create that which is required. The obstacle might be an emotion (e.g. yearning or surrender), an intellectual idea (concerning form or architecture), or simply a need to conquer some inherently virtuosic passage. Against this obstacle an action, or energy, is released to translate the written code into a sensual physicalization of sound that represents the instantaneous fusion between an object and an idea, between concrete matter and abstract matter. Therein lies the metamorphosis of matter with thought, akin to alchemy; a process that is also inherent in the "mysteries" of music, drama, and dance.

Experience Bryon (229) shows how this process links together these three disciplines and demonstrates their commonality:

> It is important to realize that one does not "do" dynamics, but creates a dynamic through action against obstacle. Likewise, one does not "do" a character but creates one through various physical, emotionally based actions against obstacle. [For the dancer] Tension is not "done," but is created through an action against obstacle.

Of course, instrumentalists, too, must act against an obstacle to produce a dynamic or change of intensity, but the work of an instrumentalist is both inherently more abstract and more concrete. The physical presence of an instrument is most obviously concrete, yet the music seems often to be related to nothing beyond itself. A singer typically occupies an even more complex position: the point of tension or resolution between the needs of the written word, the music, and movement. If a cello may be seen as an extension of the body of the cellist in performance, the body of the singer is not merely an extension of the voice, but rather they remain indistinguishable, one from the other. Whether or not a composer's objective is inherently theatrical, the voice presents a doorway through which the process of symbiosis of word, action, and sound may be evoked. In this light, the difference between an actor and a singer is merely one of emphasis rather than craft.

Bryon (230) continues to illustrate and contrast the difference between the process of realization of these inner relationships through performance and the more common act of parallelism:

> For instance, if dance is fast then colors of red are employed and emotions seem angry and the music loud. By putting a bunch of depictorial similes together, the operations of these arts are not woven but are placed in parallel, next to each other. A theme does not necessarily make the operations interrelate; it just renders the performance aspects sister products and slaves to a similar theme. This is what occurred with traditional notions of the meaning being inherent in the word. The meaning is seen as inherent in the theme and again the arts are left to depict a supposedly present meaning. To parallel the arts is not to interrelate. Fashionable contemporary terms like "hybrid" and "multi-media" often imply an interrelationship but merely parallel in practice.

The very act of working with a singer, dancer, or actor presents a composer with similar challenges. These challenges may inspire fear in the composer, because they are often beyond the compartmentalized educational objectives of institutions. Nonetheless, it was this challenge that originally inspired the Florentine Camerata in the late sixteenth century to create the longest surviving musical form, which still flourishes today: opera. Although it often seems to set out to resolve the problems of interdisciplinary relationships, opera significantly and often spectacularly fails to do so. Perhaps this very failure—along with the illusion that it is still possible—in part explains the durability of the old challenge.

The future of opera is in doubt, and that is probably a healthy sign for a medium so obsessed with its own glorious past for so long that the recent past has hardly had an effect on the big producing houses, let alone the present. Nevertheless, the centuries of development of an art-form molded around the spirit and physicality of the human voice, continues to inspire composers and singers such as Meredith Monk in ever new and exciting ways. In the liner notes to her recording of "Turtle Dreams", Monk says: "I was encouraged to work with a feeling, an idea. . .and let the medium. . . form itself. It seemed that finally I was able to combine movement with music and words all coming from a single source. . .a total experience."

5
Considerations of Style

An ability to compose in various styles has long been upheld as part of a composer's training. The availability of styles to choose from has never seemed more rich and diverse as at present. The palette is tantalizing for as many composers as it is bewildering for others. Nowhere is this richness and diversity more in evidence than with the voice. The difficulty and time required for a composer to absorb information from the sea of stylistic possibilities available should not be underestimated. There is often a further expectation that the composer will be able to create his or her own unique and original style. This chapter attempts to present some of the dangers and attractions to the composer on such a path.

The Last Romantic Artist

> *"Le style c'est l'homme même"*
> —Ludwig Wittgenstein

Schoenberg inherited Hungarian nationality, which was later converted to Czech in 1918, eventually becoming an American citizen in 1941. He was born into the Jewish faith, but converted to Lutheranism in 1898. These were choices he was able to make, until he was forced to leave Europe due to the rise of fascism. It was not always thus: Byrd wrote securely for the Catholic Liturgy in Latin until the Reformation after which he and countless others found the need to instantly espouse their new faith, at least outwardly, with an equal and undiminished fervor, instantly relinquishing their textual inspiration from the vulgate to the vernacular. Byrd had no choice if he wished to continue as a composer in England under Henry VIII.

I do not suggest that stylistic choice for an artist is equivalent to a religious choice, but both are aspects of personality that may lie deeper than rational, conscious, or logical thought. Schoenberg formally rejoined the Jewish faith later in the early 1930s, just as Byrd probably continued to practice his Roman Catholicism long after it became illegal. These are not merely historical anecdotes: The two composers' distinct moral dilemmas are echoed in myriad disguises every day for composers of the twenty-first century.

That powerful religious institutions embody the power of the state and in turn empower the state over the individual is both an historical and a contemporary fact. Perhaps Byrd's acceptance of the change of his religion was a display of the necessity of an individual to subjugate his private beliefs, at least in public, to survive as a servant of the state, which was the role of the composer for many centuries. Byrd, out of necessity, might outwardly conform to the proscribed practices of his masters, without the fear of betraying his own personal beliefs. Entire civilizations have learned to adopt similarly expedient attitudes with a change of masters, as when the subjugate Indians of Central America found their old tyrants, the Aztecs, suddenly replaced by the Conquistadors. Outwardly they had no choice but to accept the new religion, but internally, although the names changed, many of the old thoughts and practices continued, even inherited from long before the Aztecs. Religious syncretism is sometimes the only effective means of survival, and its cultural equivalent is equally effective as a means of defense against censorship.

In the last century, the continuing role of the state in relation to limiting artistic license or stylistic censorship was not just a result of right wing fascist or Nazi politics, but also of the left, as the extraordinary career and work of Shostakovitch, among thousands of others, will testify. The Soviet communists sought to control the influence of styles that they considered harmful to the state, an ancient view first espoused by Plato in his book, *The Republic*. At about the same time, the USSR's arch enemy, the USA, rejected all artists who showed the slightest allusion or tendency to Communism, in the infamous McCarthy trials.

Although I cannot be sure, I would wager a guess that neither Bach nor Mozart, Beethoven nor Brahms, Mahler nor Wagner, Debussy nor Ives, Janáček nor Bartók consciously chose their respective styles, nor was it thrust upon them by a controlling state, unlike Shostakovitch and his compatriots. The creation of their musical language was not based on a survey of the possible choices available through selective study, research, or an equivalent reading of a style-conscious consumer guide, had one existed. And here is a problem central both to comparative religion or more specifically comparative aesthetics (stylistics?) in today's educational climate: the logical extension of the consumerist ethic toward religious or artistic concerns is to enable people to perceive the possibility of choosing a religion or for artists to make choices of faith or style in the same manner as they choose other consumer goods. The acceptance or rejection of a style or idea and its value may be seen to be controlled from another parameter in today's globally capitalistic world. Idealism is no longer "politically correct," and expediency is the operative word to open doors. The only political justification for something to be created, exist, or be valued may lie in its financial potential for success.

Of course, music today has never been so rich, so diverse, so free from whatever is perceived as tradition, should a composer require such a freedom. Whereas this may be seen as an aspect of richness and fecundity, the apparently unlimited choice of styles for a composer may also be a poisoned chalice. As the composer seeks a path toward a concept of "success," the different paths toward different styles are self-defining and mutually exclusive. The proponents of style "A" do not consider the adherents to style "B" as relevant or consequential to their vision of music. Once having strayed from the straight and narrow, no return can be plausibly accepted. The field of infinite riches seems to be instead a minefield to be negotiated blindfolded for a young composer still curious, but concerned with creating a personal language.

And worse may follow, when a composer must pursue academic, public, or commercial patronage: the composer chooses which university to study at according to an often unpublished doctrine, without fear of having to confront or appraise something alien from another stylistic milieu. The composer commissioned by the public purse must skate above the shark-infested waters of "relevance" and "elitism," not to mention "popularity" itself, as if it were a fixed and immutable quality, and prove to his or her public to offer, above all, "value for money." On the other hand, the commercial composer knows well the importance and power of the owner of his purse strings, and accepts the inevitable and consequent compromises perhaps from the start. Whenever a composer seeks support, his dependent position seems open and honest in comparison to a staunch idealist position: nobody would expect a composer today to retain such a stubborn but suicidal morality. The capitulations of Byrd and Shostakovitch remain opaque, evidence of the needful complexity of human relationships faced with the problems of survival, rather than as blemishes to some idea of artistic purity. Similarly, the composer today whose overriding ambition is to maximize profit is simply passively obeying the reigning capitalist dictum, and putting all other considerations second; here there is no duplicity except and unless the same composer proclaims a stylistic or artistic insight. But the composer whose aim may be to acknowledge the influences that drove him or her to music and offer a personal response, according to an individual and instinctive understanding of artistic integrity, may now be seen as either romantically idealistic, and thus at best naïve, or perhaps even a charlatan. There seems little place for such an individual aesthetic obstinacy toward style in today's commercially driven world. The last romantic artist is long dead.

Without doubt, beyond boundaries of time and race, the availability to the composer of diverse and contrasted musical examples is unparalleled in history. However, the educational function of this presentation of diversity often seems to be to compare, judge, copy, emulate, or to reject. Music is often reduced to a table of comparative worthiness, rather than seen as having any intrinsic value in itself. This begs the question of whether there is any intrinsic value in music, other than the academic analysis or commercial "proof" of the veracity of a composition's stylistic, formal, or financial success. These values are weighed and calculated so much more keenly than any instinctive response, and yet "instinct," as in the subjugation of the conscious in preference to the subconscious methods of comprehension or creation, plays an obviously cardinal role in any creative field, both for the creator and the receptor. Nonetheless, this aspect of the arts seems hardly to be granted standing room.

However, analysts, administrators, and multi-nationals do not have the right to own or define the meaning or value of music, or proclaim an understanding of its intrinsic merits. In answering Allen Forte's concept of pitch-class sets expressed in *The Structure of Atonal Music,* George Perle (1990) offers not only a response to Forte's academic approach, but also a deeper critique based on his years of work as a composer:

> My critique begins with the subjective, intuitive, and spontaneous experience of one who has spent a lifetime listening to music, composing it, playing it, and thinking about it, and then finds himself confronted with ways of talking about and analysing music which have nothing whatever to do with what I would call this "common sense" experience. But at such a fundamental level the act of musical judgment is a private one, a matter that must be left to one's self and one's conscience. **(151)**

In the pursuit of style, there are few enough options open for a composer. One is the promulgation of the cult of individualism and its seemingly inevitable path toward conceptualism, where, perversely, originality beyond the confines of a concept into any reality is automatically suspect or made "impure" conceptually. An alternative path might be the adoption of a "school" and an exploration of its "ethical" boundaries. But history shows that the disintegration (I use the term non-pejoratively) of a "school" of thought begins at its inception, according to the dictum that rules are made to be broken, as soon as the rule itself is recognized, formulated, and established.

A veneer of catholicism seems to disguise the innate conservatism in our time. The artistic choices available are equal to, for example, purchasing a car. Unless you have unlimited financial resources, the choices open to you are far from infinite. Henry Ford's ominous dictum of offering the buyer "any color you want, as long as it's black" seems to sum up the basis of capitalist freedom, even within the arts. The restriction of areas of knowledge to experts unwilling to share their insight for fear of losing their academic "authority," and the exiling of music into a marketable, concrete medium such as the recording industry might prefer, further muddy the composer's waters.

At some stage in their training, today's composers are made aware of the choices they must make if "style" is part of a conscious, pre-compositional thought process, and that this decision is a crucial choice determining all that follows. After learning all that one is able, the only alternative might be to attempt to temporarily forget conscious knowledge and rely on an instinctive process in which sounds and thoughts metamorphose, beyond the restrictions of fashion and language, into music itself.

It is not certain whether or not these sorts of dilemmas have always lain in wait at certain intersections of a composer's development. Yet, despite a profound change in allegiances, the music of Byrd seemed to develop seamlessly through his professional life, whereas the music of Schoenberg (who, like so many, needed even to change the spelling of his name to conform to the standards of his adoptive country) and Stravinsky exemplified a semiotic and syntactic odyssey unparalleled and unimaginable before the twentieth century.

Writing for the voice offers these same dichotomies for the composer, but perhaps more intensely. A cello may remain the same instrument irrespective of culture, country, or style, but the same may not be true of a voice. Given that the diversity of singers, voices, and styles exceeds every other medium, from historical, contemporary, and geographical perspectives, does a composer "choose" to write for a certain ideal voice, sound, or style, and if so, how? Is there any way that the choice could be made truly creative rather than merely expedient?

The evolution of the voice and compositional attitudes to it over the last five centuries is beyond the scope of this book, yet, oddly, there are surprisingly common aspects that have remained universal in terms of vocal aesthetics. Gaffurius stated in his *Practica musicae*, written in 1496:

> Singers should not produce musical tones with a voice gaping wide in distorted fashion or with an absurdly powerful bellowing, especially when singing at the divine mysteries; moreover they should avoid tones having a wide and ringing vibrato, since these tones do not maintain a true pitch and because of their continuous wobble cannot form a continuous concord with other voices (1968, 148).

There is a familiarity of intention here, even beyond its modern translation from Latin to English. It is a definition of a sound, an idea of a sound, which is universally appropriate, that perhaps even survives the changing boundaries of fashion, style, and tradition through time.

Composers of all times and eras have displayed one common ability: to take whatever is available in the raw material of musicians around them and, working with them, develop it. Finding the ideal singer of any composer's dreams may be possible in time, but meanwhile there is much work to be done and much to be learned from working with whatever singers one is lucky enough to come across. Rather than sheer pragmatism, this method can be creatively fruitful, leading a composer into greater understanding and new ideas. To this objective, Chapter 8 sets out some workshop ideas for composers and singers.

All of this is a preamble to the fundamental question, What are the choices of vocal compositional style available to the composer today? I have tried to avoid offering a shopping list from which a composer may pick and choose freely. However, that is inevitably what a book such as this must supply. Later in this chapter, we will analyze some important examples of differing ways in which composers wrote for the voice within a certain style. But first what follows is an attempt to categorize those aspects of writing for the voice that are expected to be understood and acted upon by the singer.

A Shopping List

A vocal style is a behavioral idiosyncrasy acknowledged between composer and performer. It evolves as a personal reaction to a circumstance that a singer makes in relation to what may be divined as the composer's intentions, according to perceived experience. It involves making both conscious and instinctive decisions. Questions of style are usually inferred rather than designated as a part of the notated musical language of the score. The circumstance may be historical, environmental, or musical, or any combination of the three. A musical style may directly affect the type of vocal production of a knowledgeable and experienced singer in a number of different ways.

Figure 3 is a presentation of the effects of various musical situations on the voice. It compares extremes of vocal technique, from underdeveloped to over-refined in relation to registers, tone, words, and rhythms. However, the terminology is not intended pejoratively, as within certain styles an underdeveloped or over-refined technique may be precisely what is required. However, it does suggest an interpretation of the principles of Bel Canto as being basic or even central to all vocal techniques. From that discipline, if correctly applied, access to all styles is possible, whereas the converse is not necessarily true. This table is not intended as an indication of the supremacy of any technique, but is merely an indication of the universality of the basic ideas behind Bel Canto, through which maximum vocal control and flexibility are possible. The final, isolated row considers proximity as a definer of style that, given the many and varied modes of presentation, live and recorded, possible for a singer today, might be an important consideration for every composer as well.

There are however several consequences of perceiving styles in this manner. For instance, given the appropriate material and style, any voice— irrespective of training or musical technique—with a minimum of aural ability should be able to perform a song. This is hardly news to anyone who hears a radio or visits a shopping center today, but for those working with musically insecure actors in musical situations, the choice of material may be the most important consideration, rather than a crash course in music theory or stylistic perception.

For composers, Fig. 3 offers two perspectives: a brief presentation of the gamut of vocal applications, and a blueprint of what skills might be expected (and not) of singers connected with certain specialist areas. At the foot of the Table, the left hand box plots the course of a few styles in general terms. It is indicative of the extremities of some variants, rather than as a complete list of stylistic possibilities. Neither does it do justice to the variety of techniques within each style, which is self-evident to those who are intimate with the repertory. It does however aim to illustrate the fundamental aspects of many vocal styles within a single, infinitely variable framework.

It is also interesting to note the non-exclusivity of "style," as diverse styles seem to often share similar aspects. Of course, the detailed understanding of historical style is itself prone to changes of fashion, research, or merely taste. In the bottom right-hand box, music analyzed later in this chapter is subjected to the same list of parameters, and illustrates the many shared aspects apparent in diverse and contrasted styles.

These ideas illustrate how singers might react and adapt vocally to *known* musical styles, through experience or instinct. Many composers currently aim to create work in a unique style, attempting to reinvent or extend one or other basic parameter of musical language or aesthetics. The majority of all vocal scores carry little or no direct information about the vocal style required; singers approaching Purcell or Schumann, Gershwin or Dolly Parton tend to know what is expected of them. However, singers cannot know what may be expected of them by composers at the cutting edge unless there is some indication in the score. For Mozart, Donizetti, and Richard Strauss, their style was understood by all as a summary of a major contemporary aesthetic trend, and they worked directly with the singers they wrote for on an almost everyday basis. Perhaps the same may be said of composers and

ELEMENTS	UNDERDEVELOPED TECHNIQUE*		BEL CANTO PRINCIPLES		OVER-REFINED TECHNIQUE*
	A	B	C	D	E
(1) Registers	Divided, unbalanced	Use of break between registers for emotional effect	Registers balanced; smooth, even, continuous tone throughout range	Mastery over partial range, e.g., counter-tenor	Use of only one (extended) range, e.g., chest
(2) Tone	Limited palette of color and volume	Breathy, husky, or "unsupported" sounds	All colors accessible throughout volume and range; natural, controllable vibrato	Pure "white" tone without vibrato	The precedence of volume over musical or linguistic needs
(3) Words	Limited palette of color and volume	Recitative; diction at the expense of legato, or semi-singing in cabaret. Colloquial vowels and diphthongs.	Classical enunciation, pure vowels, allied with legato line	Legato at expense of diction. Musical line as primary objective	Purity of vocal tone: vocalize
(4) Rhythm	Improvisation	Rubato	Balance between notated and inferred rhythms	Limited rhythmical freedom	Absolute mathematical strictness

Additional Elements which Affect Vocal Style:

	A	B	C	D	E
(5) Proximity	Audio/visual recording; access to fine detail	Intimacy: close proximity of audience; or some amplification	Perfect balance between closeness and objectivity, involvement without embarrassment; perhaps ambient amplification	Amplification perhaps leading to distortion	Greek Amphitheater or Grand Arena presentation

Some Generalized Vocal Styles analyzed with the above

Specific Example Analyzed in Chapter 5

Rap:	1A, 2A, 3A, 4E (5D)	Britten:	11C, 2C, 3C, 4C, (5C)
Early Baroque:	1C, 2C/D, 3C, 4D (5B)	Schoenberg:	1B, 2B/C, 3B, 4B/E, (5B)
Heavy Metal:	1B/E, 2E, 3B, 4A (5D)	Parton:	1B/D, 2C, 3B/C, 4A, (5A)
Popular Ballad: (Sinatra, Bassey, etc):	1B/E.2C, 3B, 4B (5B)	Gershwin:	1C, 2C, 3C, 4B/C, (5C)
Crooning: (Crosby, etc):	1E, 2B, 3B, 4B (5A)	Weir:	1C, 2C, 3B, 4C (5B)
		Eisler:	1B, 2B, 4A/B, 5A

*NB: these terms are applied non-pejoratively

Figure 3. Variants of Vocal Style and the Effects on Singers.

singers working in certain areas of jazz or popular music today. But for the contemporary classical composer, this is less likely to be the case, and at least some indication of what is required with respect to stylistic parameters and vocal production is vital.

Some Composers' Solutions

A close study of different songs demonstrates changing relationships between text and music, and the use of the voice. As it is impractical to include complete scores, it is suggested that these examples be read alongside scores or recordings of the works.

1. Brahms: *Nachtigall,* Op. 97 No. 1

Synopsis: The nightingale's song penetrates my being. It reminds me of other music, divinely beautiful, long silenced for me. (Poem by C. Reinhold)

Consider the two phrases in Example 5.1a and their different effect on vocal production:

The first is from the beginning of Brahms's song, and has more character and is more "singable" in relation to the text. The second is uncomfortable, because it creates a technical problem for the singer: how to distribute the consonants within the legato line. If the double consonant "dr" is placed on the upper note, the crucial legato line produced on the vowels will certainly be audibly interrupted by a small silence before the "d," however skilful the singer. Additionally, the muscular tension caused by placing the tongue behind the teeth to make the "d"—simultaneously with the sudden demand to sing in a higher range— may also strangle the next vowel, causing an ugly

Example 5.1a.   Brahms: *Nachtigall,* Op. 97 No. 1.

Langsam

O   Nach - ti___ gal,   dein   sü - sser_ Schall,

Example 5.1b. Brahms: *Nachtigall,* Op. 97 No. 1.

sound, or worse. The common solution for this sort of problem is to mentally place the "dr" on the first, lower note as if it were an acciaccatura, releasing the "i" vowel on the upper note. Singers frequently have to employ this kind of technique to solve problems of legato that are insufficiently detailed or ignored by composers. Brahms understood many problems of this sort and frequently provides the singer with the detailed creative solution. In this example, the word "er," a convenient quasi-vowel sound, itself moves at the last moment up the octave to prepare for the next syllable and note, providing a solution both as elegant as it is characterful. The same solution appears over the following bar line between the words "durch Mark," where the "ch" might otherwise be similarly intrusive. The adoption of the same rhythm on "(drin)-get" and "und" is more than a structural continuation, because it helps glue together the vowels across more double consonants, "t-m" and "d-B." The opening phrase, "O Nachtigal, dein süsser Schall," is free from these potentially problematic double consonants or intrusive plosives, allowing Brahms to create a simpler melodic idea, hanging poignantly around a tritone, without any quick changes of range (see Example 5.1b).

It is also worth noting how Brahms omits the additional first melody note articulated first in the piano introduction (see Example 5.1c). It would be

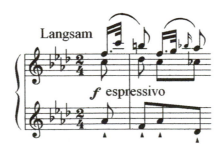

Langsam

f espressivo

Example 5.1c. Brahms: *Nachtigall,* Op. 97 No. 1.

dolce

Nein, trau-ter Vö-gel, nein!__ was in mir Schafft

Example 5.1d. Brahms: *Nachtigall,* Op. 97 No. 1.

more formally contrapuntal to do so, but the phrase would lose much of its yearning character derived from the descending semitone.

"Nachtigall" is a miniature of merely 33 bars, but it demonstrates Brahms' perfectionist attention to detail and nuance. The intimacy of the moment when the poet addresses the bird directly is clearly articulated by both poet and composer. The prolongation of the exclamation "nein!" across the bar line endows the breath afterward with an emotional function and color: the poet does not wish the bird to be disturbed by his confidence. His realization that this might be the case occurs in the necessarily breathless rest before, which interrupts his thought. (See Example 5.1d).

The poet has produced an alliterative line that follows, which at some level may have struck Brahms. The preponderance of "s" sounds becomes part of the urgency of the pleading to calm and placate the innocent bird, within the gently accelerated, conversational rhythm:

> "was in mir schafft so süße Pein/ das ist nicht dein"
> ("tr: what creates in me such sweet pain/ is not you")

Brahms slows the pace down for the next phrase, for which he luxuriates unashamedly in romantic piano harmonies underpinning the setting of "something else: heavenly, lovely tones/ that have long since faded away"; providing a shimmering climax across "nun längst," two words separated by two consonants which are semi-vowels. The legato line must be unbroken (see Example 5.1e).

The last line of the poem is repeated, but this is not merely a traditional device. The final words are "in deinem Lied ein leiser Widerhall!" which means, "in your song there is merely a soft echo." The Nightingale seems to continue her innocent tune the first time, but the echo of those "lovely tones" recurs in the repetition in the piano, ending the song on a whispered major chord.

The care and attention to detail evident in the song reflect Brahm's ability to weld his musical thought to a poem, and endow even a light lyric such as this with unsuspected depth.

Example 5.1e. Brahms: *Nachtigall,* Op. 97 No. 1.

2. Britten: *Pastoral (Serenade,* Op. 31)

This is the first song from the cycle of six disparate poetic mediations on night and death for tenor horn and string orchestra. It is a setting of the minor seventeenth-century English poet Charles Cotton. Britten was not often of the disposition to write about his creative ideas in words, but for the premiere of the opera *Peter Grimes,* written at about the same time, he produced a rare musical manifesto arguing against the methods of many of his contemporaries, for whom speech-rhythms provided an important basis for musical setting. Britten worked in a more rhetorical style, reflected in his studies and work on editions of Purcell.

Charles Cotton's poem displays an unvaried metrical simplicity and a rhyming scheme, that may be taken as either simple or banal, demonstrated in the first of the four verses:

> The day's grown old; the fainting sun
> Has but a little way to run,
> And yet his steeds, with all his skill,
> Scarce lug the chariot down the hill.

Britten's instincts or imagination achieve something exceptional, contrary to all traditional procedures (see Example 5.2). He writes across the poetic duplet rhythms by choosing a triple time signature. This ostensibly replaces the natural stresses of the language with the unnatural musical stresses. The original poem scans thus:

> The *Day's* grown *old;* the *fainting sun*
> Has *but* a *little way* to *run,*

Observing the traditional stresses inferred by bar lines, Britten recomposes this structure quite differently:

> The *Day's* grown old; *the* fainting *sun*
> *Has* but a *little* way to run,

The Days grown old: the fain-ting Sun Has but a lit-tle way___ to run

___ And yet his Steeds, with all his skill, Scarce lug___ the Cha - riot down the hill.

Example 5.2. Britten: *Pastoral* (*Serenade,* Op. 31) © 1944 in USA by Hawkes & Son (London) Ltd; Copyright for all countries. Reprinted by permission of Boosey & Hawkes, Inc.

Clearly it was not Britten's intention to use the bar lines to infer accents in this traditional way, and his use of tenuto markings at the exceptionally slow speed allows the singer to articulate more natural and subtle emphases. But there are more details that break with traditional rules or even Purcellian heightened word setting. The highest note of the first phrase, indeed of the first verse, is the first note, a top A flat, yet the definite article is hardly of any crucial importance. However, it informs the descending, yawning trajectory of the opening languid phrase, as well as the overall sense of the poem in a startling yet subtle musical way. It demands in turn a high degree of control from the tenor, who is pulled in two directions by the natural stresses of the words and the elongated accentuation of the music. This tension, when applied creatively by the singer, provides the music with a feeling of metrical depth or profundity. The poem's almost trite metrical structure is transformed into something complex and unpredictable, without semantic loss. (I do not wish to sound pejorative about the poem. Part of its charm lies in its fusion between dark images of night and death with an innocent, almost naive style. An actor speaking the poem would not accentuate the meter of the poem in such an obvious way as it is structured, but might do in part what Britten did, to create tension and variety.) Any hint of metrical symmetry is further disrupted by the expanded bars on "sun" and "skill" (as well as an unexpected tied note on "run"), which allow echoing entries in the solo horn to answer the voice, creating a subtle dialogue or commentary. Meanwhile, the slowly pulsing string chords dissect the 3/8 in cross-rhythms.

The comparatively tonal simplicity of the music offsets this complex met-rical texture, which gradually unfolds within the quietly declamatory nature of the text. It is sung as if with held breath, for fear of destroying the in-effable quality of the idea. The effect of the music, as in the poem, is of an apparent simplicity and openness, while disguising enormous sophisti-cation. Although the words supply one meaning, and the music provides an insight into the words, the synthesis of words and music here create an almost tangible, yet delicate third layer; the music "yearns" gently but passionately for that which can never be. Through the fusion of music and words we have gained an insight into both poet and composer. Preserved for one instant in creative time, across the gulf of centuries, they appear indivisible.

The harmonic language becomes darker in the second verse, which follows a similar structure to the first verse. The third verse provides a temporary relief from the tension, as both tempo and note speeds are increased, and the strings play pizzicato. Britten articulates each word of the third verse differently, and the effect of the faster speed on the words is to create a conversational style in contrast with the flowing line of the first two verses. The rising seventh falling a second echoes the strong element from the original melody ("A very little, *li-tle flock*"). Only the horn maintains its primary material, descending ultimately from an almost whispered, highest note, to a troubled pedal in the final verse.

Here the original tempo and melody returns but are transformed both in key, chord inversion, and mood. The top A flat, which began the first two verses, remains a receding memory and is never regained, while the strings now echo the dying phrases over an extremely quiet, shifting tremolo.

The last words of the poem, "Till Phoebus, dipping in the West, Shall lead the world the way to rest," are marked by a telling enharmonic change at the apex of the vocal line, as the F sharp on "West," diminuendos into a G flat on "Shall lead..." falling into silence beyond the last word.

The setting ends with the shortest postlude, double pianissimo, which briefly echoes the opening material. This "rest," as it is articulated in the music, is hardly comforting and elegiac. Despite the immediate classical beauty and poise of the song, the tension created between vocal line and text, horn and strings, rhythm and meter, is never dispelled. Neither night nor death can be avoided, but the impossible has been wished for, and the strength of feeling that yearning created remains in the form of this song, to outlive the mortality of its creators.

3. Debussy and Ravel: *Placet futile*

Placet futile	Futile Supplication
Princesse! à jalouser le destin d'une Hébé	Princess! In envying the fate of a Hebe*,
Qui poind sur cette tasse au baiser de vos lèvres;	Who appears on this cup at the kiss of your lips,
J'use mes feux mais n'ai rang discret que d'abbé	I exhaust my passion, but my modest rank is only that of a priest
Et ne figurerai même nu sur le Sèvres.	And I won't even appear nude on the Sévres porcelain

Comme je ne suis pas ton bichon embarbé,	Since I am not your bewhiskered lapdog,
Ni la pastille, ni du rouge, ni jeux mièvres	Nor lozenge, nor rouge, nor affected gestures,
Et que sur moi je sens ton regard clos tombé	And since I know that you view me with indifferent eyes
Blonde dont les coiffeurs divins sont des orfèvres!	Fair one, whose divine hairdressers are goldsmiths!
Nommez-nous . . . toi de qui tant de ris framboisés	Appoint me . . . you whose many raspberried laughs
Se joignent en troupeaux d'agneaux apprivoisés	Are gathered into flocks of docile lambs,
Chez tous broutant les voeux et bêlant aux délires,	Nibbling at all promises and bleating deliriously,
Nommez-nous . . . pour qu'Amour ailé d'un éventail	Appoint me . . . in order that Love, with a fan for his wings,
M'y peigne flûte aux doigts endormant ce bercail,	May paint me fingering a flute and lulling these sheep,
Princesse, nommez-nous berger de vos sourires.	Princess, appoint me shepherd of your smiles.
	(*cupbearer to the Gods)

   In 1913 Debussy and Ravel, unknown to each other, chose three poems by Mallarmé to set to music. Both cycles are known as "Trois Poèmes de Stéphane Mallarmé." More remarkable, the first and second poems of each set are identical. Both cycles are for voice and piano, but that of Ravel is also published with a small instrumental ensemble. (Readers should refer to the individual scores.)

   There are several aspects that immediately define the different styles and sensitivities of the two composers. Debussy, in the last years of his life, retains a stronger link with the chanson, by retaining the tradition of separate stems for each syllable, while Ravel clarifies his rhythms through necessity (because later they become very complex) by adopting instrumental-style groupings. Ravel's use of the phrase mark strongly emphasizes breathing patterns, the arching of the musical ideas, whereas Debussy relies more on the instinct of the singer, leaving these details to inference. Within their natural restraint, the two composers also display different degrees of overt emotionality, visible in the vocal line: Debussy's intervals are much smaller, moving carefully and often by step, in the context of which the opening descending minor sixth becomes a major statement in itself, a gesture of some importance, which functions as a memory when it reappears at the end of the song; Ravel curiously uses the same interval for the first word but ascending, and immediately dropping a minor tenth with the indication of a light portamento, creating a far more ostentatious gesture, more obviously dramatic than structural. The gesture, as so often in Ravel, is never repeated. The intervals that follow it are greater than with Debussy, moving more rapidly through an extended vocal range.

These characteristics are emphasized even more in the instrumental writing. Debussy, at this stage in his life, was concerned with concision and subtlety. The song treats the poem as an intimate love letter upon which we are invited to intrude, cautiously. Hardly less passionate than Ravel, the music suggests more than it demonstrates, only once rising to a forte at "nor lozenge, nor rouge, nor affected gestures." The piano writing explores many colors and details, but remains controlled, or perhaps polite, in social terms. The playful imagery of Mallarmé is transformed into many musical colors, but delicately, with a restrained urbanity, which is quintessentially Gallic.

Ravel's music here is more gestural, more public. From the outset, his was conceived as a composition for voice and ensemble, and Ravel's remarkable orchestral imagination led him toward exploring a greater palette of colors, even in the piano version. It is a more public reading of the poem, more overtly demonstrative. Part of the charm of Debussy's reading might even suggest a touch of guilt that these intimate sentiments are being disclosed, but there is pleasure even in that guilt. Instead of a private declaration of love, Ravel's song seems to be consciously, yet tastefully, showing off. He has arrived outside the window of his lover with half an orchestra, and is aware that his message will be heard not only by his lover but also by all the neighbors. He knows and cares only about the passion he feels.

Surprisingly, the piano score of Ravel displays no dynamic marking greater than mezzo forte; the extraordinary climactic outburst at "Since I am not your bewhiskered lapdog" is not assigned a dynamic at the apex of the crescendo. Ravel is of course no less Gallic than his elder compatriot, and there is a consistent delicacy and attention to detail. A count of nine pianissimos and one double pianissimo in the score hardly suggests he is really proclaiming his love from the rooftops, but reflects instead an extraordinary and almost uncontainable desire to create orchestral color on his part, and neatly serves to underline the unusual intensity and intimacy of Debussy's composition.

Both composers demonstrate an antipathy toward melismas, and remain scrupulously within the constraints of the original poem. Debussy demonstrates his musical concern with structure and balance, and as a colorist he remains in the service of these traditional compositional tools. Ravel, on the other hand, demonstrates a more dramatic leaning toward gesture, as well as a preoccupation with color as a primary tool.

With such a comparative study, there is a temptation to evaluate these two settings. However, even if it were possible to do so, it would inevitably reflect more on the proclivities of this author, than bear any worthwhile and objective outcome. If the similarities and contrasts between these two settings aid other composers to identify their own individual relationship to such a text, the influence of either Ravel or Debussy will become more definable in their own work.

4. Donizetti: *The Mad Scene (Lucia di Lammermoor)*

The vocal expression of insanity has been a constant obsession with many composers for at least four centuries. Fundamentally the genre serves to justify why someone is singing rather than speaking; for the composer there is an inherent acknowledgement that singing is an extreme mode of emotional expression, as compared to speaking. Shakespeare incorporated songs of this sort for many of his characters when pushed to this extreme state: Both the Fool and Edgar use songs in *King Lear* to feign or imitate madness; Ophelia's pathetic songs from *Hamlet* have been raided by many composers, including Richard Strauss (*Drei Lieder,* Op. 67, No. 1), Shostakovitch (*Hamlet Suite,* Op. 32a), and Elgar (*Unpublished Song*), among others, to create the desired effect in a concert hall.

A mad character in opera has full license to sing in a way beyond the normal or accepted limitations of the time; operatic "mad scenes" have often become virtuoso tours de force for the leading prima donnas. It is not without interest that operatic madness at least prior to the twentieth century seemed to be an entirely feminine condition, as attributed by usually male composers (see Clément [1989], which offers great insight on this topic). An early example in the theater was the song *From Silent Shades,* an anonymous text set by Henry Purcell in about 1682 (published 1683, from *Orpheus Britannicus,* Vol.1), also called *Bess of Bedlam.* The following list shows some of the more important mad-scenes for sopranos from the traditional opera repertoire:

1627   *La Finta Pazza* (Monteverdi) displays madness in the text
1640   *Il Ritorno d"Ulisse* in patria (Monteverdi): Iro's suicide
1732   *Orlando* (Haydn): includes a passage in 5/8 time
1825   *I Puritani* (Bellini): "Vien, diletto, è in ciel la luna; Qui la voce sua soave"
1830   *Anna Bolena* (Donizetti) "Piangete voi; - Al dolce guidami . . ."
1835   *Lucia di Lammermoor* (Donizetti): "Il dolce suono"; "Spargi d'amaro pianto"
1854   *L'Étoile du Nord:* (Meyerbeer) "La, la, la, air chérie"
1868   *Hamlet* (Ambroise Thomas) "Le voilà! Je crois l'entendre"
1899   *The Tsar's Bride* (Nikolaj Rimsky-Korsakov) Marva's Aria

The surreal and expressionist poems of Schoenberg's *Pierrot Lunaire* and his monodrama *Erwartung* may also be cousins to the genre, which has developed with perhaps slightly less gender stereotyping in the last century. Certainly the states of emotional distress or extremity have continued to beguile composers with or without the word "madness," in Berg's *Wozzeck,* Menotti's *The Consul,* and Ligeti's *Le Grand Macabre.* Unusually, Peter Maxwell Davies' *8 Songs for a Mad King* (1969) is a music-theater work for male voice and instrumental ensemble, with text by Randolph Stow and George III. Davies' success begat a sequel, which was a return yet again to female insanity with *Miss Donnithorne's Maggot* (1974).

From a vocal point of view, Donizetti's scena remains a vocal tour de force. It comprises a scene and an aria, lasting together over twenty minutes; Donizetti wrote an additional aria ("Perchè non ho del vento") for the purpose of interpolating yet more display in the scene. From the compositional point of view, the score is perhaps as interesting for that which it omits as for that which it contains. Performance practice and changing traditions may have blurred the composer's intentions, but that may also be a reflection of the way in which voices have changed over almost two centuries. The over-riding trend in the intervening period has been toward the glorification of volume and virtuosic display. The dramatic coloratura voice must demonstrate both extreme intensity and agility allied to an extensive upper range. Performances tend to also be opportunities for sopranos to show off their control of extreme dynamic changes and contrasts, from the most filigree of high notes to the full-blooded stentorian gesture, perhaps within the same phrase. The abrupt changes of dynamic on the one hand illustrate the emotional inconsistency associated with some forms of insanity, while on the other hand engage the audience by way of introducing the element of dramatic unpredictability and creating striking musical effect. The score largely omits any indication of these dynamics, which are further amplified by a necessarily constant and abundant rubato whose ceaseless ebb and flow might suggest a pulse in extremis, on the edge of expiration. The singer's objective in this respect is the interpretation of the notes and text, where and how to use the vocal-interpretive tools of dynamics and rubato. The singer must accomplish this while remaining true to the gods of continuous, uninterrupted and blended tone, legato, and line, which represent the overriding axiom of Bel Canto, of which Donizetti displayed serious mastery in his time. Some singers use such a vehicle to search for dramatic truth and illustration of character, while others aim for the public gallery, and there are all manner of shades in between.

There is some connection between this form of composition and the many extraordinary collections of miniature songs by György Kurtág (e.g., *Three Old Inscriptions,* Op. 25; *Lichtenbergs' Settings,* Op. 37). Although they apparently inhabit opposite ends of the musical spectrum, both composers compose implicitly; although the technical means by which to annotate the score with full detail may exist, Donizetti and Kurtág leave much implied rather than stated, allowing a space for the creative imagination or taste of the singer. Indeed, that may well be seen to be the most important objective of their music. This may be seen as a contrast to the explicit compositions of, for instance, J. S. Bach, Giacomo Puccini, and Brian Ferneyhough, whose objective is to control all performance parameters by writing all the detail in the score that is possible.

For that reason, the following remarks diverge from most other sections in this chapter, with the exception of the discussion of Dolly Parton's *I will always love you*. They relate not just to Donizetti's composition of the famous "mad scene" from Lucia, but also to a certain interpretation of it by one singer. Not because it is in any way definitive; such a concept seems alien to a style so dependent on creative interaction between living performer and often long-dead composer. But rather because, in the case of Donizetti and others of his time, the music on the page was not granted the same status as the performance of it, which is a concept alien to the ubiquity of music and the search for definitive recordings so prevalent in our own time. The paradox here is that, for instance, the extraordinary popularity of Whitney Houston's version of Dolly Parton's song appeared to render itself definitive, at least for some time.

The following remarks refer to the recording by Maria Callas, conducted by Tulio Serafin, with the chorus and orchestra of the RAI, Rome, recorded in 1957:

> tr: *The sweet sound, hits me, his voice! Ah, that voice into my heart descends!*

The opening phrase of the scene is deceptively naive in the score. (See Example 5.4a.) A general tempo marking is all the help given, beyond the pitches. Like Mozart, Donizetti forces the singer to gather information from

Example 5.4a. Donizetti: The Mad Scene *(Lucia di Lammermoor).*

either her instincts or the sound of the orchestra, which is marked *piano,* with a crescendo to the word "cor," and a decrescendo to the top note of the singer's phrase. Callas sings the first phrase with the gentle but anxious forward motion that the phrase suggests, yet without any sense of crescendo that might be implicated by the quickly rising phrase; something is being held back. The pregnant silence of the voice between the two phrases is beautifully contained by a poised flute melody, which will be more important later.

The second phrase suddenly surges with intensity, and Callas glissandos on the end of c1 of "ah!" up the tone to the next note, underlying the emotional surge caused by her memory. The word "quel-la" changes its rhythm, becoming dotted as a consequence, and "vo-ce" becomes accentuated, emphasized by the ensuing silence. The resolution of the final phrase could be held back or dramatic—at this stage we cannot know. Donizetti plays with our expectations in this by pondering on the same dominant D for the next five syllables. The stasis or confusion is all the more emphasized after the surges and constant movement before. He even elongates and slows down the tempo with minims on "cor di-," suspending or even teasing our expectations. When Callas eventually arrives at the top note, after the orchestral decrescendo, it is with one of the most sinewy, filigree, whispered tones imaginable, and so it remains—captive, unleashed through an unnotated pause during an orchestral silence—suggesting an intensity of emotion barely tolerable, let alone communicable. (Yet we already know the power of the voice from the second phrase, and we are greedy for it.) The final portamento down the octave resolves the phrase tonally, but certainly not emotionally, and we are propelled on. (After another silence, we hear his name: Edgardo.)

The music now has many new details, and the joint skill of the vocal writing and performance is demonstrated in the transcription, Example 5.4b, to be compared with 5.4a.

This represents a full collaboration between composer and singer; the structure and the psychological insight are Donizetti's, but the personality, the choice, and range of color are from Callas. The style in which Donizetti

Example 5.4b. Donizetti: The Mad Scene (*Lucia di Lammermoor*).

Example 5.4c. Donizetti: The Mad Scene (*Lucia di Lammermoor*).

wrote not only allowed for interpretation of this significance, but also expected the roulades and arabesques of decoration to be personalized by the singer.

One other section will serve to show how much trust Donizetti appeared to give to his singers, and with what reward. The following passage occurs around number 29 in the score (see Example 5.4c).

Callas's performance should be heard to be understood in relation to the way the voice is used to vocal and dramatic ends, but a representation is shown in Example 5.4d.

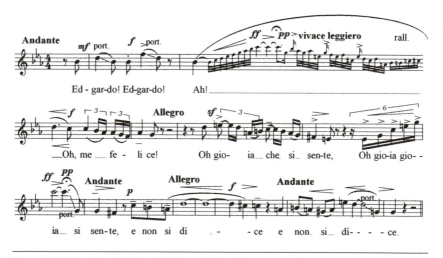

Example 5.4d. Donizetti: The Mad Scene (*Lucia di Lammermoor*).

The surges of passion followed by self-pity, the glissandi and portamenti, the decrescendi between fortissimo and pianissimo on the highest notes, the innocent playfulness of some of the coloratura contrasted with the dramatic power unleashed in other phrases, the changes of tempo and mood within a second: All of these are the qualities which endow the music with life. Yet Donizetti leaves the detail to the singer, who knows her own voice best.

5. Eisler: *O Fallada, da du hangst*

Brecht's poem was written in 1919 in the context of postwar famine and revolution. There were contemporary news reports of crowds of hungry Berliners carving up the corpses of police horses that had fallen during street fighting, which may have led to the poem's conception. Fallada was a horse in a fairytale by the Brothers Grimm. The poem was adapted by Hans Eisler in 1932 for a cabaret revue. The following literal translation scans the song line by line.

O Fallada, There You Are Hanging
I pulled my cart-load in spite of my weakness.
I came up to Frankfurt Avenue.
There I stood still and thought: Oh ever!
This weakness! If I don't make an effort
It may happen to me that I break down . . .
Ten minutes later I was only a pile of bones on the street.

I had just broken down there
(The coachman ran to the telephone)
When there rushed from the houses
People hungry to win a pound of meat
To tear from me with knives the meat from my bones
And I still was living and was not finished at all with the dying.

But I knew these people, they were once my friends!
They used to bring me sacks against the flies
Gave me old crusts and even
Admonished my coachman to be gentle with me.
Once they were to me so friendly and now so hostile today!
Suddenly they were changed! Oh what had happened to them
    to change them so?

Then I asked myself: Who has sent
Such coldness into the people?

Who has hit them so
To freeze them through and through?
Please help them! And do so quickly!
Otherwise the consequences might be beyond reason!

Eisler did more than set words: he modified or edited nearly all the texts he composed music for, especially those by Hölderlein and Anacreon. He was no less willful toward living poets, and in his settings of Brecht he also made numerous alterations to the verse, both major and minor. Inevitably Brecht regarded alterations of his work with mixed feelings, but he nevertheless accepted the composers right to change the original and wrote: "His musical setting is for me what a performance is for a play: the test. He reads with enormous care." In contrast to Wolf, Eisler's absence of literary humility or subservience exemplifies an opposite, but no less respectful relationship between composer and poet.

Brecht's original poem was entitled "O Falladah, die du hangest!" In the complete works edition (Brecht: *Gedichte VIII, 1913–56* [Suhrkamp Verlag, Germany 1965,] 102) it is structured as a surreal dialogue between a reporter and a dead horse, comprising 8 verses with a total of 50 lines. Eisler omitted all the reporter's verses, creating a monologue of 24 lines. Additionally some words have changed spelling (such as in the title), other words have been added (e.g., "*so* freundlich," verse 3), and some punctuation changed. It is undoubtedly a major overhaul of the poem. Even so, there are textual discrepancies between the text as published (Deutscher Verlag für Musik, Leipzig, DVfM 9087) and recordings by singers who worked with Eisler, such as Gisela May.

Dramatically, the original poem succeeds in placing the reporter between the victim (who pleads for help not for himself but for those who wronged him) and the audience. The device represents the imposition of Brechtian objectivity into an emotionally wrought situation. Eisler's recreation provides the traditional requirement of a morality-based music-hall song, with the singer as the subject, and thus tightens the structural message within the new medium, with words straight from the horse's mouth! It is difficult to imagine that a composer could ever exert a more proprietorial control over the work of a poet, and a tribute to Brecht's admiration for his friend that he would accept such changes.

The suffering and weariness of the horse are evident in the opening from the intervals leaning heavily through a repeated minor third in the voice. Eisler's sensitivity to the text is evident in the sudden cessation of the vocal part in bar 15 representing the effect of the deliberating dots in the text at line 5, increasing the effective gesture of the emotive line at the end of the verse, with its awkwardly rising intervals and unfinished cadence. The

Example 5.5a.   Eisler: *O Fallada, da du hangst.* Copyright acknowledgement: Deutscher Verlag
für Musik, Leipzig.

gestural effect is repeated at the end of each succeeding verse, but without
the preceding sudden silence in the first verse (see Example 5.4a).

The setting is strophic, but with a characteristic development of detail.
The final verse exaggerates the effect by augmenting the durations in the
voice, over a mock-tragic 6/8 cross-rhythm, heavily reiterated in the accompaniment. The effect of the end of the song is literally arresting, as any sense
of resolution or completion is avoided both harmonically and rhythmically:
The question as to whether we can prevent the people's decline into barbar-
ity is left hanging for us to answer. The ending, as if balanced precariously
on a precipice, brings to mind Stravinsky's *Rite of Spring,* at the end to Part
One, but the continuation or consequences of this song are unwritten. Never
was a question more forcefully put to an audience in the form of a song (see
Example 5.4b).

The tradition of the cabaret song involved a synthesis of speech and song
reflected in the blurring of distinction between the actor and the singer.
Rhythms are interpreted liberally, where the words demand pointed emphasis, and pitches are approximated in a "sprechstimme" style, where the
incredulity of the horse relating his fate so justifies, as in verse 2.

Eisler's art was a subtle one, clearly exemplifying the adage that the greatest art is that which disguises itself. His songs work on many levels; his
embracing of vernacular rhythms and functional harmonies clearly suggest
the popular contemporary cabaret context, but the work evinces great care,
precision, and subtlety of detail. If the musical language appears simple, it
is the result of extremely refined or distilled ideas: the simplicity of econ-
omy and precision, rather than innocence. The strength of the song lies

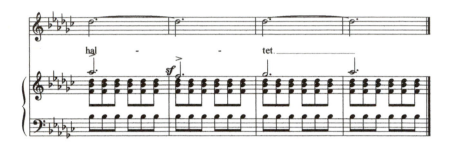

Example 5.5b. Eisler: *O Fallada, da du hangst.* Copyright acknowledgement: Deutscher Verlag für Musik, Leipzig.

within the depth of belief in the message shared by composer and poet, their political-social conscience that led to the necessity to communicate this truth as widely as possible, and their technically calculated control of the means.

6. Gershwin: *Summertime (Porgy and Bess)*

There are certain songs that have attained an almost mythical status, even beyond the concept of a classic or a standard. Occasionally they even seem to promulgate a life of their own, beyond an association with the composer, and become so identified with, by so many people, that they are raised to the status of a folk song. They may also fulfill many functions, social and ceremonial, such as *Happy Birthday* (composed by Mildred J. Hill, a schoolteacher born in Louisville, Kentucky, on June 27, 1859) and *Here Come the Bride* (Wagner's Bridal Chorus from *Lohengrin*), or they may simply speak on an emotional level beyond the boundaries of their conception, or of any other time and place, such as *Yesterday*, by Lennon and McCartney. *Summertime*, from the opera *Porgy and Bess* by George Gershwin, probably falls into this category.

Example 5.6a. Dvořák: *Songs My Mother Taught Me* (*Gypsy Songs,* Op. 55, No. 4).

The evocative nature of the vocal line is created primarily by the opening interval between the first two syllables, "Sum-mer": a descending third between E6 and C6. Whether major or minor, this is probably one of the first musical intervals we learn to use with our voices. Try saying "mummy" with the descending minor third and then a major third to experience the emotional charge that is inherently conveyed. Having made a primary subconscious connection with us with the first word, the vocal line remains suspended, lingering around and between those same notes over the following syllables, before finally falling away down through the tonic chord. The same descending interval, sometimes major, sometimes minor, recurs eternally throughout the history of music, always with the same subliminal or conscious reference (see Example 5.6a).

Sometimes the interval initially rises, but the slow oscillation or varied repetition of the interval always reproduces a similar effect (see Example 5.6b).

There is a profound change of effect with the device according to the vocal range. Brahms exploits the calm rocking between notes in the lower middle range to create the effect of a lullaby, whereas Dvořák reaches back nostalgically into memory with a larger, gestural interval and melismata. Verdi chose the same device for Desdemona's cries of despair, sung while the orchestra is tacit, in *Otello* (see Example 5.6c). The descending minor third is repeated three times with diminishing force, but the major third between A and C sharp provides another point of oscillation, or emotional doubt, in the preceding phrase.

Example 5.6b. Brahms: *Wiegenlied.*

Se - dea_____ chi - nan - - -do sul sen, la___ te - -

portando
la voz

sta! Sal - ce! Sal - ce! Sal - ce!

Example 5.6c. Verdi: *Salce, Salce (Otello).*

Un___ bel di, ve - dre - mo le - var - -siun fil di fu - mo

Example 5.6d. Puccini: *Un Bel Di (Madama Butterfly).*

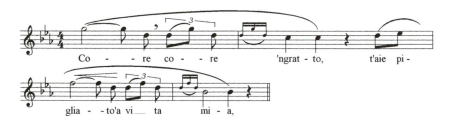

Co - re co - re 'ngrat - to, t'aie pi -

glia - - to'a vi ta mi - a,

Example 5.6e. Cardillo: *Core 'Ngrato* (Neapolitan Song).

Et de - pre - ca - ti - o - nem___ me - am.

Example 5.6f. Stravinsky: *The Symphony of Psalms.* © 1948 by Boosey & Hawkes, Inc., New York, USA. Reprinted by Permission.

SIGHT BY SI-LENT SAIL-ING MIGHT_____ I - SO-BEL

WILD WOODS EYES AND PRIM-A - ROSE___ HAIR

Example 5.6g. Cage: *The Wonderful Widow of Eighteen Springs.* © 1942 Peters Edition, Catalog Number: EP6297.

Puccini touched the same nerve with his hauntingly doomed aria of hope (see Example 5.6d). It lingers less than the Gershwin, is less rhythmically variable and more directional in construction; it is always perceptibly moving toward a vocal operatic climax, but it is undeniably another variation on the same theme.

Puccini was at some level in dialogue with his own cultural heritage, as this excerpt from a well-known Neapolitan song composed at about the same time suggests (see Example 5.6e).

Although the first interval might be changed, the device of a repeated and varied oscillation between two notes, starting with the higher, seems to occur and recur with an almost predictable frequency.

Stravinsky consciously or unconsciously made much use of the oscillation between very few notes for many of his themes, from the opening of *The Rite of Spring* onward. The opening chorus of his *Symphony of Psalms* combines this technique with the archetypal minor third (see Example 5.6f).

The device is probably as ancient as the voice itself, but in the hands of John Cage, it may take on a startlingly fresh but strangely eternal quality (see Example 5.6g).

"Summertime" is an extraordinary hybrid, stylistically borrowing from gospel and blues, jazz and late romantic, chromatic harmony, which also emphasizes the use of parallel tritones for the effect of color. Structurally it is not goal-orientated or climax-driven, and is in fact a simple (in the sense of undeveloped), two-verse strophic song. The melody itself is almost pentatonic, but for the two E's on "high" and "sky," one in each verse. The vocal range does not move beyond one octave, from E to E. The style of language (by Dubose Heyward) is also famous for its colloquial evocation of a specifically contemporary Black way of speaking. Out of all of this Gershwin created a song ostensibly simple enough to be rendered indelibly on the subconscious of millions, yet sophisticated enough to stand in a major twentieth-century opera.

7. György Kurtág: "... und eine neue Welt ..."

This song is from the series *Einige Sätze den Sudelbüchern, Georg Christoph Lichtenbergs,* Op. 37. As with all the songs in the set, it is an unaccompanied setting, thus uniquely in this chapter I am able to reproduce the entire song (see Example 5.7).

Translation:

> [Title:] ... and a new world ...
> "The American who was discovered by Colombus had a horrible
> surprise."

Glossary:

> *Keck, heiter, lebhaft:* cheeky, cheerful, vivacious
> *plötzlich erstarren:* suddenly frozen
> *wieder erstarren:* again frozen
> *noch schneller:* more fast
> *zögernd:* questioningly
> **Wieder erstarren, aber in Tempo bleiben:* again frozen, but keep in
>   time
> *(Augen und Mund weit offen):* Eyes and mouth wide open

The song, which is typical of a number of important series of songs by
Kurtág, is innovative in several ways. Kurtág explicitly denies the nature of
the collection to be cyclical, or to reflect any intrinsically structural order.
There are 14 songs in the opus and any number may be performed in an
order selected by the singer. He even suggests the possibility of repeating
one song several times within a context of other works, perhaps by other
composers. In the preface, the composer points out that the changing context
of a song may affect how its content is perceived. These concepts open new
possibilities concerning the nature of the concert song, while still reflecting
many traditional preoccupations associated with the form. All the texts are

* Wieder erstarren, aber im Tempo bleiben
  (Augen und Mund weit offen)

11-24.II.1996

Example 5.7. György Kurtág: *"…und eine neue Welt."* © Editio Musica Budapest, by permission.

aphoristic, the shortest containing three words; this particular song, one of the longest of the set, has ten words.

The character of the text is witty, and Kurtág's setting exaggerates this with tellingly acute precision. There is an intensity to the musical setting that matches the composer's evident sensitivity to both text and subtext. It represents, perhaps more than any other song in this chapter, the proximity of a composer's job to a stage director. The text alone represents a universal or objective statement that was perhaps intended to be read in private. This gives a contextual or subjective reading of the text by way of detailed and specific directions as to its vocal performance. The score represents perhaps, for the singer, the end of the creative rehearsal process enjoyed by director and actor, prior to the final more mechanical series of consolidating rehearsals. Despite the characteristically detailed instructions, a singer must find sufficient feeling for both text and context, and not merely slavishly reproduce the instructions, however detailed they seem. The energy of a live performance, and interaction with the audience, is vital to the volatile but ephemeral nature of the song, which then becomes a finely honed comic sketch.

The first two phrases repeat the first two words, but in such a way as to set up increased expectations, with the continually rising second phrase. The repetition emphasizes the inferred change of perspective that our subject is the American—that is, the original American—rather than the discoverer himself, who is more traditionally the subject of such observations. The staccato markings are like the wagging finger that accompanies an old and wise storyteller: "You think I am telling you a story about this?—Well, really it is about that!" The angular and pointed nature of the opening, teasing scalic phrases, contrast greatly with the smooth but convoluted and unpredictable second line. "Kolombus" is given a higher range, because the name is important for its universal associations and reverberations, but the highest pitches in the song are reserved for "entdeckte." The reason for this, and the pause that follows, is the play on words, the half-pun insinuated with the final word of the song. Before that, the penultimate phrase contains a cross-rhythm that cuts across the feeling of compound time that is inferred but not stated in the score. The word "böse" (horrible) invites, through its suddenly loud glissando, some traditional vocal word-painting, but another measured (implying with pulse) silence delays the punch line: The word "Entdekkung" (surprise) shares its first two similar sounding syllables with "entdeckte" (discovered), and the silence that separates the final two syllables of the last word teases us and mirrors the American's surprise, completed with a twisting of the otherwise consistent pulse during the final silence.

Despite the use of silences and pauses, and the absence of accompaniment, timing, as every actor knows, can make or kill a punch line, and Kurtág uses rhythm as a discernible pulse to both underline meanings and undermine expectations. The pitch relations too are sometimes discernibly and functionally tonal, as in the opening two phrases, and at other times less predictable, although always with a purpose, which is to place and relay, by way of range and emphasis, the most important information or word.

The willingness or necessity of the composer to transcend the usual formal boundaries of composition and enter stage-director mode is implicit in the material, and made explicit in the penultimate bar, when he directs the singer, during the silence, to maintain her eyes and mouth wide open, the visual dramatic representation amplifying the musical intention. As with all great users of comedy, the art of witticism is taken very seriously.

Few composers since Webern have displayed such imaginative and detailed synthesis between text and music, but perhaps Kurtág's unique gift is to contrive such perceptive control also at the service of a profound wit.

8. Dolly Parton: *"I will Always Love You"*

This was one of the most performed popular songs of the 1990s. It was composed by Dolly Parton and made famous particularly by Whitney Houston. It is an example of the work of a singer-songwriter, and it exploits Dolly Parton's voice in terms of ranges and strengths, incidentally fulfilling identical objectives with Whitney Houston.

It is difficult to categorize the style of song, because musical style still plays a large part in terms of racial identity in the USA. This in itself is worthy of note in relation to socio-cultural studies of the genre of song, but this is beyond the scope of this book. However, the vocal line glances back to the tradition of gospel singing at a time earlier in the century when it was beginning to fuse with jazz and blues, and more obviously latterly to soul music. Its form is not unlike an anthem such as *Amazing Grace,* and much embellished. In this case it begins characteristically a cappella, low in the vocal range and surges forward with a key change up one tone to a passionate climax and finally a reflective coda. It was unusual if not unique in the decade of its success, in its traditional dependence on melismata for emotional leverage. As in music from Couperin through Rossini to the Spiritual, the core expressivity lies in the embellishment of the tune, which thus becomes a structural rather then a decorative device. Interestingly, in the printed version published after Whitney Houston's recording, these embellishments are written in some detail into the score, although our written musical language is not yet able to reflect the subtlety of her rhythms and inflections. The difference between the written page and the singer's interpretation are of the same dimension as the difference between the score of a Chopin Ballade and a performance by Paderewski. However, the accompaniment to the song itself remains more tightly rhythmically controlled, against which the detail of the vocal part is thrown into sharp perspective.

The vocal range is two octaves, from low F#, far greater than many popular songs. The technique most associated with the song, aside from a dependence on melisma, is the use of the break for expressive purposes. Although both singers can produce the highest note "belted" with a powerful almost tenor-like power (though not tone), the natural break between the A5 and B5 provides a dramatic change of color and expressive effect, as in ". . . and I— will always love you— . . ."

The attentive listener will notice that the pitches B and C sharp with "you" are sung in a different register to the A that proceeds and follows. On the other hand the phrase on the final "you" sails up to the fifth above on an E, with the fuller sound of the lower range. It is an indication of the degree of technical control by singers at this level.

In this song the choice of key does more than define the vocal range. Both the place and use of this break seem almost to have become a necessary part to the performance of the song, although of course there is no indication of this in published material. The difference of a tone, rather than a semitone over the two notes across the controlled "break" helps the singer to control the audible change of register.

One aspect of the Bel Canto tradition trains the singer to control the *passagio* and create a seamless crossing between all registers without changes of color, and certainly without the slight jump of the larynx that is characteristic here. Because the idea is fomented early in some training that such a technique is somehow wrong or erroneous, it is not surprising that some young singers and teachers find it difficult to acquire or understand the skill involved. However, it is a perfectly natural phenomenon, and when understood and mastered, may become a powerful expressive tool, or an extra color in a singer's palette. There are many instances of the use of the technique in popular music, from Billie Holiday to Shirley Bassey. Currently the Colombian pop singer Shakira exploits the technique with every song, to great individual effect. It is applicable to both male and female voices. The technique has evolved in many different guises in different cultures, from some folksingers in the African continent to the extreme example of yodeling in Switzerland.

The specific inheritance of gospel is underlined in the type of melismata, which are predominantly by step, moving freely in between the main melody notes. In this context, the leap of a fifth mentioned above is a dramatic gesture, and the leap of an octave toward the end of the song defines its climax.

It is easy—too easy—to overlook the detail and craftsmanship of a popular song, whether it be *Du bist die Ruhe* by Schubert or this one; somehow success, whether for commercial or artistic reasons, can blind composers to the very qualities that lend an enduring quality to the connection between words and music. *I will always love you* was special both because of its newness in relation to other songs in its genre and because of its traditional aspect, in the time honored magic of the extended vowel sound speaking of something of and beyond the lyrics of a song: a quality inherent to the art of song across boundaries of style, era, and geography.

9. Purcell: *Dido's Lament (Dido & Aeneas)*

Queen Dido has just rejected Aeneas's offer to defy what he believes to be Jove's command, and stay with her. "That you had once a thought of leaving me," she argues, is proof that he is indeed a "faithless man." The chorus comment on this extreme attitude toward human relationships in the manner of a chorus in classical Greek drama. They necessarily disguise any criticism of their Queen by attributing her self-denial to her greatness. Dido is inconsolable, and Belinda is either unable to speak or is prevented from entering discussion. In contemporary terms, Dido's lament is a priori a dramatic essay on a self-made victim facing the ultimate price.

In the short recitative before the famous aria (example 5.9a), Dido takes Belinda's hand. Significantly, there is no gap between her name and "darkness"; it may be assumed that Belinda opens her mouth to say something here, but Dido will have none of it, bent on her course of self-immolation. The awkward quarter-note rest between "bosom" and "let me rest" is equally telling. Purcell relinquishes his characteristic rhetorical, melismatic flourishes, except for this word, "darkness," the abruptness and emotional force of which instill the silence of terror into her sister. For Dido, there can be only one path downward from here, and the entire recitative slides remorselessly and chromatically in that direction. The appoggiaturas on "bosom," "would," "death," and "now" leave no doubt to the extent of her suffering and anguish. The double appoggiatura on "wel-come," with the final reversed dotted rhythm on the descending fifth, dramatically represents a sob, or a cry, which surely breaks Belinda's heart, as Dido lies supine, dying on her breast. Ever the Queen, Dido regains some self-control, for her final aria. Ahead lies a descent into darkness, made tangible by the tortuously chromatic passacaglia theme that will occur twelve times underneath. Throughout, Belinda is rendered powerless and mute, even as Dido's last words are addressed directly to her. The aria is in effect a dialogue, the tension of which is created by the muteness of her companion.

Example 5.9a.   Purcell: *Dido's Lament (Dido & Aeneas)*.

Purcell demonstrates a penetrating understanding of the psychology of the moment. Debilitated and awash with self-pity, her vocal line barely is able to move even by step at first. Certain phrases in the text are repeated as she apparently reacts vehemently to the words she finds herself saying:

> When I am laid, *am laid* in earth, may my wrongs create no trouble, *no trouble* in the breast.

Dido's realization of the meaning of her words provokes a temporary surge of breath and energy, reaching higher in the vocal range, only to fall again. Such dramatic repetition may be that which an actor would employ, but it is heightened by descending melismas on "laid" (inferring "Yes, I really am contemplating how I shall be laid in the earth") and the falling fifth on "trouble" that seems an echo of her earlier sob on "welcome." She is pleading with Belinda not to suffer for her, yet the weakened repetition seems to lose conviction, perhaps as she sees the look in Belinda's eyes. At this point the music does something that drama alone would rarely contemplate, and repeats these opening phrases. Convention might suggest that the repetition

Example 5.9b. Purcell: *Dido's Lament (Dido & Aeneas).*

would involve some development by way of vocal decoration, but Purcell's music seems so intense and calculated that to do so might easily seem merely decorative and therefore superfluous (see Example 5.9b).

Dido in extremis is perhaps not entirely coherent verbally. The entire text of the second half of the aria is "Remember me! But ah! Forget my fate," but the repetitions Purcell used convey more keenly what is being said between the words. The music explores each word as if under a microscope, extracting every last significance: "Remember me! Remember me! But ah! Forget my fate, remember me! But ah! Forget my fate." (repeated) This is surely much more than a conventional baroque repetitive device; in fact it is a new structure that allows the music to speak beyond the verbal sentiments.

The first repetition of "Remember me!" on one note is almost modern and gestural in its starkness, and no less chilling for the words' recurrence another four times. The pitch D is insisted upon and returned to again and again, with ever-shifting harmonies, and even its release onto the high G barely balances with the tension it has created. The words gently reverberate through their soft consonants, a fact that many singers have seized upon to permit the legato to just hold them together with their vocal line. The silences on either side of the first repetitions emphasize her isolation, and again articulate Belinda's painful helplessness.

This final passage demonstrates Purcell's understanding of the use of selective repetition of text to extraordinary effect, far beyond the conventions of his time. Purcell again restrains himself from melismatic eloquence, except for the exclamation "Ah!" Dido is already beyond words, beyond the present, beyond life, yet her plea to be remembered remains ringing in our ears far beyond the opera's final, unworldly chorus.

Given the intensity of the music and its demands for a mature vocal control, it is scarcely believable that Purcell's only opera was originally written for a girl's school. The libretto reveals many holes in the plot and appears to have been written without much skill or sophistication. Yet the composer seized upon it with a passion and wrung out of it a new structure of extraordinary intensity.

10. Ravel: *Vocalise-Étude (en Forme de Habanera)*

The form of the vocalize as a basis for a complete composition dates back at least to Spohr, whose *Sonatina for Voice and Piano* Op. 138 of 1848 suggested an important development of wordless vocal music. Other than individual songs, the only other extended examples I have found are the *Concerto for Coloratura Soprano and Orchestra* by Glière, and a *Sonate-Vocalise & Suite-Vocalise* Op. 41 by Medtner. Villa Lobos's famous *Bachianas Brasileiras* No. 5 is only partially a vocalise. Individual vocalises in more traditional song-form have been written by many composers since, including Fauré, Honegger, Ibert, Roussel, Ravel, Messiaen, Vaughan Williams, Henry Cowell, and most famously by Rachmaninov (Op. 34, No. 14). Both this and the Ravel exist in many versions for various instruments, reflecting the popularity of the melodic writing, which is for many the principal association vocalize has with the song form. The outer sections of the Villa Lobos are often extrapolated from the ferociously rapid text-setting of the middle section of the first movement (*Aria*) for similar diverse commercial use, and interestingly Villa Lobos also uses humming in the *Aria*'s final section, as opposed to the open A vowel.

The use of a single pure vowel in sections or divisions of a composition is more common. Since Gregorian chant, which is the earliest notated music in existence, individual syllables have been extracted from words and elongated far beyond the limits of linguistic intelligibility. The expressive nature of the open vowel has presented an allure to composers from at least Perotín, through Josquin Des Prez to beyond Richard Strauss, with famous examples along the way by Handel, Bellini, and Rossini. Whereas this remains a fundamental part of compositional vocal technique, the idea of a complete work without text, exploiting the open vowel, is a definition of a pure vocalize, and appears to be a relatively recent concept.

Incidentally, a reverse-process in which the addition of words is made to existing instrumental music has an equally important minor chapter in music history. For example, the English, at the time of Haydn's visit to their country, bought several of his piano trios, but with the violin part replaced (and sometimes modified) by a voice with an invented or borrowed English text. The popularity and development of this is well documented in an article by Gretchen A. Wheelock (1990). According to her, it was not itself an unusual practice, and continued with later composers, but the unusual element here is to consider how fundamental to making music the voice was, and how, through the voice, access to a wider range of music became viable.

The attraction of the vocalize emphasizes similar preoccupations. For composers, it allows an exploration of the melodic aspect of voice without extra-musical reference, and for the audience it presents an opportunity to appreciate the voice unencumbered by textual or linguistic reference. However, the limitations of the form are clearly demonstrated in its association with romantic or late romantic preoccupations with line and melody, which accounts in part for a decrease in popularity in the later twentieth century.

For the purpose of this book, a vocalize may allow us to analyze the factors that contribute to idiosyncratic vocal composition outside of the requirements of dealing with text. Ravel was one of the finest orchestrators of all time, and his knowledge of timbre and color was equally evident in his vocal writing. Although his *Vocalise-Étude (en Forme de Habanera)* from 1907 exists in many instrumental versions, it was composed originally for a voice. The question most useful in relation to the concerns of this book is: Why is it essentially a vocal rather than an instrumental work?

The original key of F minor contains the range of an octave and a half, from B flat to F. This defines a middle voice range, accessible by sopranos of diverse types. However, the use of the lower tessitura, especially toward the end, suggests a darker voice, perhaps a mezzo or a soprano with a rich chest range. The most obvious idiosyncratic device exploited by Ravel with respect to the voice is the glissando. The final phrase of the song specifies a rising glissando (described in the score as a portamento, suggesting a lighter touch) between the Fs followed by a reversal. Other wind and string instruments are of course able to simulate glissandos, and this alone hardly satisfies the vocal criteria we are searching for. Gershwin's *Rhapsody in Blue* famously opens with an extended glissando for the clarinet over several octaves, exposing the breaks between the different registers, which add tension, difficulty, and interest to the gesture. However, vocal glissandi may be of a quality quite separate from their instrumental counterpart. The articulation of each and every microtone between the given pitches (which is "fluked" with specific instruments) given an emotional context can result in an extraordinary vocal effect. Nina Simone toward the end of her recorded version of the song made famous by Billie Holiday, *Strange Fruit* (widely available on compilations), provides one of the most moving and unforgettable vocal glissandi I have ever heard. Ravel marks the score "presque lent avec indolence," and the singer who can capture the indolence of these two glissandi goes some way to providing a quintessentially vocal effect.

There are several other vocal details in the writing. If they do not seem specifically vocal in objective, it may be more to do with the ancient derivation of all vocal music shared by string and wind instruments.

The first three of the four repeated notes that begin the second theme in the second section are articulated with both tenuto and staccato marks; they are repeated an octave lower after the key change, with an additional mordent-type acciaccatura before the fourth note. The repeated attack on the same note with an open vowel sound suggests a textual derivation, or a vocal equivalent of tonguing or bowing, yet here seems more suggestive of a kind of speaking with a vowel. It is an effect more associated with early romantic vocal cadenza figures, where a soprano duets with a flute, but here it is neither decorative nor superficial, being structurally related to both rhythmic and melodic characteristics of the composition. The three cadenzas or roulades of notes are each articulated with contrasted character and objective; they demand an agility in the midrange of the singer that is more sensual than virtuosic. It is a vocal agility that is required here, rather than strength, albeit with a specific color. The inverted mordent figure with which the vocal part opens becomes a structural device in many ensuing phrases. The use of the upper note in the mordent seems to lighten the music, endowing more playfulness than one might imagine with a normal mordent. The melody itself is of the suspended descending type, described in the section on Gershwin's *Summertime*. Ravel has stipulated all the breathing required for performance, and this dictates the various lengths of phrase structures. The melodic movement is predominantly by step, with some thirds; other intervals are used only between sequences.

The changes of register provide the most characteristic vocal aspect; the use of the lower or chest register, after long descending phrases, and particularly before the final cadenza is very effective with the right sort of soprano voice. If indolence is not far from indulgence, both may be appropriate in the creation of the almost exotic, sensual undertone with which the music seeks to seduce the listener, through the earthy tones of a female voice. There is nothing in the score to indicate that a man may not sing this work, yet it would surely be a mistake, or a travesty.

The Habanera is a Cuban dance form in origin, and this appears to be a song of seduction, another example of the "siren song" referred to in Chapter 7, however indirect or indolent in its intention. The characteristic and laconically repeated rhythm in the piano is suggestive of a nightclub, complete with decadent, sensual harmonies, completing the frame for the spectacularly underplayed, vocal tour de force.

Some More Vocalizes:

Pierre Boulez: *Le Marteau sans Maître:* IX "Bel édifice et les
presentiments" (utilises sequences sung with the mouth closed:
"bouche fermée.")
Giuseppe Concone: *Fifty Vocalises* (didactic works)
John Corigliano *Vocalize* (1999) Duration: 20' Solo Soprano; orch.+
electronics
Henry Cowell: *Vocalize for Soprano, Flute and Piano* (pub. 1964, C.F
Peters)
George Crumb: *Apparition 1, 2 & 3* for soprano & amplified piano
(*Summer Sounds, Invocation To the Dark Angel, Song of the
Nightbird*)
Gabriel Fauré: *Vocalise-Étude No.1* (1907)
Karl Goldmark: *Die Königin von Saba* (*The Queen of Sheba*); opera,
with vocalize aria sung by character by Astaroth to lure Astaroth
Reinhold Glière: *Concerto for Coloratura Soprano and Orchestra,*
Opus 82 (1943)
Olivier Messiaen *Vocalize- Étude* (1935)
Nicholas Medtner: *Sonate-Vocalise & Suite-Vocalise Op. 41* (1922–6)
André Previn: *Vocalize For Soprano, Cello And Piano*
Sergei Rachmaninoff: *Vocalize Op. 34 No. 14* (1912)
Louis Spohr: *Sonatina for Voice and Piano* Op. 138 (1848)
Joaquin Turina: *Vocalizaciones* Op. 74
Ralph Vaughan Williams: *Three Vocalises for Soprano and Clarinet*
Heitor Villa Lobos: *Bachianas Brasilieras No. 5*

Works Using Wordless Chorus:

Vaughan Williams: *Pastoral Symphony; Flos Campi*
Debussy: *Sirènes*
Holst: *The Planets;*
Puccini: *Humming Chorus* in *Madam Butterfly*
Ravel: *Daphnis & Chloe*
Glass: *Powaqqatsi*
Sorabji: *Symphony No. 3, "Jami"* (1942–51)
Roussel: *Evocations; Padmavati; Aeneas; Psalm 80*
Delius: *To be sung of a summer night on the water*
Roberto Sierra: *Idilio* (1990)

11. Schoenberg: *"Nacht" (Pierrot Lunaire)*

This song begins the second book of the cycle. As with all of the songs, it is
a setting of a translation by Otto Erich Hartleben of a poem by the Belgian,

Example 5.11. Schoenberg: "Nacht," *Pierrot Lunaire:* Used with kind permission of European American Music Distributors LLC, Agent for Universal Edition A. G., Vienna.

Albert Giraud. The cycle uses almost exclusively the technique of "sprechgesang," literally a mixture of talking and singing. "Nacht" is a depiction of a super-real world blackened by giant, gloomy black moths:

> downward sink with somber restraints,
> unperceived, great hordes of monsters
> on the hearts and souls of mankind . . .

Throughout the song, the bass clarinet, cello and piano create the illusion of constantly accelerating descent, almost overwhelming the voice at the climax midway through the song ("massacred the sun's bright rays") (see Example 5.11).

The musical language of *Pierrot Lunaire* is a representation of contrariness, structurally placing the voice against the constantly shifting interchange of instrumentation for the songs. The writing appears very detailed for the instruments, with each note allotted a dynamic, a mode of attack, and a relationship with the following note through phrasing. Repetition is eschewed in favor of continuous development or interchange of ideas.

Nacht is subtitled as a Passacaglia, of which the most obvious structural element is an ascending minor third followed by a descending major third. Classical forms of structure and development of thematic ideas seem to represent the musical ethos, in a tradition stemming back to Bach and beyond. However, despite the contrapuntal nature of the music, these elements merely supply the background, and become almost decorative, devoid of their reference to functional tonality. The compositional foreground is here represented by the voice, and it is the vocal writing that lays bare one aspect of the contrariness that endows the song (in fact all of *Pierrot Lunaire*) with such power to communicate.

Schoenberg wrote the songs for an actress, and his inspiration was to allow her to remain vocally free albeit within the confines of the chosen notes. The performer must first learn the notes, as she would any song. Having done so, she must forget she is a singer and become once again an actress, proficient in melodrama, which was one of the strongest dramatic forces at that time. The term "melodrama" is of German origin signifying a synthesis of music and drama. The contrary nature of the composition is the amount of vocal freedom allowed the singer, within a musical framework that seems overabundantly controlled and detailed. The singer of *Pierrot Lunaire* is not merely an interpreter, in the sense of the traditional lied, but needs to display imaginative and creative ability. The cross on each stem is both a negation and an elaboration of each note, allowing the singer to use her actor's instincts to infuse the text with meaning through sound, perhaps in the same way that Schoenberg originally allowed the notes to appear instinctively, without conscious reason. In this way, the text, which is all the singer has to guide her choices, becomes a structural part of the sound world, and its coloring becomes the foreground of the composition, to which Schoenberg relegates responsibility beyond a dynamic and an approximate, or more appropriately, an undulating pitch.

The dichotomy of enormous control of the background and the creative freedom in the foreground must have required enormous courage for a composer so vehemently authoritarian or even dictatorial as Schoenberg, who was simultaneously discovering an instinctual harmonic and melodic language that he could not consciously control. The adventure, in creative terms, led to his need for a search toward a reassertion of intellectual control through serialism to replace the so-called atonality evident at this time. Atonality means literally "without tone," a quality in abundance in this work, in any "pure" form.

Inferred but unnotated in the score is the different approach to text that actors have as opposed to singers, and much of this contradicts their respective training and instinct. A singer must be concerned with line, for which the vowel represents a continuous, uninterrupted stream of air. Moreover vowels always represent certain fixed pitches. Although the vowel remains the core of emotional communication for both actor and singer, the vowel for the actor represents a fluctuating object, both in duration and pitch, the ephemeral nature of which requires a fusion between musculature, and emotional and intellectual insight. It cannot be notated. For a singer, the duration of a consonant is minimized, sacrificed at the expense of line, but not comprehension, while for an actor a consonant may be understood in the same way that untuned percussion sounds relate to an orchestra.

In the days before amplification, when *Pierrot Lunaire* was written, actors and singers both had to fill large arenas such as the theater and the concert hall, with the power of their voice alone. The few recordings of theater and concert that exist from the early years of the last century testify to an "unnatural" style of delivery, from our perspective, but this exaggerated and over-accentuated (again, from our perspective) delivery persisted into many films into the 1940s, such as the Shakespeare films of Lawrence Olivier. The technique of performing text in this way, however seemingly old-fashioned, is not mysterious, but rather a universal part of our heritage. Try entertaining a five-year-old by telling a ghost story, and elements of this melodramatic style will become apparent to all. However, Schoenberg transcended this tradition, already somewhat debased even by his time, by placing it within such a highly sophisticated musical context. The result is a unique synthesis of traditional dramatic and contemporary (even today) musical elements. And therein lies another dichotomy, that to our ears the dramatic reference may seem quaintly old-fashioned, while Schoenberg's music, from almost a century ago, remains disturbingly modern.

The first three notes in Example 5.11 are marked to be sung. They represent thematically the motif of the Passacaglia, and are among the lowest notes a soprano can ever expect to sing, which is why Schoenberg supplied an "ossia." Like most "ossia," they are almost never used by a singer, perhaps as a point of honor. This excerpt shows the extremes of range and dynamics in the song, covering over two octaves within a few bars, between double pianissimo and forte. Later, the tiny gestures of rising sevenths on "Erinnrung mordend" (tr: "destroying memory") interrupt the crawling chromaticism, which returns with the ensuing climactic phrase. In these strange, otherworldly sounds, portending the doom-laden imagery, Schoenberg has turned his back on the lush romantic texture and line of *Gurrelieder* (with which he was still engaged, paradoxically), and created a unique vision, at once Gothic and contemporary.

12. Schubert: *Du Bist die Ruhe* Op. 59, No. 3 (Rückert)

Du bist die Ruh,	You are rest,
Der Friede mild,	The mild peace,
Die Sehnsucht du	You are longing
Und was sie stillt.	And what stills it.
Ich weihe dir	I consecrate to you
Voll Lust und Schmerz	Full of joy and pain
Zur Wohnung hier	As a dwelling here
Mein Aug und Herz.	My eyes and heart.

Kehr ein bei mir,	Come live with me,
Und schließe du	And close
Still hinter dir	Quietly the gates
Die Pforten zu.	behind you.
Treib andern Schmerz	Drive other pains
Aus dieser Brust!	Out of this breast
Voll sei dies Herz	May my heart be full
Von deiner Lust.	With your pleasure.
Dies Augenzelt	The temple of my eyes
Von deinem Glanz	by your radiance
Allein erhellt,	alone is illuminated,
O füll es ganz!	O fill it completely!

Rückert called his poem "Kehr ein bei mir" ("Come home to me"). Famously, Schubert set the poem, yet no song by that name exists. Instead, it is known by the first line of the poem, "Du bist die Ruhe." Schubert breathed an extraordinary combination of calmness and tranquility along with yearning into his music, which may have led him to the decision to choose "You are rest" as the song's title. As if ignoring the poet's title were not enough, the composer also pitilessly destroyed the structure of the poem. Somewhere during the process of the composition, each two poetic verses became fused as one musical verse. Yet the music seemed unfinished after the final line of the second verse, which therefore needed to be repeated, with a slight musical variation, to create a codetta.

This led to another problem Schubert encountered with Rückert's five-verse structure. Schubert set the third and fourth verses strophically in relation to the first two, thus the fifth verse supplied insufficient material to balance within the tripartite structure that was emerging. His solution was simply to repeat it, with a slight variation. Those concerned with symmetry and organic relationships may note that, in this way, without any relationship to the original poem, Schubert's superimposed tripartite structure reflects within each microcosm that which it achieves in the macrocosm, because each verse is structurally a miniature representation of the whole song (see Example 5.12a).

The song easily repays detailed consideration. The gentle alliteration of the opening poetic line lightens the legato over the repeated G, and the essence of yearning is suggested in the minor third between "der" and "Friede," faltering down a semitone before resuming the higher note on "mild." Setting verses strophically is by no means always an easy option, but here Schubert creates a seamless alloy between a single musical phrase and

Example 5.12a. Schubert: *Du Bist die Ruhe* (Op. 59, No. 3).

four different lines of poetry. Schubert's gift was for melody, and his special insight was how to ally a musical phrase with one or more poetic ideas. But his insight was essentially not self-conscious or technical, as is demonstrated by his disregard for poetic form and structure. Instead he seems to have had an uncanny ability to create a melody that amplifies the sentiments or spirit of the poem, which once heard together become indelibly wedded. In that sense, Schubert was a composer in the hallowed tradition of popular or folksongs that in our present time we might see replicated in Paul McCartney or Jerome Kern, rather than of the more lofty aspirations of Schumann, Wagner, and Wolf, who consciously and even avowedly strove toward the concept of "art." But Schubert was hardly a "naive"; he was the first classical composer to emphasize the importance of the accompaniment and elevate it to near partnership with the voice. The distinction here is between the creative process itself and the technique employed to elaborate it.

"Ich wiehe dir" is a close inversion of the opening phrase, but the melisma on "voll Lust und" provide a new surge of emotion, somewhere between the joy and the pain in question. The most inspired aspect of the melody is the final, repeated line, in which the yearning figure is followed by a sighing figure on the word "Herz" (see Example 5.12b). There is no syllabic justification for the falling interval on the one vowel, and a lesser composer might have left the first note of the word unchanged. But the unstressed falling sixth or falling fifth bring the breath of life to the line and, in dramatic terms, create and fix the character in one subtle detail.

Example 5.12b. Schubert: *Du Bist die Ruhe* (Op. 59, No. 3).

The third verse, musically speaking, moves swiftly sideways into a more intense, even trance-like state. The new semitone shift on the first two words immediately function to ease us through a new doorway; the vocal line moves by step discovering each new syllable, each new harmony with awe, as if they had never before existed. Both singer and pianist appear surprised by the outcome of this swift journey, so much so that a silence is necessary afterward to collect themselves. Schubert was a master of contextual contrast. The contained subtlety and simplicity of the first two verses, delicately emotionally poised, gave us no hint of what was to occur here.

It is difficult not to overemphasize the dramatic effect of this line, rising remorselessly as did the vision in front of the poet's eyes. Immediately afterward, the singer is reduced to a nearly whispering pianissimo, able only to echo feebly the earlier sighing codetta. In this context, the repetition of the extraordinary ascent not just confirms what may have been a hallucination, but increases its effect. The added interval of the ascending fourth before "deinem" further exaggerates what was already an extreme. The vision is a lover's vision, we thought, but the effect with the transcendent chords now seems almost religiously euphoric. At the end of this brief song, within a few spare bars, Schubert has brought together the three great Romantic themes of love, religion, and art, and fused them together before our eyes and ears.

Whereas the poem remains unspecific and enigmatic, that which was left unstated in the words has been graphically demonstrated in the music. Yet the mystery and awe remain.

On the final word, "ganz!", Schubert omits the sighing fall, which by now seemed inevitable. Even the singer seems to be left breathless, along with his audience, contemplating the vision with exultant wonder. Perhaps that is what lies beyond our own yearning and sighing.

13. Schumann: *Auf einer Berg* (No. 7 of *Liederkreis*)

This song is the seventh in the cycle of twelve Eichendorf settings, the poet being a close contemporary of the composer. It has a pivotal function both numerically and emotionally. It is the still center between two typical fast, mercurial settings (*Schöne Fremde* and *In der Fremde*). It is also the only poem in the cycle that seems to avoid the personal pronoun. It depicts a castle where an ancient knight sleeps for centuries. He is seemingly oblivious to the world outside, where we discover a romantic countryside of natural beauty. A wedding party flows by on the Rhine, and the bride weeps. At face value, the poem seems distant and objective; there is no commentary or evaluation, and the reader is left without explanation or context.

In the sparsest possible style, the music also seems to leave more unsaid than it discloses. The four verses of the original have merged into two virtually strophic musical verses, stripped of declamation or gesture. The music is sparsely textured, with only occasional dotted quarter notes relieving the otherwise laborious movement of half-notes. The monody discreetly obscures the contrapuntal nature of the piano writing, which encloses the voice within its own distant, hymn-like echoes. The piano's abnormally sustained, dying notes become almost inaudible, but just perceptibly enough create a succession of climbing dissonances through a cycle of fifths, perhaps more in memory than in sound.

We are, surely, with the strange knight, inside the vaulted, stonewalls of the castle, trapped within his memories, unable to take part in the life outside. The heavy and irregular dotted rhythm pulse is his only sign of life. We are so removed from reality that we only see the tears of the distant bride; we cannot divine whether they fall through joy or despair. Neither the knight nor the wedding party know of each other's existence; only we have the full picture, and because we have no tangible presence except through the eyes of the poet or the ears of the composer, the effect is overwhelmingly of impotent enclosure.

The opening phrase ("Up there, in his look-out,") seems all but lost in a slow revolution (see Example 5.13a). The bare descending fifth remains ambiguous as to tonality until the end of the second bar. The same yawning

Example 5.13a. Schumann: *Auf einer Burg* (No. 7 of *Liederkreis*).

interval is delicately echoed three times in the piano, descending and trans-posed. The melodic line then pushes up ("the old knight has fallen asleep") just beyond the first note only to fall back, moribund.

The answering phrase ("The rain is pouring down and the forest rustles through the portcullis"; Example 5.13b) is even less ambitious than the first, following immediately in the voice part, while the echoes of the first phrase are still dying in the piano. The density of the ever-expanding texture is only partially relieved by the delayed echoes of the descending fifths. The labyrinth of sound envelopes and stifles thought completely; there seems to be no escape for either from this acoustic environment: a word or a sound here never ceases, but rather continues modulating through infinity.

The second verse of text ("With his beard and hair grown into each other...") grinds and pushes slowly upward, step by step, with ever the same

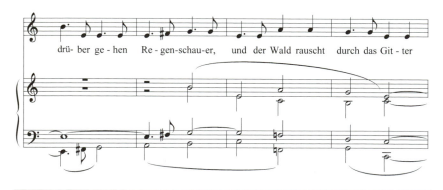

Example 5.13b. Schumann: *Auf einer Burg* (No. 7 of *Liederkreis*).

insistently repeated, descending interval. At the fourth attempt, a sequence of telling, unprepared dissonances drag the voice back through an imperfect cadence and on into stillness and the silence of a tiny interlude, itself little more than a gently echoing confusion of the preceding harmonies, before the music repeats itself all over again, for the final verses.

Schumann's attention to detail is impressive: at "Eine Hochzeit fährt da unten" ("A Wedding Party sails by"), Schumann avoids the obsessive falling interval and introduces a gentle syncopation with the new idea, to gently urge the music on and up. In the last bars of the song ("And the lovely bride weeps"), a harmonic cliché attempts to conclude, as if with a sacred "amen." But as the appoggiatura grinds inevitably into the last chord, there is no feeling of finality: we are left suspended in the dominant, and the song could as well revolve endlessly, as the knight stirs restlessly throughout his centuries of sleep.

The vocal range is confined to an octave above middle C (in the original key), and the piano writing is equally restricted, containing no material that does not appear in the voice part. For Schumann, of all composers, to write a song without piano prelude or postlude suggests an unusual relationship between voice and piano, words and music. Uniquely in this song the piano acts as an echo chamber for the singer, rather than as a supporting partner. Nothing disturbs the deathly silence beneath the song; even the attack of quiet piano chords is avoided by the use of ties over bar lines, leaving the singer often in hiatus, in place of a downbeat. The final chord on the piano lingers, dying beyond the last note of the singer. Rarely has a composer demonstrated the essential dichotomy between the sound of a piano, which cannot sustain sound, and the voice, which is about line; never have the two contrary creatures been placed together with such telling effect.

"Auf einer Burg" is an extreme example of composition by omission: so few words, so few notes, but so cunningly chosen and so tellingly placed. The lack of romantic gesture, the understatement of dynamic and texture, and the intensity of control render a fusion between poetic and musical thought in a musical language of an intensity perhaps never surpassed.

14. Judith Weir: *King Harald's Saga: "Grand Opera in Three Acts for Unaccompanied Solo Soprano Singing Eight Title Roles (Based on the Saga "Heimskringla" by Snorri Sturluson, 1179–1241)"*

The ambitious dramatic demands in the concept of this startlingly original work fomented a wide variety of vocal writing from the composer, within the intense but brief space of its ten-minute duration. The exploitation of different vocal textures, musico-textual relationships, and tessitura create not just a display of techniques, but serve to illustrate a panoply of different characters, etched with imagination onto a single, unadorned vocal line.

There is an incidental connection here between the contrapuntal suites for solo instruments of Bach, where the illusion of many voices leads to an interplay between different ranges and textures inferred to continue in a silent background, but with dramatic vocal music the underlay of words and intervention of different characters provides an almost unlimited scope for her imagination. Weir also demonstrates more contemporary techniques such as "cutting" (an analogy to film editing), a technique I term "word play," and the use of spoken voice. The latter provides wit, information, conceptualization, and aural relief from the bare, minimal intensity of the mono-opera.

In common with much late twentieth-century music for voice, there is a tendency to simplify the action of notated rhythms. Even here, with the absence of bar lines, groups of triplet quarter notes would traditionally infer accents on the first of each group. But there are many occasions when, to a contemporary composer, rhythm simply signifies duration, and the question of stress or accent is left to the singer. Example 5.14a shows the phrase as it appears in the score (1), the traditional inferences of stress (2), and a more practical realization (3). There is obviously a discrepancy between writing for instruments, where the musical instincts of the performer will opt for the traditional inferred stresses, and writing for voice, where the singer is left

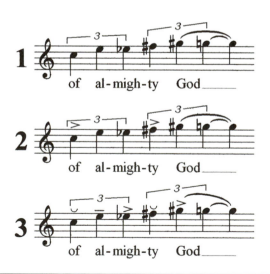

Example 5.14a. Judith Weir: *King Harald's Saga*, © Copyright 1982, Novello and Company Limited, London, England. International Copyright recurred. All Rights Reserved. Reprinted by Permission.

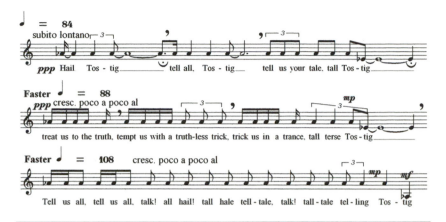

Example 5.14b. Judith Weir: *King Harald's Saga,* © Copyright 1982, Novello and Company Limited, London, England. International Copyright recurred. All Rights Reserved. Reprinted by Permission.

to redistribute the accents. In order to avoid misunderstandings, composers might do well to indicate their intention in this respect.

After the opening declamatory setting, in the following passage marked Fanfare (Example 5.14b; p. 3 in the score), Weir exploits a new relationship between text and music, that I call word play. The meaning of the text is subordinated to its sounds. The ensuing Fanfare, almost entirely on one note, creates a startling effect, especially after the more traditionally expressive lines that preceded it.

When the librettist is also the composer, as in this case, the text is bound to reflect musical preoccupations, and vice versa. Furthermore, a composer is perhaps more free to discover the possibilities of the use of non-semantic text to dramatic effect. The passage that follows uses a text of dubious "literary" worth, yet of enormous sonic and dramatic significance: "Hail, Take, Kill, Win, Sail, Fight, Go, Go." Each word is elongated and explored on the vowel with cadenza-like melisma in an extraordinary display of energetic vocal accuracy and velocity. The choice of entirely monosyllabic words allows both composer and singer to elaborate the vowels in an extreme way, without obscuring either individual meanings or semantic relationship.

A little later, the words "Put out to sea sail far over the sea" (p. 6) provide a basis for a more leisurely melismatic treatment, reflecting the imagery of the words, where the wider spacing of intervals enforces a more leisurely pace.

Weir's playfulness and dramatic wit is displayed in a tiny section that follows (Example 15.14c), where Harald's two wives are each given just a tiny phrase to declare and contrast their personality. It provides an irresistible stimulus to the imagination of the singer/actress, able to employ contrasts in tone and color as well as tessitura. The dynamics suggest a fine, subtle range of colors rather than a comic routine. It is unusual to find this amount of wit and playfulness in contemporary vocal music.

A more blatant sense of humor soon appears. Rarely can even Wagner have imagined one of his heroines representing an entire army, yet in the following section, we hear the marching of the army, bi-syllabically, in the soprano's low register, interspersed with fast cadencial figures (see Example 5.14d). The increasing excitement of the army soon leads to a breathless development of the idea to tri-syllabic and later a quarto-syllabic treatments, with increased speeds, all in this muscular style.

The appearance of the Messenger on page 8 of the score is a new device for intercutting between scenes, borrowed perhaps from cinematography. His

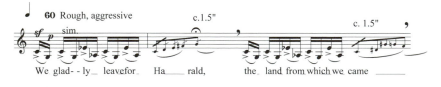

fervent interruption to the army maneuvers is marked "rapt, shimmering," and provides both aural drama and defines his character all within a few notes, as he brings the bad news to his King.

Weir's mono-opera encompasses a wealth of vocal techniques, from the spoken word, through recitative and highly decorated passages, to miniature arias. It is both a catalogue of imaginative extraordinary vocal effects and a telling fusion between drama, text, and music. Despite the extremity of vocal effect, the music remains faithful to the text in the sense that in performance it remains perfectly possible to enounce each word intelligibly, indicate its meaning, and follow the unfolding of the story. Without diminishing the difficulties of performance for a soprano, which are many, it also displays a masterful understanding of the differences and similarities between vocal and instrumental composition.

15. Wolf: *Mignon (Goethe Lieder No. 9, Kennst du das Land)*

Wolf's famous song is a passionate invocation of the romantic ideal of a distant but known locality, perhaps as a metaphor for home or heaven. Although he never set the work of contemporary poets, Wolf was steeped in literary culture, and surpassed all other composers in his scrupulous adherence to text, structurally, semantically, and perhaps psychologically. He allows himself no deviation from the poem's original structure, no repetition of words or phrases, unless they appear in the original. Speech rhythms are the basis for the word-settings, which treat melismas with utmost caution. With such respect toward the poems, clearly Wolf's aim is to present the text in a musical way that allows it to be understood with the perceptive skills and technical clarity of an actor, informed by the composer (perhaps as stage director), through the voice of a singer. The song pushes the Lied further toward opera than any other Romantic composer, and is, in a sense, a monodrama. The singer here needs enormous physical, musical, and vocal resources and control, as well as a certain vocal and emotional maturity. Not surprisingly, it exploits a large range of almost two octaves up from B flat (in the original key).

Wolf's intense temperament was anathema to the concept of strophic setting, and the three verses of Goethe's poem provide three clear sections of music, clearly developed with increasing tension and passion. Each verse begins with a vocal phrase that clearly articulates the differences between chest and middle-voice ranges, exploiting the contrast between the two colors (see Example 5.15a).

The first four words are on one note, with "das" given a semitone slow mordent emphasized by the slight syncopation, echoed by an enharmonic shift in the accompaniment. The word most emphasized for Wolf is "that (...land)," a musical representation of emphatic parentheses; the director

**Langsam und sehr ausdrucksvoll
(Slowly and with great expression)**

Example 5.15a.   Wolf: *Mignon (Goethe Lieder No. 9, Kennst du das Land)*.

has given the actor his note. The next three words, in faster rhythm, are suddenly a sixth lower, with another semitonal shift leading up through a diminished fifth to "blühn," a tone below the first note, back in the middle range. The process is repeated but, as ever with Wolf, developed, so that the mordent on "Im drunken" is now a whole tone, followed by two more upward intervals to the D flat on "Gold-" as a climax to the phrase. The final syllables plunge lower than before to the lowest note of the song, ensuring no triteness between the ends of line rhyme.

The singer, from the outset, seems to be in a dialogue with herself. (The context of the words might preclude a male voice.) The idea of a psychological dialogue, perhaps between conscious and subconscious, is a recurrent technique with Wolf and in later composers such as Berg (*Altenberg Lieder*), Schoenberg (*Erwartung*), and Peter Maxwell Davies (*Eight Songs for a Mad King*). The genesis of the form can be traced back to archetypal, theatrical depictions of madness, such as Purcell's *Mad Bess* and Donizetti's *Lucia di Lammermoor*.

The structure of the music as it develops seems to demonstrate more of these schisms, that a pre-Freudian age might have deemed unwholesome. The harmonies themselves hint at the emotional instability beneath the apparent placidity of the perhaps extreme home key of G flat major, which here has a warm but cloying quality. It soon becomes clear that another emotional division is opened up between the piano and the voice; the first outburst from the piano is marked "Belebt, leidenschaftlich" ("animated, with passion"), yet when the voice enters with an echo of the phrase, it bears the marking "Ruhiger" ("more calmly"). The singer's nervous system seems to be represented by this piano music, raging through albeit uncontrollable passion. The formula is repeated, and the singer's schism with the pianist seems to represent her efforts to withhold or suppress the pianist's instinctive response. The piano impotently drifts away through unresolved discords and into an enigmatic silence, as if beyond verbal or even musical utterance, pondering the imponderable. The penultimate line of each verse is "Dahin! Dahin. . ." ("Do you know it?"), and with their setting the music suddenly explodes through three rising phrases, marked "leidenschaftlich hingebend" ("surrendering to passionate emotion"), in an almost uncontrollable frenzy of harmonic and rhythmic energy, before returning to repeat the process more emphatically with each succeeding verse. Wolf has surpassed the role of accompaniment in his writing for the piano, which has become inextricably an equal partner, or even an alter ego for the voice.

The words in Example 5.15b represent a phonetic gift to a composer bent on climax, especially in poly-consonantal German: the softened attack on "Da-" is followed on the second syllable by, in effect, a mere vowel change to "-hin." The voiced consonant "m" eases into the next word through a dark vowel, and the double consonant "-cht" is negated by the first vowel of "ich," and the final two words have a grateful simplicity. Wolf seized on these details to create one of the most unforgettable gestural exclamations in all Lied.

Example 5.15b.   Wolf: *Mignon (Goethe Lieder* No. 9, *Kennst du das Land).*

The composition is a keen psychological analysis of an actor's possible interpretation of the text, and clearly displays the character's intensity of feeling along with her fear of acknowledging such depths. Within the tightly controlled structures of the music, the many psychological and emotional divisions are clearly portrayed within the singer as well as between both performers, and doubtless many psychologists might suggest its suggestion of schizophrenia. In its portrayal of such extremity, it has more in common emotionally with German expressionism than romanticism, however rooted it seems to be in the earlier style. Wolf revealed his awareness of the unusual range and demands the song made, even within his own oeuvre, in choosing it as one of the few of his own songs that he orchestrated.

6
Singers on Composers

This book is essentially and inevitably a composer's view about singers. This chapter uniquely attempts to view some of the problems and benefits of the collaboration from a singer's point of view. I have asked a number of singers a series of questions in relation to working with composers. It is hoped that their comments will prevent composers about to embark on collaborations to have to reinvent the wheel, as well as avoid falling into too many overpopulated pits.

There are many issues not covered by the small range of questions necessarily chosen. Similar dialogues or interviews might make an interesting vehicle for research to be considered as workshop activities in addition to those listed in the final chapter.

My special thanks to those singers who responded so generously to my questions: Linda Hirst, Cleo Laine, Sarah Leonard, Frances Lynch, Jane Manning, Lynda Richardson, Sarah Walker (and her husband Graham Allum who answered on her behalf), and Kate Westbrook.

Singers' Biographies

Linda Hirst is world-renowned as a performer of contemporary music. She is also recognized as a leader in performance education. In 1980, she co-founded Electric Phoenix, and subsequently this ensemble developed an international standing for its commissioning and performance of new repertoire. She has worked with Sir Simon Rattle, Pierre Boulez, Oliver Knussen, György Ligeti, Luciano Berio, and Hans Werner Henze. She has collaborated with several of the United Kingdom's most celebrated composers, presenting the world premieres of their works. In autumn 1999, she was awarded an honorary fellowship of Dartington College of Arts and in Autumn 2000, she was awarded an honorary doctoral degree from the University of Huddersfield. She is Head of Vocal Faculty at Trinity College of Music, London.

Dame **Cleo Laine** is one of the most celebrated singers of our time. Cleo commands a dazzling array of vocal styles and is the only singer ever to receive Grammy nominations in the Female Jazz, Popular, and Classical categories. Cleo showed early singing talent which was nurtured by her Jamaican father and English mother who sent her to singing and dancing lessons. In her mid-twenties she seriously applied herself to singing and auditioned for the hugely successful British band, The Johnny Dankworth Seven, led by the acclaimed John Dankworth. Cleo toured extensively with the band and in 1958, she married Dankworth, which strengthened their bond as personal and professional collaborators. She annually tours the US and is a frequent guest on American television. She has been honored by Queen Elizabeth with a D.B.E.

Sarah Leonard is one of Great Britain's most versatile sopranos. She is closely associated with contemporary vocal repertoire and has worked with many leading composers, including Birtwistle, Boulez, Bryars, Dusapin, Ferneyhough, Kurtag, John Harle, Richard Rodney Bennett, Klaus Huber, Lachenmann, Ligeti, Michael Nyman and Sciarrino. Opera performances include *Dr. Faustus,* Giaccomo Manzoni, La Scala, Milan; *To Be Sung,* Pascal Dusapin, Théâtre des Amandiers, Paris; *Das Madchen mit den Schwefelhölzern,* Helmut Lachenmann in Stuttgart and Vienna; *Dirty Tricks,* Paul Barker, Spitalfields Opera, London; and *Al Gran Sole carico d'amore* Luigi Nono, Hamburg State Opera. She performs regularly with many chamber ensembles, including the London Sinfonietta, Ensemble Modern, Schoenberg Ensemble, Musikfabrik, Ensemble Recherche and Ensemble Intercontemporain. She frequently gives song recitals.

Frances Lynch was born in Glasgow in 1959 where she studied singing at the RSAMD, and went on to study voice and contemporary music and electronics at City University, and the Guildhall in London. Her career has spanned a number of fields from pop to the most extreme forms of contemporary classical music as a performer, teacher, composer, and music director. As a performer she has toured her one woman voice and electronics programs worldwide—her current program, "SHE," includes work by György Kurtág, Judith Weir, Roger Marsh, Karen Wimhurst, Judith Bingham, Fabrizio Casti, and Paul Barker among others. She is Artistic Director of "Vocem Electric Voice Theatre," a company producing experimental projects in contemporary music-theater in the UK and Europe. They have a long-standing relationship with Judith Weir, and have worked with Maurizio

Kagel and Luciano Berio. As a solo artist she has premiered many new works: *A Night at the Chinese Opera* by Judith Weir, with Kent Opera; *Songs for the Falling Angel—A Requiem for Lockerbie* by Keith McIntyre (artist), Douglas Lipton (poet), and Karen Wimhurst (composer) for Scottish Television and the Edinburgh International Festival; and works by Paul Keenan, Thomas Ades, Alejandro Viñao, Elizabeth Sikora, Leo Kupper, Vic Hoyland, Christodoulos Georgiades and Polly Hope, among others.

Jane Manning, soprano, has more than thirty years international experience in an exceptionally wide-ranging repertoire, and still enjoys an active performing career. She has given more than 350 world premieres to date, and has worked closely with composers such as Bedford, Bennett, Birtwistle, Boulez, Cage, Carter, Lutyens, Knussen, and Weir. Her catalogue of CDs includes the major song cycles of Messiaen, all Satie's vocal music, and works by Berg, Dallapiccola, Ligeti, and Schoenberg with conductors such as Boulez and Rattle. Her two books: *New Vocal Repertory: An Introduction,* and *New Vocal Repertory 2,* published by Oxford University Press, are in regular use at conservatories and universities throughout the English-speaking world. She was awarded the OBE in 1990, and an Honorary Doctorate from the University of York in 1988. She has completed six years as Honorary Professor at Keele University and is a visiting professor at the Royal College of Music, London.

Lynda Richardson has sung frequently for the ROH Covent Garden, the ENO, and Scottish and Welsh Operas. Her specialty is contemporary music, and she has performed as a soloist in most European countries, Scandinavia, the US, Canada, and the Middle East. She is well known as a concert and session singer, and has sung on innumerable film soundtracks, BBC radio, TV programs, and TV jingles. Lynda currently teaches at Mountview Academy and is Head of Vocal and Choral Studies at the Centre for Young Musicians, London. She arranged the music and conducted 400 singers in the Commonwealth Parade for the Queen's Jubilee, and conducted Bernstein's "Chichester Psalms" at St. Johns Smith Square, London.

Sarah Walker has built an extraordinarily wide repertoire, ranging from Bach and baroque to twentieth-century composers such as Berio, Boulez, and Birtwistle. She is much in demand on the concert platform worldwide where she has worked with conductors such as Solti, Kleiber, Norrington, Masur, Rattle, Gardiner, Muti, Harnoncourt, Mackerras, Rozdestvensky, and Haitink. She has sung in opera houses all over the world, including The Royal Opera House Covent Garden—where she made her debut as Charlotte in Massenet's *Werther* opposite Alfredo Kraus, The Metropolitan Opera New York—where she debuted as Micah in Handel's *Samson* with Jon Vickers in the title role, the Vienna Staatsoper, Le Châtelet in Paris, Geneva, Brussels, Hamburg, Munich, Chicago, San Francisco, Lisbon, Madrid, and many others. Sarah Walker was made a C.B.E. in the 1991 Queen's Birthday Honours.

Kate Westbrook is a singer and librettist. Her musical career began in the mid-1970s when she joined the Mike Westbrook Brass Band. She has toured widely and recorded more than twenty albums. Kate's vocal range embraces Contemporary Music, Opera and Music-Hall, as well as Jazz and Popular Song. She sang the role of Anna in *The Seven Deadly Sins* by Brecht and Weill with the London Symphony Orchestra, arias by Rossini with the Mike Westbrook Orchestra at the Proms, and songs by the Beatles with the Westbrook Band in "Off Abbey Road." Her latest recording project is Cuff Clout, a neoteric music-hall, in which her lyrics are set to music by eight composers from the worlds of pop, rock, jazz and classical music.

Has your collaboration with the composer ever resulted in a change to the music, and if so, with what result?

Jane Manning: Usually [it is] a question of practicality, especially regarding misjudgments of tessitura. Male composers (including the well-established and experienced ones) very rarely seem to understand how high a soprano really sings, or what it feels like to try to enunciate a text AND sustain a line way above anyone's normal speaking range. One gets fed up with being blamed for the composer's awkward setting of the text (comments such as "the singer's vibrato obscured the words" are very unfair in most circumstances, and are often made by people who don't even think about the problem). I have indeed occasionally requested a composer to put something down a bit. Being kept at the extremes of one's range limits the possibilities for finer nuances, colors, and dynamics. Also phrasing: young composers occasionally expect limitless breath. Humming their own lines gently in a lower range while writing does not adequately indicate the reality of an energized full-blown performance!

Also there's the question of margin of error. I really hate it when the piece's main "hazard" occurs at the end of the work, so that one spends all the time dreading that moment, which could spoil the whole experience in a flash! An example would be a very long "dim al niente" in an awkward part of the voice on an uncomfortable syllable (at a register break or with a pile of percussive consonants to negotiate!). Or a long, gradual build-up, by step, with no rests whatever, at the top of the staff, getting louder and louder in relentlessly sustained notes, ending in a long held climactic note. This kind of writing tires one out, and even a mildly high note seems a terrible effort in context. Re-entering pianissimo after a longish tacet, before which was a loud exposition, is also hazardous, unless there's a loud instrumental moment to cover throat clearing! Young and less experienced, or the permanently secure and considerate composers will be receptive to suggestions to modify these potential nightmares. I've often succeeded in getting small changes made—the result is a happier performer and a better performance. And the performer will be happy to repeat the work in future—an important consideration!

Sarah Leonard: I have asked composers to change minor details such as to shorten the length of very long notes to give the throat muscles a rest, and enough time for a breath before singing again. A young talented composer wrote me a song for inclusion in a recital. He was inexperienced with vocal writing and set words far too high for my voice. He willingly changed the phrase to lower notes so that the words would be understood. His individual style still came through.

Lynda Richardson: Composers normally want to "get it right," and are open to hints as to what's going to make the singer's job easier—such as not expecting lots of fast "patter" words high in the soprano range, or agreeing to change certain pitches to suit somebody's range.

Frances Lynch: Almost always. Sometimes composers ask me to improvise material—sometimes based on world music ideas, or sketches of their own, etc.—which they record and work with even before they begin work on the piece—e.g., Alejandro Viñao; and others, like Judith Weir, sometimes create scores where the vocal part is finished, but the electro-acoustic part we develop with her approval. (I'm currently doing this on a new piece for solo voice and tape—*I was born in a small village* adapted from her opera *Blond Eckbert*.) Other composers sometimes present a score they feel is finished, and then I suggest changes to the vocal part (usually this refers to them using high registers in my voice too much, which is a bit of a turnoff for any audience—particularly if it's loud), and sometimes they change a lot of things after they've heard me sing it—sometimes even after several performances. Composer Karen Wimhurst, with whom I work a lot, began changing a lot of things in rehearsal, but now knows me so well that everything is perfect for me right from the start! A recent piece by Roger Marsh that I am working on at the moment has been altered in order to suit the composer partly—changing instrumentation, cutting some drums out and making them vocal, etc., but he has given me the task of cutting to improve its impact—which of course I do with his approval. The best experiences now with Vocem Electric Voice Theatre are when composers work and develop material with us over a few years—like Karen Wimhurst, currently developing through sketch and improvisation *Carmen—Silent Movie Opera,* and composer Andrew Lovett, who is writing a multi-media opera *Abraham* with librettist Mike Levy. After a week of work in progress our approach to performing the music and text provided many ideas for a radical rewrite by both parties, and this work is ongoing for the next few years. This kind of long-term development forms the most exciting partnerships, and the most fruitful for both composer and performers. Basically, there is almost always an effect on the composer, working directly with a performer—in my experience we help each other to do a better job.

Linda Hirst: Peter Sculthorpe rewrote the song *A Star's Turn* for me in '99, making much of it a 4th lower. He then inscribed in the copy for me. The simple reason was it lay too high—I was the singer and I was at ease lower, which was the right feeling for the music, and the actual pitch was less important. When studying *Revelation and Fall* for Peter Maxwell Davies and London Sinfonietta, I phoned Max and said I didn't have a high E flat. His reply was "it doesn't matter—sing it as high as you can." In fact in the heat of performance it came out quite well and was very short anyway. If a composer does not INSIST on all notes being absolutely as first written, there is far more chance of a success, both in terms of collaboration, and effort from the singer to get it right.

Kate Westbrook: Because I am an untrained singer—self-taught—it has always resulted in a change, because I have always had to say: change the key, can we change this line so it sings better in my voice? I'd like to use this color here so can we move this line to this register so I can use that particular color. Of course, with Mike [Westbrook], when we work on a project together we are discussing it all the time, which is very valuable. But even with other composers that I have worked with, I find the same things happen, because they are writing for me, so it's rather a different process from a classical singer being given a known piece of music, with a known approach and a known range.

Cleo Laine: I have had several pieces written for me by classical composers interested in jazz. Richard Rodney Bennett wrote two pieces for me that had strict tempo, "sing as written" and improvisation, a mixture of disciplines that I enjoyed. This was also the case with Don Banks and George Newton who introduced me to the avant-garde world with different improvisatory sounds—such as clucking, blowing, and using my falsetto-contralto voice liberally.

John Dankworth, who knows my voice better than anyone, writes for me and accepts how I interpret the music. If I protest some things are impossible he tells me to work it out. Only once have I rebelled and told him a voice could not, or rather a tongue could not, get the words out at that speed. He ceded the point. Each of them likes a voice that is able to sing what is written freely when required.

Have you ever refused to sing a new work, and if so, why?

Jane Manning: Yes, but only a very few times. (No names!) Once or twice because of the impracticalities I've already mentioned, and where the composer would not be receptive to any suggestion of adjustments.

(A work was actually conceived for an entirely different voice—one very famous composer simply didn't understand that a normal lyric soprano doesn't have a whole octave above the staff to draw on, or to make "harmonics"!) Also for such an unidiomatic setting of a foreign text that its stress and meaning were completely destroyed. (I eventually reworked the text underlay radically so that it could be done, albeit not very satisfactorily.) One case only where the words were deeply offensive and embarrassing. (I do not embarrass easily and might even find this possible now in view of differing levels of acceptability these days!)

One important case where I was required to vocalize on gasping in-halations and raspings virtually throughout. Horribly uncomfortable and vocally damaging, and after several attempts, I simply could not get round the problem or see how it could possibly work, especially in volume control. The composer has never forgiven me! Another time I was confronted with a piece of great vocal virtuosity and complexity at only a fortnight's notice. I would have needed much longer to get it up to the standard that would satisfy me, and so I stood my ground. This also did not go down well with the composer—but the organizer/ensemble were sympathetic.

The final reason would be that I didn't like or respect the music. Very rare, as most of my friends are composers I respect a great deal, but one is occasionally besieged by people who will never be soul mates and whose work illustrates this. Over the years I've become a bit better at wriggling out of potentially awkward situations!

Sarah Walker: Yes, a couple of times in the case of recently composed, not newly commissioned work, but only when the quality of the music was just not good enough and the need to pay our mortgage was not so great . . . Someone of Sarah's talent range can get near to making a silk purse out of a sow's ear, but then, why should she be asked to? There are people who can write good music.

Frances Lynch: Yes, there have been times when scores have been unreadable—which is simply a waste of my time—I send them back; and when a composer has not allowed enough time for me to prepare the work to my usual standards. (I work mainly from memory, and usually prefer to study a finished work months in advance in order to give the audience the best possible chance of hearing the work interpreted and not just read.) This has not happened for many years, as I avoid people like the plague who have reputations in this regard—however, a composer recently didn't finish a work for a Vocem event performance which was a developmental piece being written in rehearsal—as we were working for another company we felt obliged to do something for them—so I wrote the rest of it on the morning of the first night, and we semi-improvised it (something I have had to do before now!)

Linda Hirst: Yes—a piece by a composition student, which was misogynistic, obscene, and lacking in any expressive content. There have been pieces which are clearly not for me—too high and light, too slow and sustained in recent years, and as time goes on, I am more careful about what I can accept.

Kate Westbrook: I don't think it has ever arisen, because either I have written the libretto or text. If it is just a line within a piece I don't like, I could say so, but I have never said no. If it was something I disagreed with philosophically, or morally, I wouldn't sing it. But I am in a slightly strange position, I suppose, because I am not quite the "hired gun" that a lot of singers are because I am coming at it from a left field, so to speak, and I don't have the skills that many composers need, so I have to initiate a lot of things myself. If you have limitations you still have to find a way to do what you want to do.

I joined Mike's band, having been a fine artist, as a tenor horn player in a street band he had. So I only gradually started singing in the band as time went on; he thought it would be fun to do a song here or there. Then I really started working on my voice and I found that I had a rather sort of thin middle range and a very bad break—everybody has a break and young singers learn to work over that. But I have never really been able to surmount that, so I worked very much in the lower area of my voice, and that's what interested me, and I have gone down and down and down, so I can sing in the same register as a man. But then I do have a high voice, but it's more like a male alto, it's a different sound altogether. So I use that in improvising a lot, but I don't use it very much in delivering texts, because my clear, articulated voice is in my lower register.

I was going to do some Eisler songs, but I did them down the octave, and the conductor/pianist I was rehearsing with, at the first rehearsal looked up at me and said, absolutely appalled, "Christ! Your voice is low!" I knew he didn't like it, but we had to do this big concert in Paris, but they liked it. When I did the *Seven Deadly Sins,* the only time in my life I have done anything so grand, with the LSO at the Barbican, I was given the score for lower voice, but I had to take the soprano one, and put it down an octave.

Have you ever discovered new things about your voice through collaborating with a composer?

Jane Manning: I've tried very hard to think of an exception but the answer is a resounding NO! It's always the other way round! (I've always had a very analytical and technical approach to my singing and find that composers are mostly eager to know more about how the voice works.)

Sarah Walker: No. Singers of Sarah's experience know more about their voices than anyone, with the possible exception of their teachers. In Sarah's case, the great Hungarian teacher Vera Rozsa was, and is today to some extent, the only person Sarah would turn to for vocal advice. In this instance it's because Vera is such a great musician that musical and technical problems are indivisible. Solving a technical problem rarely comes up unless there is a musical need.

Sarah Leonard: My voice and I can do far more than I realized!

Lynda Richardson: No. Although I did discover how to do vocal harmonics when doing a contemporary piece, but it was the conductor who showed us, rather than the composer.

Frances Lynch: Of course—the great thing about working in the current scene is that variety is the key—they are all looking for different sounds and techniques—I would say that everything I have learnt about flexibility, style, ornamentation, and expression, not to mention aspects of technique which I have to develop to cope with their work (range extensions, funny noises, etc.) have come directly from the composers I work with. Sometimes I get a work sent to me that can take years to work out how on earth to do it—e.g., *Aubade* by Tom Ades—apparently impossible range-wise—then suddenly I found the key to the technique in my third year of facing it, through my theatrical interpretation, and was able to do it very easily. I persist like this with pieces that I feel are really great; I get determined to be able to do them and it makes me raise my game.

Linda Hirst: Yes—far too many to write down. A few examples: working with Georgy Ligeti on *Aventures* and *Nouvelles Aventures*—every time we do this, there are new things one discovers, and when a composer talks of music and its meaning rather than notes on a page, one is open to discovery all the time, in the search for the right feeling or color to put in the voice.

Kate Westbrook: I think that happens almost every single time I start a new project, because there are always so many problems that I have to find a way of overcoming or circumnavigating. Then so even at my great age, I am finding new things all the time.

Do you have any advice for composers and singers who wish to collaborate?

Jane Manning: Being married to a composer gives me special insight, and I can see both points of view! For me the collaboration has mostly been a rewarding one. Mutual sympathy is essential—everyone is protecting his or her own insecurities. It's good to remember that things can change as one develops—and the composer is also developing. It's easier when both singer and composer are at a similar stage, but people should be prepared to share their expertise and be patient. A clearly presented score is a good start! Also one doesn't want to be fussed at a first rehearsal. Trust is important.

There are of course a number of subtle social and personal reasons why I wouldn't wish to work with some composers again. One of today's most important foreign composers is such a notorious bully, never satisfied (that old Continental Professor syndrome!), that I make sure he's far away before I perform anything of his—I'm not alone in this!! I was forewarned, and have never had the bruising experiences others have told me about.

On the lower level there are those I've avoided from the outset. The question of personal taste can also be colored by experience—the nicest composers can turn out to be neurotic and querulous, yet unable to communicate what they *do* want. Nothing is more maddening than the student composer who much prefers the breathy, naive untrained voice of his 19-year-old girlfriend, which he erroneously describes as "pure," to a normal female trained voice. Psychological factors are crucial in the working relationship.

It's always a delight to find a composer (e.g., Judith Weir) who is practical, clear-minded, courteous, and considerate, and conveys her wishes cogently in her scores. Ambiguous or perverse notation can cause minor annoyance and hold things up, and a composer who confronts one with a huge list of "notes" just after the final run-through on the day is deservedly unpopular.

(On a very personal level, there is such a huge array of gifted composers around that I wouldn't make a special effort to program works by some of those who, when I was a young beginner and premiered their works, passed me over for subsequent performances for someone they deemed to be more prestigious, yet had zero commitment to new music. Loyalty counts for something as far as I'm concerned, although there are often mitigating circumstances. But anyone who happens to have slated my husband's music will get no help from me!!)

Unsolicited scores are another thing. The only one I've ever sent back by return was utterly simplistic and banal, and accompanied by a letter denigrating many of the composers I was most associated with, whom he must have known were close friends. I gave him a flea in his ear! I usually try to be encouraging.

(Some of these things of course apply to all performers, not just singers, but the emotional aspect is crucial with such an organic instrument as the voice—it is somehow more upsetting to make a foolish noise, or misfire on an exposed high note than it is to crack a note on a woodwind instrument, for instance. The human side cannot be ignored.)

Sarah Walker: This is impossible in a general way, which is what it must be in book form, save encourage the collaborative process. Interfere in each other's area as much as you can get away with and hope to remain friends.

Sarah Leonard: It is a good idea for singers to trust composer's instincts and not be too judgmental to begin with. Learning something with new ideas in it is a leap of faith for everyone concerned.

Lynda Richardson: Be as open-minded and flexible as possible and try to give each other what they ask for. It's an exciting situation which can lead to benefits all round. You can't collaborate with a dead composer!

Frances Lynch: Yes, show each other mutual respect and learn to trust each other absolutely. If you can't—don't work together. That way, you will never have any problems.

Linda Hirst: Mutual admiration and respect, and as much knowledge of each other's ability and inclination. A desire to work together, and early meetings before writing begins, to explore range, color, temperament, interests, intellectual leanings, special talents, no-go areas, personality, etc. A piece I enjoyed in all stages began with a conversation about my godmother and her relationship with my mother who was a much less patient person than the former. It was a small incident I described, but it became a marvelous little solo scena for me to sing.

This was personal, but absolutely not the only way to feel part of the work—other pieces have been partly or completely written before seeing them. Simon Holt came to meet me to ask the range, and used every single note of it, which was a challenge, and exciting.

Kate Westbrook: I have noticed with composers other than Mike—it doesn't really come up with him, in that we might say to each other at four in the morning, "Don't you think we should do it like this?"—that, in general, they can get quite tense if they think you are going to ask them to change something. So I think it's terribly important for the singer to be sympathetic to the composer's rather "dog-in-the-manger" attitude about what they've written. It's perfectly understandable that they have written something and they want an interpreter, rather than someone to start altering it. So I think the very first thing for a singer who doesn't have all the conventional skills, is that they should forewarn a composer and say, these are my best colors, this is where I can be scary, this is where I can be sweet, so that it becomes a process of exploration, which they can embark upon together, instead of somebody having written something and getting very uptight when they don't think it will be delivered as they conceived it.

The process of collaboration has many aspects for me. In *Platterback,* I had the idea, wrote the text and left it on the piano for Mike, who was very busy doing something else. At some point he looked at it and said he didn't think he could accept it, but I left it on the piano another month, and he started working on it. I think he probably asked me to change one or two words and he asked me to write a little bit more for another section. Eventually, the result was collaboration that worked very well, and we now perform that together with three other people.

Sometimes, Mike writes a piece of instrumental music, which I love particularly, and I try to write some words for it. That has happened quite a few times, then one can really make the words fit perfectly, because even the most wonderful composers sometimes don't make the word "come crunchy" on a melodic line.

Good Friday, 1663 has a libretto by Helen Simpson, adapted from her own short story. Mike wrote the music, and then when I started performing it, by doing all but one of the characters, I would say, could you change the line here, so that the phrase falls completely in the right spot for that particular word, and so on, so that my collaboration occurred much later in the process.

What makes words singable?

Kate Westbrook: A line that has to be sung is not like poetry; a line that has to be sung has to have a "singability" about it. But then sometimes, you do want to work against the grain, and make something really difficult. For instance, there is this line in *Platterback,* toward the end: "A dog with humped back/ it's spine showing through." I knew it was going to be a tongue-twister, but I wanted to keep it in, because I liked the "pt," "k," "sp" sounds all going on in the line. I was afraid of it being a sentimental line, so I wanted it to have something a bit spiky in it, even in "it's spine." In Cole Porter's *Love for Sale,* he must have decided to have a tease for singers in "Let the poets pipe of love—I know every type of love," so any singer afraid of "popping" into the mike is going to have to deal with it. On the other hand, I can see why Queen used the word "Galileo" in the song. It is such a delicious sound; it has an in-built thrill to it.

One thing I find with a lot of classical singers–and I don't know whether the composers go mad with this, if the text is important to them. They just don't love consonants enough; they love vowels and use them to make beautiful sounds. They are often trained not to risk the beautiful sound being damaged by a nasty little consonant. But sometimes you have to make an ugly sound, even with a vowel, and maybe you have to love consonants, or the thing is just a meaningless exercise, isn't it? I love all consonants, perhaps some more than others.

7

Conclusions and a Way Forward

Composers approach writing for the voice from various viewpoints. They may be looking for a certain sound, or an opportunity to play with language, or be interested in using the voice as a dramatic vehicle. The composer's own predilections will inevitably color how the voice is heard and seen. This chapter summarizes the various approaches to the voice with the objective of allowing more informed choices to be made. It attempts to sum up many of the strands in earlier chapters of the book, and indicate a few of the inherent possibilities and trends for future development.

The Ultimate Challenge of the Voice

Nicholas Cook (1998) argues persuasively that the idea of "music alone," without reference to anything but itself, is a theoretical concept rather than a reality. Music, he emphasizes, will happily align itself with any and all other media or arts. Although he argues against a musico-imperialistic position, the composer working with the voice—music's most common and enduring ally—is inevitably confronted with the tantalizing possibility of creative relationships and values far beyond the scope of a traditional harmony or theory textbook. This is indeed food for the imagination, allowing full reign to any composer's ambition, whether motivated as a grown-up-child-at-play or as the creative spirit who tries to discern order or harmony amidst life's chaos.

Music is infinitely able to reinvent itself and metamorphose all that it comes into contact with. The number and quality of relationships between music and all-that-is-not-music are similarly inexhaustible, and worthy of a separate book. However, the voice remains the most common interconnecting door between music and the "outside," and is paradoxically either a well-trodden path or a virgin landscape, according to the disposition of the composer as regards his or her received perception of tradition. The relatively recent academic discipline of melopoetics has begun to explore and discuss the infinite variety of issues concerning the inter-art discipline for music and text. *Word and Music Studies,* a book of nineteen essays presented in 1997 at the founding conference of the International Association for Word and Music Studies (WMA) in Graz, Austria, represents the first flowering of this new discipline.

The voice offers creative access to many extramusical areas through three complementary but contrasted areas: music and words; the sound of the human voice; and visual aspects of performance.

Music and Words

It might be stated most radically that music has never existed without words. Curiously, two of the most important periods when it may be said that "music alone" was sought and valued, the Netherlands School in the fifteenth century and the Darmstadt School in the middle of the twentieth century, both provoked a precocious outpouring of words to explain, analyze, or justify the composer's view of music's inviolably fundamentalist position. The Netherlands school *was* concerned with text setting, and provided a vehicle for exploration concerning music's need to allow words to speak for themselves, or to be heard as abstract sounds as the conveyers of musical ideas. The problem of linguistic intelligibility in musical setting has been a perennial concern for church authorities. Desiderius Erasmus (1466–1536) wrote these words some 500 years ago, criticizing contemporary composers: "Modern church music is so constructed that the congregation cannot hear one distinct word" (Lee 1970).

Frequently mentioned in *die Reihe,* a series of influential pamphlets published by the Darmstadt School from the 1950's, is the term "musical purity." It is an unfortunate phrase that suggests a moral or religious tone, and infers music's superiority over its frequent allies, which somehow render music unclean. It may now be understood not so much as an avant-garde posture, but rather a circular completion of the argument that began with the early Christian authorities who were scandalized at music's ability to dominate and even subjugate holy writ. Their fear was that music might sully the pure religious message and subvert the ignorant congregation into sensuality and licentiousness. The will to political power and religious dogma often lurk just below the surface of our words, often returning to haunt us.

At other times, words have represented an indissoluble part of a constantly evolving musical language, from their inclusion in all musical scores to program notes and program music, from theoretical treatises to the setting of words as lyric or dramatic material. The age-old argument—whether the voice or the music is preeminent—is the subject of countless discussions and books as well as at least one opera libretto (Strauss's *Capriccio*). These discussions often miss, by default, the interdependence and instability of words and music in relation to each other, which counts for at least a part of their joint allure. The question of preeminence or hierarchy between words and music is irrelevant in the context of their voluble relationship, which may be comfortable or combative, obvious or subtle, dominating or subservient—in different styles, individual works, or even within the same work. The composer's urge to control will usually vie with the axiom of ambiguity that underpins our verbal expression and communication, and the ensuing friction may be just that which breathes longevity into a work.

Words open the structure of music to intellectual understanding, while music "speaks" to us both more precisely and more ambiguously than language is able. The necessity of words to explain music reflects our own dependence on the need to name something in order to know it. The continuous striving for superiority between words and music reflects the divisions in our perception between rationality and emotionality, instinct and reason, thought and feeling. But the subtlety lies within the discovery that neither words nor music uniquely inhabit any one of these areas, but reside within both in fluid and unstable proportions. It is the dynamic between the two that provides the creative energy that so often beguiles us.

The composer fascinated with language often makes a choice to write copiously about or in support of her or his work, or to incorporate the words into the body of the music's score, or into the sound and language itself.

The Sound of the Human Voice

The human voice was the sound first recorded on the earliest phonograph in 1877 by Thomas Edison. This new ability to hear our own voice was at least a symbolic preface to many fundamental twentieth-century concepts—from theories about the subconscious to post-modern deconstructional processes that consciously interpose the voice of the writer between the reader and the subject. The voice remains the most common, potent, and powerful tool of musical communication, and functions to a limited extent independently from linguistic understanding or intention. Although superficially a vocal style may reflect a certain country, era, or tradition, many singers today increasingly approach the voice from a plurality of different methodologies and are able to control the superficial color and adapt to the needs of a multitude of references. "Crossover" in this vocal sense is currently practiced by singers associated with all the musical disciplines and styles, and seems an area likely to increase over the next generations. The "core" vocal sound has remained unchanged for millennia and represents a unique reference to our history and certainly for our musical future, irrespective of increasing dependence on amplification, technological innovation, or digital voice simulation.

Nevertheless, there exists an important divide between musicians and the public regarding the primary target for the singer: creating a unique voice or subjugating the voice to the material to be performed. The inherent "grain" or tonicity of the voice remains an abiding and overriding obsession for some, while for others the art of communication carries much more value through the artistry of performance. This is the major area of dispute in terms of vocal appreciation both professionally and among the larger public: for some, the sound of the voice may be enough to thrill and engage, whereas for others this is merely an envelope containing that which is to be communicated through the singer's artistry, that may itself overshadow any concerns with vocal limitations. As a result some singers hardly ever approach different styles of music with different vocal styles, since their sole concern is about their sound, and any music is merely a vehicle for that, while others continually search for colors, timbres, and nuances in their voice that they feel bring a veracity to their realization. The same phenomenon may be observed with some famous actors, who are content to replicate their screen image irrespective of character and situation, while others (often called "character actors," a term curiously used disparagingly) metamorphose themselves, subjugating their id in their search for dramatic truth. On those rare occasions when both concerns seem to be equally mastered and displayed, both singer or actor and their voice rise to an altogether higher and exceptional level of artistic ability.

The composer obsessed with vocal tonicity may be drawn toward the lyric and dramatic traditions that have sustained this fascination for many centuries, whereas the composer excited by his or her own and the audience's reaction to a communicative singer may perceive how the music plays a more complex role than as merely the vehicle for the singer's voice. There is a parallel, controversial and provocative area for composers: some composers seek the holy grail of perfection in terms of the realization of notational values, while others will forgive inaccuracy (if necessary) at the expense of insight and communication. It is always rare to encounter both perfection of accuracy and the energy of insight.

Visual Aspects of Performance

To watch a singer while listening invokes the multitude of possibilities of corporal and spatial communication. The pop video remains a contemporary testimony to the innate "multimedia" nature of singing, perhaps taking off from where opera could not grow in its long-established developmental trajectory toward ever-bigger voices and grander arenas. Perhaps pop concerts may be considered the most successful form descended from opera today, and the contemporary significance of the pop video is treated seriously and in depth by Andrew Goodwin (1992). At a certain level, all performance arts are essentially theatrical. Nicholas Cook (1998) pointed out that even the orchestra displays an inherent theatricality, often assumed or monopolized by the role of the conductor, who communicates and commends it to the audience, even through his or her back.

Through the close-up lens of the camera, the theatricality that remains uniquely vocal in performance has in recent generations expanded to include both the areas of corporal intimacy of the performer and public grandiosity in terms of spectacle, including the infinite spectrum between these extremes. Allied with technology, the vocal performer has succumbed to ever greater intrusions into personal intimacy, while at the same time performances have been experienced by larger numbers of people than any concert hall or stadium could accommodate. Opera singers have particularly suffered under the unforgiving scrutiny of the close-up camera, whereas popular singers are often specifically groomed for this. All performers of music may be aware of their responsibilities toward performance and presentation, but singers above all have become victims of the elusive fashion expectations of size and appearance that modern media continues to demand.

The composer fascinated by these concerns may be drawn toward extra-musical areas, such as theater, film, performance art, dance, music-theater, multimedia, and opera, where the visual and aural mediums exhibit complementary or symbiotic relationships.

Conclusion

Together, these three areas indicate the unique plurality and diversity of creative choices leading directly from a composer's collaboration with a singer. The ultimate challenge for any composer is to regard these not as mutually exclusive choices, but compositely as aspects of the same discipline, inferring some kind of extended contemporary theory of "gesamtkünstwerk," realizable through a sophisticated and elaborate music-theater, interactive recording, or both. If contemporary singers are for the first time beginning to approach the voice as an instrument able to function across a spectrum of styles and situations rather than as a slave to one, then contemporary composers are confronted with an extraordinary and exciting challenge to begin to understand the complexity, subtlety, and individuality of each singer and his/her unique potential.

Music may be seen as a model to encourage awareness and sensitivity on a holistic level. Professional performers, including singers and actors, may quickly learn that their discipline is affected by physical, emotional, and psychological events in their life. A singer's voice will reflect every event in the life of the person. To some, it appears almost as a barometer, while to others it may appear as the generator of their well-being. Whether as cause or effect, it remains for many an early and formative experience of the nature of interconnectedness. Musical performers are privileged to work in an area that uniquely combines intellectual, emotional, psychological, and physical disciplines, in approximately equal importance. Composers, on the other hand, often seem to exhibit tendencies that depend on a restricted palette, and may be consequently labeled as cerebrally, romantically, or monetarily motivated. Yet, because the performance of any musical work must involve all four disciplines, the composition must contain the relevant information, if only by inference. Composition as conscious play or control of the performer's intellect, emotion, psychology, and physicality is a logical if perhaps an awesome ambition for any composer. Through working or collaborating with a voice, a composer at least has an opportunity to tackle the bigger themes of unity and division that profoundly underline our sense of being modern.

How Our Audience Hears

I cannot claim to present the reactions of the unknown public, as I was able to integrate the voices of at least some singers into Chapter 6. Yet as composer and musician I am also part of an audience, perhaps even the most important member of an audience in my composer's imagination. Hence I grant myself license, however undemocratically, to address at least one point of view of the great public at large.

The lack of consensus today concerning what constitutes beauty in a voice may be simply a result of aesthetic subjectivity. It may alternatively be symptomatic of a more profound problem: a result of our decreasing ability as a species to discern between certain sorts of sounds, by which I also infer a degradation of the auditory sense through time in evolutionary terms. It might seem that during certain eras there has been something approaching consensus regarding vocal standards, or at least that disagreement was not so precipitous. For instance, the seventeenth and eighteenth centuries, although very recent from an evolutionary point of view, may arguably have displayed a much more unified qualitative vocal appreciation, ultimately leading to the concept of Bel Canto. Although the reasons may have had more to do with common social, cultural, and educational opportunities in Europe at the time, nevertheless there remains the possibility that as a species our auditory sense is in decline in the same way that our olfactory sense has declined in evolutionary terms.

It is currently generally accepted that the area of the brain that deals with speech also deals with the visual sense, whereas the area that deals with singing is concerned with the aural sense. In Chapter 4 I quoted Patsy Rodenberg's view that the written word has long superseded the spoken word, which has led to an ever-diminishing importance or understanding of oratorical abilities and the vocal techniques that fueled the hallowed and ancient art. Politicians today necessarily cultivate their image in preference to their linguistic content, reflecting our increasing dependence on visual information. In classical music, the visual sense of the score has become the primary basis for the wealth of literature on the subject, and in popular music, both live performances and pop videos are witness to the multi-media basis for this "new" music.

The extent of sound intrusion and pollution in our city life has occurred parallel to the development of an increasing facility to produce more decibels when listening to recorded or broadcast music. This has proved habit-forming and has resulted at least in part in a dependence on amplified volume, which at extreme levels obliterates a thoughtful or emotional response to musical stimulus in preference to something more basic: The physicality or animality of sound has become the overriding pursuit of certain areas of music production. An obvious example is popular films, where clichés of rumbling bass sounds habitually compete with rhapsodic string and fanfaric brass sounds at the threshold of auditory damage. Their clichéd existence paradoxically undermines the evocation of any "dangerous" emotions, such as fear or horror by supplying a high degree of "comfort factor" through the very recognition of the sound-type and its formulaic application. The reliance on cliché was a similar byproduct of minor composers during the early growth in popularity of opera before the reforming quest of Gluck. As a result, much film music of today has been reduced to little more than sophisticated and visceral sound effects.

The degree of volume used in the cinema, the rave club, and in stadium concerts far exceeds the imagination of earlier composers of symphonies or operas. Yet the organizations concerned with the concert and the stage, even when dealing with traditional repertoire, find themselves having to compete with the public's expectations created by these events. If the performers cannot be made to play or sing louder, opera houses and concert halls are ready to amplify them. In short, a great number of the public is left aurally unsatisfied at less than potentially dangerous or really damaging decibel levels. This trend is entrenched by the ubiquitous operatic obsession with vocal volume at the expense of other qualities, such as expressivity, sensuousness, timbre, and the real variety, weaknesses, and vulnerabilities of the human voice. The voice is often reduced from the most sophisticated and complex instrument of musical and non-musical sounds to a machine for screaming (undifferentiated white noise) in some forms of heavy metal, or for producing homogenous vowel sounds in international opera houses. Orchestras, too, that within a generation of memory proudly displayed different national characteristics among certain instruments, have themselves long since homogenized, increasing the recognition and "comfort factor" for audiences in the same way that certain hotel chains purport to do for tired and overstressed international business executives. Our age does not tolerate difference in this respect: Globalization seems to be the purveyor of greyification rather than celebration.

The universal expectation and dependence on high volume is surely an indication of a decrease of refinement in our ability to hear and discern between sounds, whether natural or man-made. It seems to be an unavoidable byproduct of living in a noisy environment, where the function of not hearing or being alert to sound is a protective device for survival. In such an environment, gentle and subtle sounds cannot be distinguished as valuable, and our opportunities to develop this sense seem to be decreasing. Perhaps this partly explains the schism that began to show in classical music at the turn of the century, when certain composers and musicians were intent on refining and redefining their musical detail or complexity, but unable to take a public with them, as had been more the norm in the nineteenth century. Musicians may be among the first and the last to witness the evolutionary degradation of their auditory capacities.

Male and Female Voices: Reason versus Emotion

Assumptions about gender attributed to vocal qualities betray ancient prejudices. From the Sirens in Homer's *Odyssey* to the invention of the telephone and phonograph, the disembodied female voice has been a symbol that engenders male fears, vulnerability, and mistrust in some perhaps even more acutely than the unvoiced or silent female body. The myth of the Sirens has remained a seminal text for almost 3000 years; the telephone, invented in the 1880s, was the first instrument to both physically "free" the female voice from her body (even the earliest operators in the USA were female) and simultaneously provide a unique workplace for would-be suffragettes.

The early years of the recording industry found technical problems in recording and reproducing the upper female range, that had no counterpart with male singers. There were some interesting consequences: Barbara Engh (1994) takes this into account when discussing Theodor Adorno's seemingly sexist and inexplicable remark (in *The Curves of the Needle*, 1928) that unlike the male voice, the female voice cannot be successfully recorded "since it requires the physical appearance of the body that carries it." This reaction of such a sophisticated individual as Adorno to new developments in technology shows how even a distinguished listener can be misled, but a further observation may be useful here: Far from freeing us from the "bondage" of myth and superstition, science and technology often seems to be a vehicle for reawakening dark areas of the psyche, merely providing a new vehicle for conveying the same ancient and irrational points of view and experiences with the additional "justification" of scientific rationality.

The embodied female voice has traditionally been the vehicle for (usually male) composers, librettists, and playwrights to express extreme emotions, including insanity and ensuing suicide. Many feminist analyses have demonstrated how song, and in particular opera, has repeatedly asserted through repetition and inference that men are essentially rational and therefore responsible, whereas women are essentially irresponsible because of their emotional and unstable nature. While putting to one side, of course, the nature of war—undoubtedly one of *man's* proudest testimonies to their rationality—the case for the prosecution is never more clearly enounced than in the Freemason-inspired "comic" opera of Schikaneder and Mozart, *Die Zauberflöte,* where both evil and hysteria are personified in the extreme pitches of The Queen of the Night in counterbalance to the tranquility and peace of Sarastro's Kingdom of Light and Reason. Despite the adjectival paradox between light and dark in vocal as opposed to philosophical terms, many Sarastros have lamented privately how it seems the devil always gets the best tunes. Expectant audiences still today dote on the Queen's top Fs even to the expense of any other notes, and customarily fidget through Sarastro's profound aria, especially when it is taken too lugubriously.

The gender-based argument concerning the source of stability and instability, rationality and irrationality as defined by reason and madness is, however, an oversimplification, as Roland Barthes (1985) pointed out: "In relation to the writer the composer is always mad (and the writer can never be so, for he is condemned to meaning)"(300). Reason is then, by definition, a linguistic or semiotic adjunct, rather than a sexist association. Although some composers have suffered famously from insanity, evidence for their instability may be less easily found in their music. If irrationality is a characteristic of all music, this may reflect on the limits of music's relevance or the importance of non-rational thought in life. It might also be suggested that music's a-rational (as opposed to irrational) character becomes tempered, with the addition of rational language.

Many commentators have managed to neatly circumvent all these arguments by pronouncing music itself as essentially an "effeminate" art, and therefore prone to develop the same "weakness" in the beholder. Plato, in *The Republic,* offered advice about which musical modes might cause unwanted characteristics of gender to develop in boys and girls. Later writers, such as William Prynne Histrio, in his *Mastix or the Players Scourge,* published in

London in 1633, have proved even more categorical in their condemnation of certain aspects of music:

> Such Songs, such Poems as these [are] abundantly condemned as filthy, and unchristian defilements, which conteminate the soules, effeminate the mindes, deprave the manners, of those that heere or sing them, exciting, enticing them to lust. To whoredom, adultery, prophanes, wantonnesse, scurility, luxury, drunkennesse, excesse: alienating their minds from God, from grace and heavenly things: and Syren like, with their sweet enchantments entrap, ensnare, destroy mens soules, proving bitter portions to them at the last, though they seem sweet and pleasant for the present (267).

The obviously hysterical tone of this document is itself of interest in a discussion of its gender-based assumptions about rationality and instability. It might be easy to dismiss such sentiments as a single case of extreme religious Puritanism, but for the fact that all ages and cultures seem to contain those who articulate with differing intensity their fears concerning the perceived effect of music. Nearly two centuries later, William Cobbett wrote in his *Advice to Young Men and (Incidentally) to Young Women, in the Middle and Higher Ranks of Life* (London, 1829): "A great fondness for music is a mark of great weakness, great vacuity of mind: not hardness of heart; not of vice; not of downright folly; but of a want of capacity, or inclination, for sober thought."

The articulation of such fears is often a precursor to a censorial or even destructive threat. The (long-haired) "degenerate and effeminate" rock musicians and singers in the middle of the twentieth century shocked and put fear into the parents of their own generation; before them, politicians from both left and right sought to control so-called undesirable elements in the music of composers in Germany, the USSR, and the USA, and more recently in Afghanistan, for fear of contamination. An interesting phenomenon is that the sociopolitical movements that display such fear of music and its effect are often those with a poor record, or little interest in, the emancipation of women. The Ayatollah Khomeini made these comments about music and its destructive nature:

> Music is no different from opium. Music affects the human mind in a way that makes people think of nothing but music and sensual matters. Opium produces one kind of sensitivity and lack of energy, music another kind. A young person who spends most of his time with music is distracted from the serious and important affairs of life; he can get used to it in the same way as he can to drugs. Music is a treason to the country, a treason to our youth, and we should cut out all this music and replace it with something instructive (Quoted in Lebrecht 1982).

Whether the motivation for this ancient and ubiquitous fear is religious, social, political, or gender-based in derivation is a subject beyond the scope of this book. What remains beyond a doubt is the ability of merely the sound of the human voice to reach parts of our psyche and provoke instinctive responses and reactions within us for which we may not be aware. In this respect, the female voice remains arguably dominant. As the poet Ambrose Philips wrote in his *To Signora [Francesca] Cuzzoni* (25 May 1724):

> Little Siren of the stage,
> Charmer of an idle age,
> Empty warbler, breathing lyre,
> Wanton gale of fond desire,
> Bane of every manly art,
> Sweet enfeebler of the heart,
> O, too pleasing in thy strain,
> Hence to southern climes again;
> Tuneful mischief, vocal spell,
> To this island bid farewell;
> Leave us as we ought to be,
> Leave the Britons rough and free.

The first voice a baby identifies with and responds to even before it is born is of course its mother's. Could it be that in man's urge "to put away childish things" (I Corinthians 18), we affirm that the power of this attraction must be, on some level, subdued or even throttled?

Awareness of the voice long predates linguistic understanding; it is the sound of the voice to which we are forever "bound," in Homer's sense, even as life begins. That sound may be rediscovered in disembodied form elsewhere. The voices of boys before puberty remain on some level remindful or disturbing to us: a fact suggested by the distant and (to us) unsavory sexual mores of the Ancient Greeks, the use of boys playing female roles on the Renaissance stage, and the later extraordinary stellar fame of the emasculated castrati, instigated by the Roman Catholic Church. The otherwise distinctive and contrasting arts of opera and pantomime maintain one aspect in common; the habit of cross-dressing between leading men and ladies remains, even in a traditional setting today, potently contemporary in its effect. In the history of opera, gender swapping occurred, reflecting changing social requirements or restrictions in different eras: the prohibition of women on the baroque stage in some countries necessitated the development of male imitations. The counter-tenor and male alto found their niche in baroque opera and this simultaneously coincided with the development of the castrato singer in those countries who did not object to the idea of castration for the sake of art, in preference to using real female actresses. There can be no doubt that this illustrates a contradictory pseudo-morality at work in this period of female prohibition and male dismemberment. Later, in the classical era as the vogue for the female voice grew, a trend was established for women to play young male, gallant, or pageboy roles. This idea continued until the last century: the famous eroticism of Richard Strauss's music in *Der Rosenkavalier* is more disturbing for many, given that the two lovers are in fact women in the audience's eyes, if not those of the characters. Mozart's famous aria of male adolescent yearning, *Non so più cosa son* from *Le Nozze di Figaro* could arguably not be realized believably by a male singer of sufficient maturity to do service to the sophistication of the music. In traditional British pantomime even today, the interchange is in both directions, where women achieve the virile male prerogative as a Prince, and men impersonate with ease the ungainly and ridiculously Ugly Sisters. A wider range of character types is rarely to be found: more serious impersonations by men of women remained furtive or clandestine, until the twentieth century. The reversal of reality in this pantomimic role-play allows us a rare opportunity to examine our reactions to the "disembodied," or rather "re-embodied" vocal sounds, and analyze our instinctive responses during the apparently harmless act of laughing, which might otherwise prove provocative or "uncomfortable."

There is both a male and a female aspect to every voice. They coexist as different forces in balance, reflecting personality traits. Very often one remains hidden, as in the case of the mature, broken male voice that seeks to hide the child's voice that he retains, but seldom displays in public.

The unsuspecting composer may approach these sexist concerns or gender traps with naiveté or arrogance, but whether the concerns figure consciously or unconsciously as a part of the creative process, he or she may sooner or later be subject to these reflections, considerations, or even judgments. The choice of which voice to write for or the gender implications of the textuo-dramatic material must remain of necessity the prerogative of the creator, but the significance it evinces and the consequences and repercussions will always be open to evaluation, and later re-evaluation.

Going for a Song

The composer who writes for the voice is always in some way contributing to the vast and seemingly limitless repertory of song. Although it remains arguably the most ubiquitous and important musical medium, and—despite the title of this section—it is certainly not always the cheapest, the history of song may by no means be thought of as a linear or progressive development. There have been many affirmations followed by counter-affirmations, statements of objectives followed by counter-objectives. Composers and performers in the twentieth century expanded the boundaries of the form as well as its application through various media perhaps more than ever before. The result, as so often in history, is not a consensus of opinion about song throughout all or even any one artistic community. The subject is worthy of a book in itself, but this section is an attempt to summarize a few of these divergent opinions as they affect composers.

Attempts to define the nature of song exhibit cyclical historical preoccupations, reflecting different perspectives of both its social functions and the professional preoccupations of the author. Plato's objective in *The Republic,* for instance was essentially political: he emphasized music's useful application in the responsible development of "good citizenship" through its ability to forge or influence character. Goethe's objective, as we shall see, reflected his own literary preoccupations; he sought to emphasize the dominance of rational or linguistic communication, inferring a subservient role for music. Composers may often be equally unaware of their subconscious objectives when working with voices or text; arguably, composition necessitates a complex dialogue between rational and subconscious motivations. Perhaps the only worthwhile definition for a song for a composer is the one being worked on at the time. A singer's perspective of a song, in any era, may be more practical or utilitarian: as a vehicle to communicate with and to profit from, or as a tool to discover and derive creative and performing energy.

Song has three concurrent definitions: as a fusion of words and music; as an integral part of the structure of some forms of poetry (e.g. in classical Greek culture); or as the natural utterances of certain birds, mammals, and insects. Furthermore, the word is often used by young children learning to play music on an instrument, suggesting a deep unconscious connection between abstract and representational musical forms. Curiously, there seems to be no name for an equivalent genre of instrumental music, except by definition with the instrument's name, as in the cumbersome "a piece of piano music." Mendelssohn's *Songs Without Words* expressed a romantic and lyrical aspect to his piano music, and Chopin's Nocturnes are sometimes described as lyrical compositions. Dramatic elements might be thought to conflict with the nature of song, yet some commentators such as Edward T. Cone (1974) perceive the relationship as complementary: "If every song is to a certain extent a little opera, every opera is no less an expanded song" (21). Neither does the word "song" carry any connotation concerning intimacy or spectacle: a song may be a private act of seduction by a lover with his guitar to his beloved, a public performance involving a soloist and a grand orchestra, or the semi-spontaneous outburst of thousands in a sports stadium.

There are also examples of songs that are hardly acceptable even under the first definition of a fusion of words and music. A vocalize may be thought a specific form of song without words more comfortably than a voice "impersonating" instrumental music, and many composers since Berio and Stockhausen have experimented with phonemes and vocal sounds with perhaps only oblique reference to language itself. In any case, the use of abstract vocal sounds such as "fa-la-la" is probably as old as song itself. There is a constant line of development in this playing with phonemes, from the sixteenth-century madrigal to twentieth-century "scat" singing. Some early Italian and English madrigals were a verse-repeating form, which often used "fa-la-la" in the refrain, e.g. *My Bonny Lass She Smileth* by Thomas Morley. *Matona Mia Cara* by Orlando di Lasso uses an interesting variant: "ton, ton, ton; tiri, tiri; ton, ton, ton, ton, ton." Some sources suggest the singers would have simultaneously danced while singing, thus these songs are sometimes called "Balletts." Dance music, too, was not so far from the inspiration of the jazz singers and composers who developed a singing style that emulated some aspects of instrumental playing (See Excerpt 2.10 from a concert work by Johny Dankworth).

Even the notion of a song as a form merely involving voice and text seems inadequate if both voice and text are independently expendable. More precise are the names of the many subgenres of song, which accentuate specific characteristics. For example:

> Anthem: represents a specific collective and cultural perspective
> Antiphon: a short sentence sung or recited before or after a psalm or canticle
> Aria: illustrates an emotional reaction to a dramatic circumstance
> Aubade: morning song
> Ballad: relates a story
> Barcarole: a boat song supposedly derived from Venetian Gondoliers
> Blues: a traditional and formulaic song of protest or complaint
> Canticle: a bible hymn
> Carol: celebrates a specific religious event with crude and simple musical qualities
> Catch: humorous rounds
> Coronach: originally a Gaelic funeral song
> Dirge: a mournful song
> Dithyramb: a wild choral hymn originally from ancient Greece
> Ditty: a short simple song
> Drinking song: usually to accompany revelry
> Epithalamium: a marriage song
> Folk songs: often anonymous in origin and kept alive by an oral tradition
> Glee: an unaccompanied song for men in more than three parts

Hymn: collective expressions of faith
Lullaby: communicates the feeling of security and sleepfulness to
    children
Paean: a hymn of praise or triumph
Patter Song: exploits an abundance of words and syllables
Prothalamium: a song proclaiming a forthcoming wedding
Round: unaccompanied vocal canon
Roundelay: a short simple song with a refrain
Serenade: an evening song
Shanty: a song with alternating solo and chorus
Threnody: a lament; wailing song

The abundance of these subgenres testifies to the complexity of the genre, its flexibility and its importance; their diversity explains the difficulty of a successful generic definition.

A history of song, such as by John Koopman (1999), is obviously an invaluable resource for understanding how time and different cultures have contributed to the wealth of variety of definitions and applications of the genre. Goethe's famous preference for Karl Zelter's settings of his poems over Schubert's highlights some of the difficult relationships between words and music, between poets and composers. The schism between linguistic intention and musical expression has maintained an important trajectory in music history, from Aristophanes's dismissive or ironic remark that any words might be good enough for music, through the many medieval Christian dictates against complexity obscuring the nature of sacred music, to Brecht's extraordinary acknowledgment of his begrudging preference to the textual editing of his musical partner, Eisler. But to narrow the history of song down to musico-textual bartering would be to miss the obvious predominance of the singer, who must transcend these concerns and create a third and all-enclosing structure. One tradition of song, from at least the troubadours until today, honors poet, composer, and singer as one and the same person. The collaborative aspect of song is perhaps less of an equal partnership than might be thought, if only in that it will always be the singer who has the last word, makes the final decisions, perhaps despite whatever hierarchical arrangements have been previously agreed by the other two collaborators.

The fourth wall of song, as in theater, is the audience. Its perceptions may obviously be more strongly colored by the singer than the earlier collaborators. It is the voice and performance of the singer that provides the window through which an audience first perceives the song, and for many that first experience remains the only source from which any response or judgment may be made. In this sense, the singer may seem to personify the

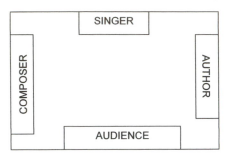

Figure 4. The Four Walls of Song.

song, becoming a flesh and blood representation of the most ephemeral, collaborative art form. If the collaboration between author and composer is doomed to inequality, then their differences are of little consequence in the face of this subsequent alchemical transformation.

The analogy of the four walls bears further exploration (see Figure 4). Although this diagram is merely representational of an audience's perspective, clearly the composer and author are only obliquely visible to the audience. That as a species we are increasingly dependent on visual communication has been discussed earlier. Whether the audience's attention is on the linguistic-rational side of the brain or the musical-instinctive side is evident in the diagram. However, the diagram does not convey the more complex relationship between words and music, also discussed earlier: both move potentially freely between the extremes of rationality and instinct.

The third definition of song extends its importance beyond our species. Biomusicology is the study of the biological basis for the creation and appreciation of music. Researchers in this field present various strings of evidence supporting two hypotheses: music making is a primal human enterprise and the art form includes many virtuoso performers throughout the animal kingdom.

Recent in-depth analyses of the songs sung by birds and humpback whales suggest that, despite their vocal potential to exceed human choices, their song making reflects many human preoccupations with musico-linguistic structures. Male humpback whales, for instance, spend half their life apparently singing in preference to any other activity. Studies have found similarities between their rhythms and those of human music. The vocal range of a whale may exceed seven octaves, but stepwise movement is preferred to large leaps, and the A/B/A system of the baroque "da capo" aria is apparently a favorite structural device. There is also evidence of rhyming refrains, which may aid their ability to remember the complex material. The pentatonic scale, which has been the foundation of so much human music, is utilized by the hermit thrush, and birds as a species compose songs reflecting similar human preoccupations with notes, rhythmic variation, harmonic patterns, and pitch relationships.

It would seem song making is both an instinct and necessity for many living species, with a discernible commonality of structure and intention. If the definition remains elusive, the extent of activity in this area throughout all of nature defines it, for some, as a primary function of life. From this perspective, perhaps all human music making may be heard as a branch of song making, whether or not the human voice is heard.

Toward a Compositional Theory

The aim of this section is to clarify and differentiate comparative levels of structural syncretism between music, words, and visual performance elements. The objective is to allow composers to see the voice as a starting point with which to enlarge the scope and language of music into the many types of performance art and beyond.

The composer engaged in writing for the voice is inevitably confronting extramusical issues, challenging a comprehension of the network of interdisciplinary areas. As well as making music, the singer uses words and can move. Some composers may be content to allow the instinct of the performer or director to be led by the inferences of the score, whereas others may understandably wish to exercise some conscious control of these extramusical ideas, or at least develop their cognitive faculties to allow for informed choice. Many cross-arts studies have been made, examining distinct interrelationships between the performing arts. But my aim is to suggest an analytical framework that may specifically provide a composer with some tools to compare levels of complexity between the three disciplines.

I propose three levels of complexity. The levels may demonstrate distinctive characteristics, but they are not exclusive. Examples may be found of works that apparently remain within one level, and others that cross all the levels. On a constructional level, there is certainly a potential for a graded progression in any direction between the levels. It also needs to be stated that there is no pejorative intention, in that "quality" or any other means of judging the "value" of an artistic product is simply irrelevant here.

Three Levels for Music

It may be seen that music functions along a spectrum with sound at one end and structure at another. This implies a reliance on time as the vehicle, because a sound is a time-based event, perceived at the moment of creation, whereas structure relies on a comparative analysis of events taking place at different times, perceived through memory. This spectrum may be distinguished by the theories of foreground and background proposed widely by the writer and theorist Hans Keller (1986). The basis of Keller's approach is the idea that, to communicate expressively, music has to work "two-dimensionally"—that is, there has to be an interaction between its "Foreground" (by which Keller means the music actually played and heard) and a "Background," which is not in fact present in the music as heard, but is created in the mind of the listener as the piece progresses. Specifically, this Background consists of the sum total of musical expectations aroused in the listener during the course of the piece, reflecting their conscious and subconscious musical experience. These definitions are distinct from the definition of the three levels I propose, but are useful when we compare similar structural spectrums in language and movement.

A musical composition on Level One is constructed from unambiguous references to acknowledged styles. The "tension" in the music, where it exists, is derived from the interplay between the traditional parameters of melody, harmony, and rhythm within an identifiable stylistic boundary. Examples might be a hymn tune or dance music; an early Haydn string quartet, or an early Beatles's song.

A musical composition on Level Two will involve at least one additional element, which may have implications on some or all Level One type events, which are thereby highlighted or contextualized. Such an additional event may be a certain rhythmic freedom that may not be notated, a temporary direction to improvise, or an event that in some way challenges or stretches the obvious stylistic boundaries of tonality and pulse. The consequence is a sense of ambiguity or anachronism. Examples of ambiguity might be the controlled improvisatory sections in some of Lutoslawski's scores, or the manufactured soundscapes on the Beatles's famous *Sergeant Pepper* album. These examples demonstrate enrichment or deepening on the level of communication, whereas the imposition of a disco beat onto Mozart's 40th Symphony is a different example of a Level Two activity, which seems to restrict the original musical language, and create a dichotomy. Some systems music that takes classical or romantic chord progressions and places them within a mechanically rhythmic framework, defunctionalizing them from their harmonic context, also provides a dichotomy, but that may be more subtle or enriching.

A musical composition on Level Three may imply the subjugation of Level One events by the application of a larger idea that dominates all the material. At an extreme point at the end of this Level, the distinction between Foreground and Background both within the musical structure and the listener's perception may be negated. The music subsequently may seem

Example 7.1.   Three Levels of Musical Complexity.

extreme and uncompromising. Examples on this level are Stockhausen's *Stimmung,* where a static harmonic series provides the vehicle for foreground events, Schoenberg's *String Trio,* and many works by Webern, where the contrapuntal technique so enriches the foreground area of events that little or no background is perceivable. The same may also be said of some of the sacred choral works of Machaut.

Example 7.1 presents three invented phrases which demonstrate more clearly one perception of these different levels through three treatments of the same idea. The first example, aside from a chromatic nature, is not so far from any traditional melody, and represents Level One. The second example represents Level Two. It treats the pitches both developmentally and in a more free and improvisatory manner, the rhythmic freedom representing here the "additional idea," but the link with Level One is clear. The third example represents Level Three. The imposition of a rhythmic formula—or two contrary formulas to be precise—all but obscure the original melodic gesture, which becomes merely a vehicle for a rhythmic gesture. These are but examples; the same level of complexity may be applied to any one or all parameters of music simultaneously. Although the three examples are clearly related for ease of comparison, the idea may only ever appear in one level.

Three Levels for Words

Words may be said to function along a spectrum with phonetic sound at one end and linguistic meaning at the other. The complexity from a listener's point of view is that these extreme functions are centered in different parts of the brain; we habitually find it difficult to hear language as sound, when we are intent on meaning, and respond only subconsciously to this part of the communication. In order to concentrate on the sound of a spoken language, we must in some way repress the cognitive instinct, which may be easy if we are hearing a language we do not understand. It is on this level that we may enjoy songs and poetry in languages that we do not speak.

The treatment of any text is a contexualization of it. The following invented text will serve to demonstrate how any text may be treated in three levels, which are distinctly related to the three levels already described in music:

> A: We have reached the end. There is nowhere else for us to go.
> B: I see something ahead. It may be a light.
> A: There's no point in your pretending. It won't change anything.
> B: If I could just reach out and move this...

In Level One, this dialogue occurs in a soap opera, between two trapped people. Clearly, the words of each reflect two opposing reactions to the situation. Both characters are trying to impose their own view of the situation on the other. They are reacting emotionally toward each other with more energy than they utilize against the physical danger itself. In this context, the words are unambiguous in their meaning, and there is only one level of communication taking place. The physical reality of their situation, their stress and distress is evident in both voices.

In Level Two, the same text occurs as a part of a radio play. Although there has been a suggestion of some physical disaster, it is not as present in our imagination as the voices are. Both voices are speaking in a dreamy sort of way, emotionally perhaps disconnected, or slightly "high" in some way. The words may suggest a disagreement, but the tone of their voices suggests there is no friction between them. What are we listening to? Are these two people trapped in a tunnel, or are they lovers in bed, post-coitally? The director is playing with our sensibilities; the last line here seems suddenly and vulgarly funny. And yet it is only the music of the language that has changed, not the text.

The ambiguity of the scene comes from a deliberate use of the language on two levels, relating to opposing physical and emotional reactions in different contexts. On a musical level, the information conveyed through the way the language is being used is much more conscious because we have no visual information. As with Level Two in music, the imposition of another element (the stylized sound of their voices) has the effect of changing all Level One information.

In Level Three, the text is presented in the theater. Two actors speak, but in a very special manner: A speaks only the consonants, while B speaks only the vowels. It is evidently very difficult, and when they fail, they go back to the beginning of a sentence and start again. Although we are aware that words are being used, their presentation in this manner pulls our attention toward the sound-structure of language, and away from semantic structures. Of course, we end asking why they are doing this, but the reason may not be at all connected to the original text, as was the case in the other two levels. In Level Three, the imposition of an idea or a technique has the potential to destroy the significance of Level One or Two, and present an abstraction or distillation of an idea.

Three Levels for Visual Performance Elements

Movement, as a part of a performance, may be said to function between the extremes on the spectrum—between the minimum that is necessary to achieve any specific objective to a point where the movement is in itself the objective, and is necessarily demonstrative. From a composer's or musician's perspective, the movements of the players in a classical string quartet are no more than is necessary for the objective of producing the required sounds or communicating ensemble through gesture. "Playing to the gallery" expresses the notion of exaggerating certain gestures, to communicate visually some aspect of virtuosity. There is a cliché in circus performances when the strong man drops his weight, or fails to lift it twice, demonstrating both the weight in hand and the extremity of the accomplishment, when achieved. He may have been able to lift the weight as if it was a paper bag, but our enjoyment is dependent on our perception of the difficulties involved. Certainly musicians by the nature of their role do not get second chances, but many performers strive to display the difficulty involved and their mastery of it, while others pursue the art of concealing art.

Movements in Level One will vary greatly according to context. Level One may be considered to be movements that are appropriate or instinctive to the context or style, the restrained movements of the classical string quartet for example. However, in the field of rock music, a more demonstrative visual language may seem "natural," as in Pete Townshend's famous windmill arm-smashes on the guitar with The Who. But it is not merely a matter of musical style: many rock bass guitarists remain as still and concentrated as some chamber music players, as they lay the unmoving rhythmic and harmonic foundation to the structure, whereas many classical soloists cannot resist playing to the gallery. In short, a Level One visual presentation satisfies the appropriate expectations of the viewer of any given context.

In Level Two, an additional element is placed that may reflect on some or all of the other elements. A trombonist playing a solo in a concert may

FUNCTIONAL SPECTRUM	MUSIC *sound...structure*	WORDS *sound.......meaning*	VISUAL ELEMENTS *minimal...extravert*
LEVEL 1	Basic, traditional relationships of melody, harmony, and rhythm, etc.	Words and meanings in an emotionally unambiguous context.	That which is appropriate or instinctive to the context or style.
LEVEL 2	One additional ingredient that affects the interpretation or perception of other material.	An additional element or layer of meaning or intrusion of sound, which affects the perception of meaning, invoking other levels of meaning or ambiguity.	An additional element that contextualizes or highlights other material.
LEVEL 3	Application of a larger idea or structure that potentially obscures other levels.	A decontextualization or abstraction of words which ultimately tend to concern themselves with phonetic structures or gestures at the expense of syntax.	The application of a big idea or "frame" causing an abstraction, an elaboration or a negation of synthesis on many levels.

Fig. 5. Three Levels in Relation to Music, Words, and Visual Performance.

play entirely within Level One limitations. If the composer asks him to wear shades with the black-tie outfit, an extra element is added that has repercussions on how his performance is perceived visually, and Level Two is invoked. If he starts speaking through the instrument, there is a Level Two of music introduced. Perhaps an example of Level Two presentation in rock music terms is Jimi Hendrix's famous gesture of setting fire to his guitar.

A Level Three visual presentation introduces one or more elements, which potentially may subjugate all other elements. Samuel Beckett displayed mastery of this when Winnie appears at the beginning of *Happy Days* buried in the ground to a point above her waist, or when the three characters at the beginning of *Play* appear with only their heads visible outside of an urn, and when Mouth in *Not I* has a fine spotlight projected exactly on that part of her anatomy at the expense of all others throughout her monologue.

Figure 5 summarizes the three levels as they are perceived within and between the three disciplines.

The aim of this comparative analysis is to provide a composer with some basic tools with which s/he may understand relationships between extra-musical disciplines that are encountered when composing for a singer. It is a perspective that I hope allows for all possible degrees of compositional decision-making and control, irrespective of any particular aesthetic or style. It also articulates the complex nature of any performance and exposes the spectrum of techniques shared between theater and music, of which the voice remains the most enigmatic partner.

8
Educational Activities

This chapter presents some workshop outlines and proposals, with the aim of developing creative collaborations between composers and singers in educational institutions. There are a number of ways that singers and composers may be brought together to work: through composer and ensemble residence programs; out-reach programs of festivals, theaters, and concert halls; initiatives by schools, colleges, and universities. Because age and ability may vary greatly, this chapter offers general suggestions and objectives for projects within a course or program. It is left to the teacher to adapt the ideas to his or her particular students' needs, abilities, and situation.

When organizing a course or seminar, it would be ideal to involve an equal proportion of singers to composers, with members slowly circulating within the group during a semester or throughout a year. However, an imbalance of numbers is more likely to be usual for such a course. The overworking of composers is less likely to be a point of concern in this situation than the physical burdens placed on singers, which suggests a higher ratio of composers may create problems. A related concern will almost certainly arise from any associated teachers of singing or even coaches, where typically great mistrust is commonly felt over the "safety" of singers in contemporary repertoire. Reminding those concerned at this starting point that most opera singers who have ruined their voices have done so by singing Puccini, Verdi, and Wagner (badly), or indeed through bad teaching, just as so many rock singers have caused permanent damage by shouting, might be neither wise nor effect the desired outcome.

Whereas it is beyond the scope of this book to solve such institutional problems, it may be of value to endeavor to start any negotiations from the area of necessary mutual trust and responsibility between singers, composers, and teachers. For instance, composers should always respect a singer's disinclination to sing something they are unhappy with (for example, vocalizing on the inhaled breath), before consulting with a teacher; but singers and their teachers in turn might try to understand that composers from different eras have always asked new things stylistically from the voice, and should not themselves be afraid to play or experiment with their voice: The cultivation of an instinctive curiosity in all things vocal is essentially a healthy attitude.

Reynaldo Hahn was a composer and singer in France and gave a series of lectures about the voice and singers in 1913–14, in which he said:

> . . . nothing in the domain of vocal sound or sound vibrations in general is useless: The briefest utterance, the least sound, the slightest noise, contains some kind of lesson; and one of the most severe charges that I bring against singers is that they are not curious about everything that concerns their art, that they make no efforts to glean information from every corner. (1990, 25)

Finding the perfect balance between the fears and needs of all concerned may be an unlikely but prized objective, but an essential part of the day-to-day management of such a course; a limited amount of friction may well be necessary to change prejudices, expectations, and improve understanding on all sides.

The main requirements for the participants are enthusiasm for composing or singing, curiosity, a good ear, practical analytical techniques, an ability to make responsible creative decisions, and a lack of fear concerning personal and collaborative creativity. These qualities may, in turn, often be seen to develop out of the workshop. The role of the course leader is essentially as an enabler or catalyst with at least a minimum understanding of the basic objectives, benefits, and inherent problems between singers and composers. The most important benefit of any such course is the practical knowledge gained by the students: being told that high notes are difficult to enunciate is less valuable than hearing the same pitches and words work in one voice, but not in another; a composer being told that he or she may be insensitive to verbal nuance will be always less effective than hearing a singer who is a good actor finding and expressing meaning in a text that the composer never imagined; being told that the role of the singer when working with a living composer may elevate the creative position of a singer from servant to partner does not convey the excitement of a collaboration where neither composer nor singer are any longer certain where their personal responsibility and ownership of material lies in respect to the final work, which has become jointly their own. To some extent, all the composers should expect to use their voice (however inappropriate the sound) when demonstrating their ideas, and all singing participants should be invited to improvise or compose, without fear of ridicule. Listening, analyzing, and discussing at every stage within the group are essential aspects of the workshop dynamic. In this respect, the various stages of rehearsal and informal/formal performance may be seen as fundamentally research tools, a fact that may influence the administrators of the institution who are concerned with measuring the value and importance of any such course.

It is perfectly plausible that these workshops may be accomplished with young composers or those with little experience in written music. The act of composition is essentially improvisational and only secondarily a written form. Many great songwriters have acknowledged a limited notational ability, and some have even suggested there may be an advantage to the dependence on instinct rather than analytical processes. In this situation, composers should be encouraged to write and record their ideas in any way possible with the objective of fixing their ideas in memory rather than as a score for the singer. The communication between composer and singer (if they are not the same person) is then by necessity and demonstratively verbal, which may be neither less valuable nor precise than a score.

Working methods may be as varied as the outcomes: composers may experience working directly with the sound, improvising with the singer, or intermittently do so in between rewrites outside of class. Singers also may well find some relief in discovering that the process toward achieving a performance may be shared and creative. The sheer necessity of working together may help the composer understand the value of clarity and explanation in the score. In all working circumstances, a sense of alertness and curiosity should be fostered. Although each project may seem goal-directed, an important secondary objective is to allow any aspect of vocal and compositional technique to arise into the collective consciousness at any moment.

There are two distinct processes involved in any workshop: working/creating and reflecting/analyzing. The working dynamic of these exercises is essentially directed toward creating the energy of mutual curiosity and discovery. The workshop is not the place to be constricted by ideas of what is *right* or *wrong*, *correct* or *incorrect*. On the contrary, the restrictions of each exercise are placed rather that the illusion of absolute freedom may be discovered within the proscribed limits. If the process or work is "successful" by any agreed criteria, this is always more important than the breaking or exceeding of these limitations. The reflective or analytical dynamic is more subtle and complex: it may be public, one-on-one through working pairs or with the workshop leader, or private. Although forum discussions will generally take place at the end of a workshop, the analytical process obviously involves intermittent surfacing during different stages, or may continue beyond the workshop when the singer or composer continues to ponder about an issue raised during the work, and arrives at a subsequent workshop with a more developed idea or alternative solution.

One word of warning to those new to the workshop experience: students and adults, especially musicians, are habitually terrified of making mistakes publicly. Creating a safe and unthreatening environment is essential preparation to achieve the required working dynamics. Although much of this responsibility depends on the personality of the workshop leader, two ideas or principles may be of value:

1. Playfulness is an essential word in theatre and music, as well as our primary method of self-education. It defines an attitude and a relationship between all those involved.
2. Making mistakes and learning from them is the most efficient way of discovering what works and what does not. The fear of making an error is tantamount to creative paralysis.

Street Songs

Objectives: To explore the different effects of situation, environment, and psychology on compositions for the voice.

Parameters: Songs must be performable by a singer or preferably a group of singers either in the open air or in an enclosed public space.

Methodology: Discussion; improvisation; trial within the group; performance in the street; analysis; refinement.

Evaluation: The desire level of audience interaction and involvement should be clearly articulated before the event; the event should then be objectively and discreetly scrutinized by members not involved in the composition or performance. If the results, however unexpected, are in any way positive, objectives may be enlarged or redefined.

Observations: What works in the street may not work in the concert hall or theater and vice-versa; exploring one area helps define the limitations and possibilities of another. Street songs explore language, performance technique, visual presentation, and musical concerns without the usual subtleties or nuances associated with the concert hall. Basic questions such as how do you attract an audience and then maintain their interest reflect universal compositional concerns: just because a concert audience is trapped in their seats is no guarantee that their concentration or interest is won. The only cautionary area is that singing outside is tiring and acoustically unrewarding for singers, and thus unison group singing may be more appropriate. Shopping centers offer both better acoustics and worse noise contamination, although when a manager agrees with the idea, interesting and challenging opportunities often arise.

Related topics of interest include audience interaction; singing unaccompanied; use of amplification; psychological or physical vulnerability; acoustical requirements; restriction and freedom; theater; costume; presentation.

Composing on One Note

Objectives: Control and understanding of the importance of color and timbre, dynamics, intensity, velocity and range in vocal composition.

Parameters: To choose a single pitch and explore the expressive vocal qualities in a particular voice.

Methodology: Selection of text or sounds; the composer explores the possibilities with the singer.

Evaluation: Comparison of results between different pairs.

Observations: The voice is an extraordinarily flexible tool of expression. Many composers with a traditional education perceive the selection of notes as the crucial activity of the composer. This exercise places other compositional parameters at the forefront of the composer's consciousness and also allows the singer to explore other tools of vocal expressivity than their range. And in the end, one note has to be chosen: which is the best for this voice (and would it also be best for other voices)?

Example: Ein Ton; Lied by Peter Cornelius (1824–1874), a song composed on the note "B."

Songs without Words

Objectives: To liberate the composer from the inherent necessities and restrictions of linguistic comprehension in vocal composition and to explore the voice as a source of sounds.

Parameters: To invent vocal sounds without linguistic meaning and utilize them expressively.

Methodology: The composer and the singer each produce a catalogue of interesting possibilities, from which a selection is made and a structure is created. This exercise is ideal for individual work, especially in the early stages.

Evaluation: Comparison and discussion of outcomes.

Observations: From vocalize to invented sounds or languages, the non-linguistic possibilities of the voice are infinite, but not without problems to overcome. These include how to engage the attention and emotion of the word-orientated singer or audience, the motivation of the composer, and concerns about notation. A study of the International Phonetic Alphabet (see Appendix 2) is recommended for advanced students.

Addendum: The idea of poems without words is a natural extension to this idea, and encourages a cross-disciplinary, creative aspect to language in common with music.

Words without Songs

Objectives: The interrelation of music and text in a text-dominated situation; different speeds of text delivery and the effect on the musical setting.

Parameters: The setting of lists of words to be articulated at speed.

Methodology: Preselection of texts; enunciation by singers to explore the problems of speedy but clear delivery in different vocal ranges.

Evaluation: Whether the objectives of clarity and interest by the composer and the singer are met, and where their individual abilities and responsibilities end.

Examples:

1.   *Catalogue Aria* by Mozart from *Don Giovanni*
2.   Wolf: *Ich hab in Penna* (Lied)
3.   *Machines Agricoles,* cycle by Milhaud

Addenda: The use of a single word for an entire composition also produces interesting and related problems for singers and composers, e.g., Mozart's *Alleluja* from *Exsultate jubilate,* K 165.

Identical Texts

Objectives: The perception of textual diversity of understanding, and variety of interpretative responses to the same text.

Parameters: A single text is chosen as the basis of compositional material for each composer. It might be a good idea that the text is chosen by a singer, as in a commission.

Methodology: Singers and composers are invited to speak the text in front of the group, after which a general discussion begins to uncover the richness, diversity, and ambiguity of meaning or interpretation. A continuous process of understanding how each creative decision impinges on the next, defining, limiting, clarifying, or divulging expressive intentions and "meaning."

Evaluation: Continuous comparison and discussion.

Observations: Allow a singer to choose a text; some singers are curiously and erroneously uninterested in issues about text, and the responsibility to choose for the group may help the singer to understand the complex process of singing better. All the composers in the group then set the same text. The interest lies in analyzing how each team has reacted differently to the same textual starting point.

Examples:

Chansons:
Green (Verlaine: Fauré/Debussy)
Mandoline (Verlaine: Fauré/Debussy)
Claire de Lune (Verlaine: Fauré/Debussy)
En Sourdine (Verlaine: Fauré/Debussy)
Spleen (Verlaine: Fauré/Debussy)
Soupir (Mallarmé: Ravel/Debussy)
Placet futile (Mallarmé: Ravel/Debussy)

Lieder:
Ganymed (Goethe: Schubert/Wolf)
Harfenspieler Lieder (Goethe: Schubert/Wolf)
Lieder de Mignon 1–4 (Goethe: Schubert/Wolf)

English Song:

Shakespeare:
Blow, blow thou winter wind. Set by Thomas Augustine Arne, Frank
    Bridge, Madeleine Dring, Erich Korngold (Op. 31, No. 3),
    Sir Hubert Parry, Roger Quilter (Op. 6, No. 3).
Full fathom five. Set by Frederic Ayres (Op. 4, No. 2), John Banister,
    Robert Johnson, Michael Nyman (*Ariel Songs,* No. 3), Igor
    Stravinsky (*Three Songs from William Shakespeare,* No. 2), Michael
    Tippett (*Songs for Ariel,* No. 2) Ralph Vaughan Williams
    (partsong, from *Three Shakespeare Songs,* No. 1), Charles Wood.
O mistress mine, where are you roaming? Set by David Amram, Amy
    Marcy Cheney Beach (Op. 37, No. 1), Theodore Chanler, Ernest
    Farrar, Gerald Finzi (Op. 18, No. 4), Percy Grainger, Mary Howe,
    Erich Korngold (Op. 29, No. 2), Thomas Morley, Herbert Murrill,
    Sir Hubert Parry (*English Lyrics,* set 2, No. 1), Roger Quilter
    (Op. 6, No. 2), Sir Charles Villiers Stanford (Op. 65), Ralph
    Vaughan Williams, Richard Henry Walthew, Peter Warlock.

Alfred Edward Housman:
Is my team ploughing? Set by George Butterworth (*Six Songs from A
    Shropshire Lad,* No. 6), Ivor Gurney (*The Western Playland,* No. 6),
    Charles Wilfred Orr, Ralph Vaughan Williams (*On Wenlock Edge,*
    No. 3).
When I was one-and-twenty Set by Robert F. Baksa (from *Housman
    Songs*), Sir Arnold Bax, Sir Arthur Bliss, George Butterworth

(*Six Songs from A Shropshire Lad,* No. 2), Henry Balfour Gardiner, C. Armstrong Gibbs, Ivor Gurney (*Ludlow and Teme,* No. 6), John Jeffreys, Charles Wilfred Orr, Sir Arthur Somervell (*A Shropshire Lad,* No. 2).

Time Limits

Objectives: Fast and instinctive creative responses, the experience of producing ideas under pressure; control and understanding of difficulties in performance.

Parameters: Depending on the number and quality of individual working spaces, short time limits of 10, 20, or 30 minutes work best. The songs are necessarily short, even incomplete.

Methodology: Preselection of text; timed individual work composing, then rehearsing within similar time limits with the singer, followed by informal performance.

Evaluation: Post-performance discussion.

Observations: Writing a song in ten minutes, or half an hour, is not an arbitrary task, but part of the real-life experience for many media composers. It demands a high degree of discipline and craftsmanship. Writing a song that may be mastered by a given singer in ten minutes or half an hour is equally or perhaps even more demanding in terms of discipline and craft. It should be remembered that the result should not be boring for composer, singer, or the listener.

One Breath

Objectives: To explore the duration and action of breath on the voice in different musical and textual situations.

Parameters: The duration of the composition is limited to a single expiration of the performer.

Methodology: Composers work alone before collaborating with the singer.

Evaluation: Discussion during and after the process.

Observations: How long is a breath, what can be achieved by a singer within such a short span? How does what the singer is asked to do affect the breath supply—how may it be prolonged or foreshortened?

This is a good vehicle for singers to begin to lose any fear of improvisation.

Writing a Song for Children to Hear

Objectives: To explore how a composer may need to adjust the musical parameters and techniques to suit the perceived necessities and abilities of certain audiences.

Parameters: Decisions should be first made concerning the proposed age and abilities of the young audience.

Methodology: Collaboration between singer and composer leading to informal presentation performance in front of invited children.

Evaluation: Directly by the audience in open discussion.

Observations: It is of course impossible to predict audience reaction, and attempts to do so border on condescension and arrogance. This is a complex task that requires a great deal of imagination and technical control.

Addenda: Writing a song for children to sing is an excellent exercise for understanding the voice and abilities of the young.

Improvisation

Objectives: For a composer to work directly with a voice without a score; for the singer to react quickly and creatively to instruction; for the onlookers to learn about communication between singers and composers, the hazards and strengths of verbal communication in terms of sound. Other objectives are to discover something about the voice of the singer and the mind of the composer.

Parameters: Either with or without preparation, a composer works with a singer to a given time limit. It may take place in front of the group who must remain attentive and quiet, or without the onlookers. The session should end with an informal "performance" of the piece, however short.

Methodology: The composer sits at a keyboard, if required. Using words and demonstrating ideas, the composer gives an idea to the singer of how to begin with a sound or phrase. Clarity of direction is essential, as is willingness to try anything, and a certain boldness of spirit, especially by the singer, who acts as joint composer. The discussion that follows should focus equally on the process involving the interaction of singer and composer and the product. It might be advisable to allow all the onlookers to speak before the singer and composer join in the ensuing discussion.

Evaluation: Words are often the métier of singers, and may be offered easily or even profusely. Composers who are taciturn may find the process testing, especially in front of colleagues. The ratio of words to actual singing should ideally be small, and the process depends on rapid, instinctive decisions and reactions from both parties.

Observations: Singers with some experience or special courage may improvise in front of the group without the aid of a composer to great effect, demonstrating both imagination and vocal ability. Questions of style in any predetermined form might best be avoided; a "free" style of improvisation liberates all from the concerns or restrictions of correctness or incorrectness. It is preferable to attain a noncompetitive sense of trust within the group before attempting this exercise. The results might be compared at a later stage with the product of a "closed" session and a report from both the singer and the composer on the process.

Further Projects

The following composition projects are directly related to techniques discussed in the text. There is probably little to be gained from them without recourse to a singer willing to try out or demonstrate the ideas. Furthermore, the diversity of voices, even within a type, demands that these exercises be somewhat tailored for a specific singer. All the projects may require finding or devising short texts, which may introduce cross-curricular work. Alternatively, many projects may be equally successful with "nonsense," phonetic texts, or as a vocalize.

The Break

Compose vocal music that deliberately exploits the division of voice into the three registers. Instruct the singer to demonstrate or exaggerate the different colors of each register. The contrasts must be justifiable through the text and the musical intention.

For instance, it might be possible to write a trio for one voice, with each character sharply defined as to character or mood. Alternatively, the ranges might be used consecutively to suggest some kind of journey or emotional progression.

A complimentary exercise would be to compose something using a similar vocal range that requires consistency of tone and color throughout.

Vocal Categories

This requires access to different voice types, though not necessarily simultaneously. Each singer should present and perform a short song or excerpt, which they believe demonstrates an aspect of his or her own voice. The composer is then invited to compose something that further exaggerates this aspect or exploits the opposite effect.

- A bass singer demonstrating the lower range may be asked to use extreme notes that are not available in full voice, but the color must be appropriate to the composition. The use of falsetto notes exploits an opposite effect.
- A soprano may sing fast coloratura passages, demonstrating flexibility and accuracy. The composer may respond with ideas that are yet more rapid, or produce a sustained, lyrical line that demonstrates an opposing effect.
- A tenor may demonstrate a heroic, romantic, and dramatic scena, to which a composer responds with music that represents weakness and vulnerability, or alternatively requires precision and flexibility.

The objective of each exercise is to help define the advantages and disadvantages, strengths and weaknesses of different voice types. In this respect, to compose something that a singer finds extremely difficult is not necessarily a failure of the composer. In that situation, the composer might revise or find another singer who is able to master the specific technique required. In this way the composer will be able to compile a series of different vocal aspects applicable to different voice types.

Legato and Leaps

The composer should devise a vocal line that exploits leaps across or between registers. The same figure may appear in different places with changes in articulation, justified by the text or the compositional intention. The objective is to discover how articulations such as legato, staccato, and portamento affect the singing apparatus. The difficulty will be to compose similar musical gestures that work equally well with different articulations.

Air and Breath

These exercises explore the effect of organized breathing on the vocal line. The composer is directed to produce a long vocal line, where although there will be no rests, breathing will be possible but "hidden" to suggest a single, unbreathed phrase. Here, any text will need scrutinizing in detail by the composer for double and triple consonants that may impede the illusion of longevity and smoothness. Similarly, changes of direction or large intervals may affect where breaths are possible or impossible. Dynamics will also play a large part. Without forewarning, the project leader might demonstrate with a singer that a small crescendo directly before any breath carries the intention of continuity across the gap, hiding the breath from the audience's attention.

Dynamics

These exercises help to demonstrate the effect of different ranges on dynamics. If the composition sets out to define 12 categories of dynamics, the composer may soon find that these definitions are difficult to gauge or sustain by any singer. The speed of change will affect the result as much as the changes of range. It might be better advised to choose four dynamics (pp, p, f, and ff) and find compositional justification for applying them at the bottom, middle, and top of each vocal register. This will help the composer to discern the different effects between a forte in the sopranos' middle range compared to a forte for instance on a high G. Both terraced dynamics and crescendos and diminuendos on sustained notes will demonstrate something of the art and subtlety of vocal dynamics.

Flexibility and Stamina

It may not be solely extremes of dynamic, tessitura, or speed that tire a voice. Singing constantly in one register may eventually cause muscular tension and impede the singer's performance.

Most voices excel either in agility or volume, rarely both, and never simultaneously. An exercise for a composer in this regard involves first choosing or determining which quality is most pertinent to the prospective singer, through observation in performance. The composer should then deliberately exploit the singer's strength in a composition, which also contains a small degree of the other quality to an extent that the singer is equally capable.

It may be appropriate in this and some other exercises that the singers not be told of the technical parameters being exploited until after or toward the end of the project, so that the singers do not become too self-conscious concerning any particular qualitative judgment that the composer makes about their capabilities. The discovery of erroneous judgments by composers is an important part of a collaborative creative process and not simply a negative outcome. It takes a long while to discover and understand the strengths and weaknesses of some voices.

Composing between the Notes

The composer is directed to explore as many types of links between notes as possible, using all manner of small and large intervals to explore the possible effects of different glissandi and portamenti, as well as clean changes between notes. The setting of a text will additionally alert the composer to the way that consonants may interfere with or provoke any intention. It is suggested that some of the examples given in Chapter 2 are studied, listened to, and analyzed, before attempting the exercise.

Music and Language

These exercises are all directly related to text and music. Given texts and different languages are all equally useful.

Precision and Ambiguity. In order to demonstrate ambiguity or precision of emotion, objective, and intention, a neutral text should be found that does not explicitly demonstrate any particular mood or emotion. The composer's task is to produce a single setting that has a variety of different contexts, exploiting contrasted or opposing emotional states. Without changing the notes, the setting might have three or more versions, with annotations that suggest perhaps the character's anger, insecurity, or sensuousness. Three singers are then selected, without knowledge of each other, to work with the composer and present the different versions.

An extension of the exercise allows the original composition to remain without any specific emotional annotation, and the singer is invited to use his or her imagination and technique to create various interpretations.

Irony or Double Meaning. A text should be found that is explicit in its emotional intention, and the composer should be asked to set it in such a way as to suggest the character really feels the opposite. For instance, a text that declares love might be set so as to suggest the character singing is insincere; or a confident and strong text might be set to suggest the character's underlying insecurities, doubts, and weaknesses. Can music turn a "yes" into a "no" or a "maybe"?

Vowels

Setting texts that utilize similar vowel types, a composer is able to explore how different vowels affect changes of range in a vocal line. The composer should be encouraged to explore a wide vocal range and repeat text wherever necessary. Setting each individual vowel sound for a vocalize may demonstrate why the traditional vocalize used the open "A" sound. But much fun may be had creating phrases to be set to music that exploit families of similar vowel sounds, for example:

1. The ease with which each inky pin impinges is infinitely rich.
2. Attack a round apple as a madman and have a grand bash.
3. You use your awful fourth paw for forward or fall from your course.

Diphthongs

The singer is invited to sing a popular song, but with classically pure vowel production, minimizing diphthongs. Cathy Berberian's recordings of The Beatles's classic songs make interesting examples. An excerpt from a Handel aria performed with colloquially exaggerated diphthongs may be equally amusing. (Berberian has also used this technique on her recordings.) The composer is invited to set a text indicating, exaggerating, and controlling

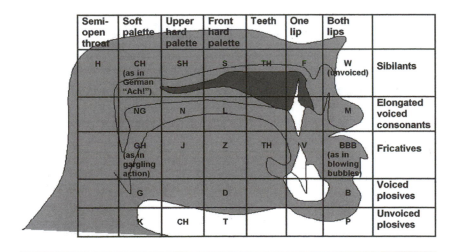

Semi-open throat	Soft palette	Upper hard palette	Front hard palette	Teeth	One lip	Both lips	
H	CH (as in German "Ach!")	SH	S	TH	F	W (unvoiced)	Sibilants
	NG	N	L			M	Elongated voiced consonants
	GH (as in gargling action)	J	Z	TH	V	BBB (as in blowing bubbles)	Fricatives
	G		D			B	Voiced plosives
	K	CH	T			P	Unvoiced plosives

Fig. 6. Vocal Placement.

their use, in a way appropriate to the objectives of composition and character; for instance, a character pretending linguistic street credibility.

Consonants and Sibilants

The composer and singer are invited to categorize different sounds as to where they are produced. The result might be something like the image in Figure 6. This diagram is useful in identifying where and partly how the sounds are made, and may be useful as a preliminary study toward the international phonetics alphabet, supplied in the Appendix.

The composer is then invited to compose with families of sounds, or progressively through the structure of the mouth. Singers with an ability to improvise often enjoy this sort of body-centered, abstract improvisation. The act of conscious discovery of those tools that we use every day, once begun, may become quite compulsive also for composers.

Vibrato

The conscious control of vibrato is an advanced vocal technique, and therefore exercises for composers in the area might only be possible at later educational stages. The understanding of differences between a "natural" vibrato, a tremolo, and a wobble is best explored through attentive listening at concerts and in recording, while the demonstration of them would only be possible with a singer of secure technical maturity and sensitivity. However, it may be possible for a composer to explore the effect of non-vibrato sounds, to compare with a well-produced "natural" vibrato. The introduction of vibrato at the end of emotive and prolonged syllables is a common feature of many popular singers' art, and might profitably be analyzed through recordings.

Text Underlay in Scores

Every text produces individual considerations, and visual clarity of intention by the composer for the singer is the primary objective. As an exercise, composers may be invited to set an existing text (perhaps solely to a rhythm) and compare their decisions with the published version.

Appendix 1: Vocal Nomenclature

Even with the individuality of each voice taken as basic, there may be still some use to these groupings:

Soprano

Best tessitura is often the high register; a consequent weakness in the middle voice; often a good chest range. Of all the voice types, the soprano range is the most diverse, from dramatic coloratura (Queen of the Night), through light lyric (Despina) to Dramatic (Tosca) and Wagnerian (Isolde).
NB: The tessitura of the writing is often more significant than merely the extreme pitches.

Sub-categories:

Soubrette: light, younger voices and characters, e.g., Despina (*Cosi fan Tutte*), Susanna (*Le Nozze di Figaro*), Musetta (*La Bohème*), Bella (*The Midsummer Marriage*).

Lyric coloratura: extreme high notes and fine agility, e.g., Blonde (*Die Entführung aus dem Serail*), Gilda (*Rigoletto*), Norina (*Don Pasquale*), Titania (*A Midsummer Night's Dream*) Lulu (*Lulu*), Cunegonde (*Candide*).

Lyric: sustain long lines, more substantial voice than above, e.g., Pamina (*Magic Flute*), Micaela (*Carmen*), Mimi (*La Bohème*), Ellen (*Peter Grimes*), Marietta (*Die tote Stadt*), Monica (*The Medium*).

Dramatic Coloratura: a more powerful and wider range, with the ability to sing coloratura, e.g., Anne Truelove (*The Rake's Progress*), Lucia (*Lucia di Lammemoor*), Violetta (*La Traviata*).

Spinto: bigger emotional range, long lines in heavy ensemble, great stamina, e.g., Cio Cio San (*Madama Butterfly*), Desdemona (*Otello*), Elizabeth (*Tannhäuser*).

Dramatic: more powerful voice with sustained dramatic singing, Leonora (*Fidelio*), Aida (*Aida*), Ariadne (*Ariadne auf Naxos*), Marie (*Wozzeck*).

Heavy Dramatic: long, powerful, sustained vocal lines over a large orchestra, e.g., Isolde (*Tristan und Isolde*), Brünnhilde (*Der Ring des Nibelungen*), Turandot (*Turandot*).

Mezzo-Soprano

Unacknowledged at the time of Mozart, this soprano may favor the middle of the voice over the top, although some have extensions into brilliant high register allied to a virtuosic display, as in Rossini's heroines.

Sub-categories:

Lyric: rich middle with flexibility for coloratura, e.g., Cherubino (*Le Nozze di Figaro*), Angelina (*Cenerentola*), Sextus (*La Clemenza di Tito*), Komponiste (*Ariadne auf Naxos*), Erica (*Vanessa*).

Dramatic: greater vocal strength, e.g., Carmen (*Carmen*), Dalila (*Samson et Dalila*), Eboli (*Don Carlos*), Fricka (*Die Walküre*), Lucretia (*The Rape of Lucretia*), Madame Flora (*The Medium*).

Alto

The most rare of female voices brings typically an earthy calmness to a lower tessitura for the middle voice, an extended lower range and reduced high range.

Contralto: mature with strong, low range and heavier sound, e.g., Ulrica (*Un Ballo* in *Maschera*), Azucena (*Ill Trovatore*), Erda (*Der Ring des Nibelungen*).

Male Alto/Countertenor

Typically, a baritone type but with a naturally strong falsetto, to which the middle voice is blended. A rich baritone voice often lurks underneath. Many baroque roles originally sung by men are today sung often by mezzos. Oberon (*A Midsummer Night's Dream*), The Sorceress (*Dido & Aeneas*), Orfeo (*Orfeo ed Euridice*), and the Handellian roles such as Giulio Cesare.

Tenor

The light and heroic tenors are two different voices. In the light tenor, the middle range blends with the falsetto to create a lyrical and flexible upper register.

Sub-categories:

Buffo: flexible, good diction, comic ability, e.g., Pedrillo (*Die Entführung aus dem Serail*), Beppe (*I Pagliacci*).

Lyric: flexibility of voice and ability to sustain legato lines, e.g., Alfredo (*Traviata*), Tamino (*Die Zauberflöte*), Tom Rakewell (*The Rake's Progress*), Albert (*Albert Herring*).

Italian: more robust with easy top C, e.g., Il Duca (*Rigoletto*), Edgardo (*Lucia di Lammermoor*), Rodolpho (*La Bohème*), Italian Singer (*Der Rosenkavalier*).

Youthful Heroic: ringing, strong top with staying power, e.g., Don José (*Carmen*), Cavaradossi (*Tosca*), Peter Grimes (*Peter Grimes*).

Heroic: Able to impact over a full orchestra, e.g., Florestan (*Fidelio*), Otello (*Otello*), Siegmund (*Die Walküre*).

Baritone

Baritones have a strong, rich middle voice. The light baritone can mix easily from his high down to his middle voice, creating an agile, youthful sound. The heavy baritone can carry the weight of his middle voice up to F and less frequently above.

Sub-categories:

Lyric: flexible throughout range up to G, and ability to sustain a legato line, e.g., Figaro (*Il Barbiere di Siviglia*), Papageno (*Die Zauberflöte*).

Cavalier: more weight, less flexible, with attractive and strong stage presence, e.g., Eugene Onegin (*Eugene Onegin*), Il Conte (*Le Nozze di Figaro*), Don Giovanni (*Don Giovanni*), Billy Budd (*Billy Budd*).

Character: power and high register, ability to sing Verdi and Puccini, e.g., Rigoletto (*Rigoletto*), Escamillo (*Carmen*), Tonio (*I Pagliacci*).

Heroic: big and heavy, often cruel and powerful, e.g., Macbeth (*Macbeth*), Iago (*Otello*), Wotan (*Die Walküre*), Wozzeck (*Wozzeck*).

Bass

The open musculature and voluminous air required for the lowest male voice to maintain a substantial volume demand often a large physical frame. Something extra-human is audible in the saintliness of Sarastro (*Die Zauberflöte*) and superhuman in the appetite of Boris Godunov.

Sub-categories:

Buffo: flexible, with wide range of expression and excellent actor, e.g., Leporello (*Don Giovanni*), Bartolo (*Il Barbiere di Siviglia*), Bottom (*A Midsummer Night's Dream*).

Bass-Baritone: darker, slightly more dramatic, and ability to sustain a legato line, e.g., Figaro (*Le Nozze di Figaro*), Claggart (*Billy Budd*).

Basso Profundo: deep and rich, e.g., Gremin (*Eugene Onegin*), Filippo (*Don Carlos*).

Appendix 2: An Application of the International Phonetic Alphabet

The following table provides a convenient reference tool derived from applying the IPA to the English language, or to other Romance languages as necessary.

symbol	word	language	symbol	word	language
ʌ	cup	eng.	θ	corazon	sp.
a	far	eng.	f	fast	eng.
ɛ	pet	eng.	g	get	eng
e	chaotic (approx.)	eng.	gs	exil	fr.
	era	it.	ɣ	luego	sp.
ə	about (approx.)	eng.	h	high	eng.
	ville	fr.	k	cold	eng.
i	see	eng.	ks	lax	eng.
o	dove	it.	l	lungo	it.
ɔ	fought	eng.	ʎ	figlia	it.
ø	peu	fr.	j	yonder	eng.
œ	surf (approx.)	eng.	m	man	eng.
	oeuf	fr.	n	name	eng.
u	doom (approx.)	eng.	ɲ	onion	eng.
	mucho	sp.	ŋ	sing	eng.
y	lune	fr.	p	pour	eng.
ã	ensemble	fr.	r	red	eng.
ɛ̃	teint	fr.	s	see	eng.
õ	ombre	fr.	z	zeal	eng.
œ̃	un	fr.	dz	adze	eng.
w	suave	eng.	ʒ	vision	eng.
j	you	eng.	dʒ	jar	eng.
ɥ	puis	fr.	ʃ	show	eng.
b	bet	eng.	t	tan	eng.
β	hablar	sp.	ts	Tsar	eng.
ç	ich	ger.	tʃ	church	eng.
d	doom	eng.	v	vast	eng.
ð	other	eng.	x	loch	eng.

Bibliography and Further Reading

Adler, Kurt. *The Art of Accompanying and Coaching.* Minneapolis: University of Minnesota, 1965.

Balk, H. Wesley. *The Complete Singer-Actor.* Minneapolis: University of Minnesota, 1977.

Barker, Paul. *Devising for the Theatre.* London: Crowood Press, 2002.

Barthes, Roland. *Image/Music/Text.* Translated by Stephen Heath. London: Fontana Paperbacks UK, 1977.

Bartolozzi, Bruno. *New Sounds for Woodwind.* London: Oxford University Press, 1967.

Barzun, Jacques. *Classic, Romantic, and Modern.* Chicago: University of Chicago Press, 1943.

Bernac, Pierre. *The Interpretation of French Song.* London: Cassell & Co., 1970.

Bernhart, Walter, Werner Wolf, and Steven Paul Scher. *Word And Music Studies. Defining The Field. Proceedings of the First International Conference on Word and Music Studies at Graz, 1997.* Graz: Rodopi Bv Editions, 1999.

Brook, Peter. *The Empty Space.* London: Granada, 1977.

Bryon, Experience. "*The Integrative Performance Theory: An Anti-Hermeneutic Approach for Opera.*" Melbourne: Doctoral thesis, Department of Music, Monash University, Australia, 2002.

Budden, Julian. *The Master Musicians: Verdi.* London: Dent, 1985.

Bunch, Meribeth. *Dynamics of the Singing Voice.* Austria: Springer-Verlag/Wien, 1982.

Celletti, Rodolfo. *A History of Bel Canto.* Translated by Frederick Fuller. Oxford: Oxford University Press, 1991.

Celletti, Rodolfo. *La grana della voce.* Milano: Baldini & Castoldi, 2000.

Clément, Catherine. *Opera, or the Undoing of Women.* London: Virago, 1989.

Cone, Edward T. *The Composer's Voice.* Berkeley, CA: University of California, 1974.

————. *Music: A View From The Delft.* Chicago: University of Chicago, 1989.

Cooke, Nicholas. *Analysing Musical Multimedia.* Oxford: Oxford University Press, 1998.

Dunn, Leslie C., and Nanvy A. Jones, eds. *Embodied Voices.* Cambridge: Cambridge University Press, 1994.

Fischer, Jens Malte. "Sprechgesang or Bel Canto: Toward a History of Singing Wagner," in *Wagner Handbook,* ed. Müller, Wapnewski & Deathridge. Boston, MA: Harvard University Press, 1992.

Fuchs, Viktor. *The Art of Singing and Voice Technique.* London: Calder, 1985.

Gaffurius. 1496. "Practica musicae." *Musicological Studies and Documents.* Rome: University of Rome. 1951–, vol. XX, 1968, pp.148ff.

Garcia II, Manuel. 1841, 1847. *Traité complet de l'Art du Chant.* Rev. ed.: *Nouveau Traité sur l'Art du Chant.* 1856. Reprinted. 1872. Translated and edited by Donald V. Paschke. *A Complete Treatise on the Art of Singing.* New York: Da Capo, 1975 (Part I), 1982 (Part II).

Goodwin, Andrew. *Dancing in the Distraction Factory: Music, Television and Popular Culture.* Minnesota: University of Minnesota Press, 1992.

Grotowski, Jerzy. *Towards a Poor Theatre.* London: Methuen Drama, 1969.

Hahn, Reynaldo. *On Singers and Singing.* Portland, Oregon: Amadeus Press, 1990.

Hughes, Spike. *Mozart Operas.* New York: Dover, 1972.

Husler, Frederick and Yvonne Rodd-Marling. *Singing: The Physical Nature of the Vocal Organ.* London: Hutchinson, 1976.

Kayes, Gillyanne. *Singing and the Actor.* London: A. & C. Black, 2000.

Kerst, Friedrich. *Mozart: The Man and the Artist Revealed in His Own Words.* New York: Dover, 1965.

Koopman, John. *A Brief History Of Singing and Unsung Songs.* (*http://www.lawrence.edu/fac/koopmajo/brief.html*) 1999. Lawrence University, Appleton, WI.

Legge, Anthony. *The Art of Auditioning.* London: Rhinegold, 1988.

Manén, Lucie. *The Art of Singing.* London: Faber Music, 1974.

Manning, Jane. *New Vocal Repertoire.* Oxford: Oxford University Press, 1994.

————. *New Vocal Repertoire, Vol. 2.* Oxford: Oxford University Press, 1998.

Marchesi, Mathilde. *Bel Canto: A Theoretical and Practical Vocal Method.* New York: Dover, 1970.

Meyer, Leonard B. *Music, The Arts and Ideas.* Chicago: University of Chicago Press, 1967.

Payne, Roger. Quoted in an article by Natalie Angier: *"Sonata for Humans, Birds and Humpback Whales."* New York Times, January 9th, 2001.

Perle, George. *"Pitch-Class Set Analysis: An Evaluation." Journal of Musicology,* Vol. 8, No. 2 (Spring 1990): 151–172. California: University of California Press.

Pleasants, Henry. *The Great American Popular Singers.* New York: Simon & Schuster, 1966.

Potter, John. *Vocal Authority: Singing Style and Ideology.* Cambridge: Cambridge University Press, 1998.

————. ed. *The Cambridge Companion to Singing.* Cambridge: Cambridge University Press, 2000.

Prawer, Siegbert. *The Penguin Book of Lieder.* London: Penguin, 1964.

Punt, Norman A. *The Singer's and Actor's Throat.* London: Heinemann, 1952.

Reich, Steve. Quoted March 1991 in interview with Jonathan Coe in *The Wire* (UK Music Magazine), #85. London, England.

Reid, Cornelius. *Bel Canto: Principles and Practices.* New York: Coleman-Ross, 1950.

————. *Voice Psyche & Soma.* New York: Joseph Patelson Music House, 1975.

————. *The Free Voice.* New York: Coleman-Ross, 1965.

Rodenburg, Patsy. *The Need for Words.* London: Methuen Drama, 1993.

Rushdie, Salman. *The Ground Beneath Her Feet.* New York: Henry Holt and Company, 1999.

Salzman, Eric. September 2001. Posting to C-opera e-mail list.

Shreffler, Anne C. *Webern and the Lyric Impulse.* Oxford: Oxford University Press, 1994.

Stanislavski, Constantin and Pavel Rumyantseu. *Stanislavski on Opera.* New York: Routledge, 1998.

Stanislavsky, Constantin. *Stanislavsky on the Art of the Stage.* Translated by David Magarshack. London: Faber & Faber, 1980.

Storr, Anthony. *Music and the Mind.* London: Harper Collins, 1992.

Strunk, Oliver. *Source Readings in Music History.* London: Faber & Faber, 1952.

Tosi, Pierfrancesco. 1723. *Opinione de' cantori antichi, e moderni o sieno osservazioni sopra il canto figurato* (Bologna, 1723, facs, ed. New York, 1968. English translation by John E. Galliard. *Observations on the Florid Song.* London: Wilcox, 1743; 2nd ed. Preface by Paul Henry Lang. New York: Johnson Reprint Corp., 1968. English Translation by Edward V. Foreman. *Opinions of Singers Ancient & Modern, or Observations on Figured Singing* (Masterworks on Singing Series, Vol. VI). Pro Musica Press, 1993.)

Wheelock, Gretchen. *"Haydn's Instrumental Works 'Englished' for Voice and Piano." The Journal of Musicology.* California: University of California Press, Vol. VIII, No. 3, 1990.

Willet, John, ed. and trans. *Brecht on Theatre.* New York: Hill & Wang, 1978.

Index